HITLER'S LAST LEVY

HITLER'S LAST LEVY

THE VOLKSSTURM 1944–45

Hans Kissel

Translated by
C. F. Colton, MA

Additional material and translation by
Duncan Rogers

Uniform plates by
Stephen Andrew

HELION & COMPANY

Helion & Company Limited
26 Willow Road
Solihull
West Midlands
B91 1UE
England
Tel. 0121 705 3393
Fax 0121 711 4075
Email: publishing@helion.co.uk
Website: http://www.helion.co.uk

First published 1962 as *Der Deutsche Volkssturm 1944/45: Eine territoriale Miliz im Rahmen der Landesverteidigung*

© Verlag E. S. Mittler & Sohn GmbH, Hamburg

This expanded English edition published by Helion & Company Limited 2005
English edition, including all artwork © Helion & Company Limited 2005

Designed and typeset by Carnegie Publishing Ltd, Lancaster, Lancashire
Printed by The Cromwell Press, Trowbridge, Wiltshire

ISBN 1 874622 51 5
EAN 973 1 874622 51 2

British Library Cataloguing-in-Publication Data.
A catalogue record for this book is available from the British Library.

For details of other military history titles published by Helion & Company Limited contact the above address, or
visit our website: http://www.helion.co.uk.

We always welcome receiving book proposals from prospective authors.

Readers may wish to note that the original paintings from which the colour
plates in this book were taken are available for sale.

Contents

Publishers' Note

This book was originally published in Germany with the title *Der Deutsche Volkssturm 1944/45: Eine territoriale Miliz im Rahmen der Landesverteidigung*. The text of this English language edition is substantially identical except for the addition of a section concerning uniforms and equipment. The number of photographs has been substantially increased. The majority of military terms have been retained in their original German, and readers are directed to the glossary for English definitions.

Please note that it was decided to include a number of photographic images due to their historical scarcity, despite the fact that their quality is less than desired. It is hoped that the reader shares the publishers' opinion that a poor quality image of a very rare subject is better than none at all.

The publishers' would like to extend their thanks to the following individuals and organisations, without whose help publication of this book would have proven impossible: Stephen Andrew; Friedrich Baier; Bildarchiv ASL, especially Norbert Kandling; Bildarchiv Preußischer Kulturbesitz; Bundesarchiv, especially Frau Martina Caspers; Alexandr Grinev; History in the Making Archive, especially Ian Baxter; Verlag E. S. Mittler & Sohn GmbH, especially Herr Thomas Bantle; the Museum of Modern History, Ljubljana, Slovenia; Emil Nagel; Ullstein Bilderdienst, especially Herr Jörg-Ulrich Lampertius.

Interested readers are directed to our companion volume, *In a Raging Inferno: Combat Units of the Hitler Youth 1944–45* by Hans Holzträger (ISBN 1–874622–17–5) for detailed information and photographs concerning the HJ units which fought alongside, and sometimes as part of, the *Volkssturm*.

Foreword

Shortly before the end of the war, in autumn 1944, millions of German men were called into the ranks of the *Volkssturm* by law. Of these, as many as 100,000 served as *Volkssturm* soldiers at the front. 10,000 died a soldier's death, faithfully fulfilling their duty, in the belief that they fought for a just cause. A still greater number were wounded.

Via exposure in the wider circles of the public domain, these men are owed a fuller picture of their participation in the war, put into a historical perspective. It is for this reason that this author has produced a history of the German *Volkssturm*.

This work has only been made possible because the Bundesarchiv in Koblenz, the Zentralnachweisstelle, Kornelimünster at Aachen, the Berlin Document Center of the US Mission in Berlin, the Institut für Zeitgeschichte in München, the Search Service of the German Red Cross as well as countless other contributors assisted the author. All the institutions and individuals who supported the author's work are gratefully thanked.

Hans Kissel
Frankfurt am Main, April 1962

CHAPTER ONE

Territorial Militias

The past provides countless examples of militia armies. Examples of these should serve as an introduction, and in the following brief sections of the many sided forms of such military units are examined.

Kolberg 1806/07

In 1806 the surrender of the Prussian fortresses without a fight had "much embittered the population and caused the great mass of them to be deeply suspicious."[1] The population's attitude allows one to understand why in Kolberg Joachim Nettelbeck, acting as representative of the town's population, turned to the military commander of the town, 65 year-old Colonel von Lucadou, and instructed "that the Commandant should come to an understanding with them over the defences of the town." The townsmen had resolved that the fortress would not be handed over, especially as they had been, "from time immemorial, the natural and lawful defenders of the town."[2]

The Colonel, who until then "had no visible belief that a successful defence of the town was possible", and who "lacked the power to take steps necessary for such a defence"[3] eventually, albeit unhappily, placed the fortress in a state of defence, following the intervention of the townsmen.

However, Nettelbeck failed to receive any intimation of the role to be fulfilled by the five companies of townsmen available to him. Lucadou was completely imbued with the spirit of the Ancién Regime, and believed that the defence of the town was solely a matter for the military. "I do not wish to utilise the citizens."[4] He merely allowed the townspeople to lay out, on their own initiative, some defensive works outside the town, to prepare the flooding of selected areas, to improve the provision of firefighting equipment, and to stockpile supplies. At the end of March 1807, some months later, he finally approved their participation in 'inner fortress duties', by which the townsmen served as sentries and guards on the inner walls and towers, as well as replacing fallen artillerymen. It was not until Gneisenau replaced Lucadou at the end of April that the wishes of Nettelbeck were realised, and the citizens were planned to be deployed as soldiers. However, such a deployment was not carried out as the changing circumstances did not allow it. It was scarcely possible to continue to hold the fortress, and when the surrender was signed their besiegers did not have to take weapons out of their hands.

Tyrol 1805

In Imperial Austria stood the so-called military border, in which volunteer formations in the Tyrol, militia from the earliest times, held the first line of defence of the homeland, and thereby considerably increased the fighting strength of the regular army without demanding too much financial or personnel support from the state.

Thus in 1805 the Tyrolean militia, throughout the year, carried the burden in battle of the membership of their land as part of Austria. The first battle at the beginning of November 1805 for the Scharnitz defile on the Bavarian-Tyrolean border affords an illustrative example.

The Austrian commander occupied not only the Scharnitz defile with militia, but also fieldworks at Leutsach, which lay to the northwest of it. The men fought courageously. In addition he protected his right flank with a levy of women and girls, as well as older members of the militia, utilising the steeply overhanging precipices below the Brunnstein to employ prepared avalanches of stones to halt the enemy advance decisively.[5]

With the Imperial Commission of 8 June 1808 the Landwehr, an institution aimed at strengthening the regular army, was called into being throughout all Habsburg lands. In the main its organisation remained restricted to battalion-sized formations. Training occurred on Sundays and holidays, as well as once a month when larger manoeuvres took place, during which locations were selected on the basis that no man should have to march more than three miles to return home. In 1809 the Austrian Landwehr, with 153 battalions, finally came into action, and acquitted itself very well.

The Tyrol and Vorarlberg 1915

A particularly noteworthy territorial militia was created in the Austrian territories of the Tyrol and Vorarlberg as soon as the First World War broke out, the so-called *Standschützen*. In late 1914, when signs of the breakdown in the alliance with Italy began to manifest themselves, and regular defences were deemed insufficient to defend the land borders with Italy, the *Standschützen* was created from members of the traditional *Schützen* groups. Membership was on a voluntary basis, and in consideration of the conditions of the territories in question, the troops were organised by valleys and districts into companies and battalions. The volunteers belonged to various age groups – from 15 years of age to more than 70 – and degrees of fitness for service. Officers and NCOs were, in the old Tyrolean custom, chosen by the *Standschützen* themselves.

On 18 May 1915, only six days before Italy's declaration of war, an Imperial decree called the *Standschützen* to the colours. They hurried to their shooting galleries, where, so far as this had not yet happened, the battalions were formed, and the elections of the officers and NCOs were undertaken. Within 24 hours the battalions were transported to the border area, although many of the men were still attired in national dress. In this manner 53 battalions containing about 40,000 volunteers were called up and sent to the border.

On 23 May the commander of the Tyrol's defence could thus send the battalions into their improvised positions. A shortfall in military training, in particular the instruction in the use of machine guns of mainly Russian origin, would have to take place *in situ*. Above the actions of many other brave soldiers shone the unforgettable iron determination of the *Dreizinner*, Sepp Innerkofler, who hastened tirelessly through positions and appeared on the most difficult peaks, his paths and footprints giving the enemy the impression that the positions were defended by much larger numbers of men than was the case. Innerkofler finally met a brave death on his mountain.

The army commanders were full of the highest praise for these militia units and their men. Their readiness for action, founded on their love for their homeland and the Emperor, combined of course with their abilities as marksman, meant that on the Tyrolean front during the first crisis-filled months of the war, they halted the Italian army and retained their positions, sometimes even being able to launch attacks themselves.

Britain 1940

In mid-June 1940 Britain found itself in a very serious situation, following the overthrow of France, possessing only relatively few badly-equipped divisions for the defence the country. Thus it was convenient that as early as 14 May 1940 Britain had begun to organise Local Defence Volunteers, who later received the designation the Home Guard.

By September 1940 one million men had been enrolled, men who were either too old or too unfit for service in the regular armed forces, or men in reserved civilian occupations, or who were too young for active service. The officers were mainly retired regular officers or Territorial Army officers. When men of such experience were not available, other men with suitable military experience were employed.

The principal weapon was the rifle. However if in short supply other weapons were utilised – sports or hunting rifles, pikes, lances, swords or even golf clubs. Uniforms were initially unavailable, so only armbands were worn. By mid-1941 all members of the Home Guard were uniformed and mostly armed with rifles, many units also possessing light machine guns.

Normally the members of these units continued in their civilian occupations. Their military duties and training were fulfilled in their spare time or when an alarm was raised. They did not receive any wages.

One of the basic tenets of the Home Guard was that in every street of every town, in every factory or school, in every village or industrial complex, a group of local men would stand resolutely in defence, killing or otherwise disabling all enemies that appeared to them. Enemy movements would be impeded by road blocks, barricades, craters, ditches filled with burning oil, or mines. The tactics of these groups was defensive – they were trained in the art of delaying tactics, sabotaging equipment and particularly in the destruction of enemy transport. Special units would operate in woodland or other isolated spots where the enemy may bivouac or spend the night.

Britain was not invaded, and the Home Guard was not seriously tested; however, their training exhibited two principal purposes – to fight with the greatest determination, causing the attacker's heavy casualties, and to cause confusion amongst the enemy.[6]

Soviet Union 1941

In the summer of 1941 the Soviet Union created a 'People's Army', alongside the mobilisation of its regular armed forces. These militia divisions were aimed at supporting the Red Army in their fight against the advancing Germans. As in the 17th Century, when militia units under the command of Minin and Posharskij fought against Russia's enemies, and as in 1812, when formed in response to Napoleon's invasion, so also in 1941 the entire population was mobilised in a defensive role.

In Leningrad:

> 20 divisions of Red Militia were created from 300,000 workers, in order to prevent the entry of the enemy into the city. At the same time workers in the factories were organised in such a way that at any time the maximum number of troops could be employed in the defence of the city, without the rhythm of armaments production being interrupted.[7]

In Moscow 11 militia divisions were created, although they were sent into action against the German tanks with little more than mess tins on them at times. Workers militia units were sent into battle in many other places as well.

> The divisions of the People's Army fully and completely fulfilled our hopes, and courageously and steadfastly fought the enemy. Some divisions formed from Moscow workers were rewarded with the title 'Guards Division' for their bravery.[8]

Definition

Based on these various examples we should now finally propose a definition of the term 'Territorial Militia'. In all cases were available regular forces too weak for an adequate defence of their homeland, so that supplementary militia formations were required to reinforce them.

'Militia army' and 'regular army' are alternatives. When units of the regular army are available under arms, even during peacetime, units of the militia are normally only available latently, really only existing on paper. Militia units normally only assemble in peacetime for training purposes or in a state of emergency, taking up arms, so long as due notice is given, in time of war.

The distinguishing features of the two forms of an army, militia army and regular army, are defined by the terms 'temporary' and 'standing under arms'. Both can be recruited via conscription or on a voluntary basis. Similarly, the length of training required is without importance; a militia army can be assembled for specific training or merely on a transitory basis due to the situation prevailing at that time.

So-called enlisted cadres, which usually only retains small cadres of command and specialist troops permanently under arms, and whose units only increase to full strength in time of war following a levy or call-up, thus belong to the category of militia units.

Finally, the localised purpose of most militia forces awards them the character of a 'Territorial Militia'.

A fascinating photo showing armed German civilians before the official formation of the *Volkssturm* – members of the *Wehrappelle* (lit. 'armed roll-call') created by *Gauleiter* Hartmann Lauterbacher of Hameln at a march past, 11 August 1944. They appear to be wearing completely plain white armbands. Lauterbacher can be seen at far left. He managed to escape from Allied captivity twice, finally reaching Argentina in 1948. **Museum of Modern History, Ljubljana, Slovenia**

Members of the Tiroler *Standschützen*, November 1944. Nearly twenty battalions of *Standschützen* had been formed during the summer 1944 as a preliminary home-defence measure, drawing on the long-standing shooting clubs that already existed in the region. **Museum of Modern History, Ljubljana, Slovenia**

CHAPTER TWO

Creation

Following the successful offensives of the Soviet armies during the spring and summer of 1944, combined with the invasion of France by the Western Allies, the problem of the defence of the Reich's borders had to be considered.

The events of 20 July 1944 had shown that not only was there a civilian opposition to the Nazi regime, but that one also existed in the senior ranks of the Army's officer corps; one which "considered the overthrow of the catastrophic leadership of Hitler and the termination of the senselessly continuing war necessary", and was prepared to remove the *Führer*, whom the majority of the population in 1933 had voted into office.[9] However, the bitter consequences following the Armistice of 1918, the Casablanca Conference in January 1943 with its demand for "unconditional surrender", the Quebec Conference with the Morgenthau Plan, and not least the failure of the Allies to fully co-operate with the German resistance movement, in combination with the German people's lack of expectation that the Nazi regime could be successfully overthrown and a bearable peace concluded, meant that the German population felt itself 'cast adrift in a boat'. "Unconditional surrender," said the US General Wedemeyer in the *Wedemeyer Reports*, meant that, "significantly, both the Germans who opposed Hitler and the vast majority of the population had no choice but to continue fighting to the end."[10]

If one did not wish for unconditional surrender, then one must continue to fight. There were at least two reasons for believing that to continue fighting was not hopeless. Firstly, people placed great hope in the announcement of secret 'wonder weapons'. Based on the albeit limited evidence seen, it was not believed that such weapons were simply propaganda and lies. Secondly, it was perceived that the relationship between the Western Allied democracies and the Communist military autocracy was strained to say the least, and that one had only to hold on long enough in order for this alliance to fall apart. The serious differences of opinion over the Balkans between London and Moscow were evidence of the strained relationship.

Consequently, if the senior military command busied itself with the problem of the defence of 'Fortress Germany', despite the hopeless situation, then they will fulfilling their duties as soldiers.

From a military point of view it was evident that there was a question as to whether the availability of personnel and materiél made it possible to form a front beyond the borders of the Reich, in addition to defending the Reich itself, particularly due to the weakness of the infantry arm. Should such an eventuality come to pass, it was hoped that the enemy penetration into the Reich could be delayed as long as possible in order to allow sufficient time for the deployment of the 'new weapons' or for political developments to take place.

It is now unfortunately impossible to say whether the consideration of such military possibilities was discussed in the highest levels of command, because the relevant documents are lost, and the people in question are no longer alive. The following picture emerges from documentation still available, including literature produced since the end of the war as well as questions asked of the various people 'in the know'.

Generaloberst Guderian's book *Erinnerungen eines Soldaten* reveals that as soon as he took over the office of Chief of General Staff of the Army following 20 July 1944, approval was received from Hitler for the restoration of the German defensive fortifications in the East. These included the so-called Heilsberg Triangle, the fortifications in Pomerania, the fortified front of the Oder-Warthe bend, and permanent positions along the Oder.

> Together with the General of Engineers at OKH, General Jacob, I provided a construction plan. I ordered the reformation of my former disbanded Fortress Detachment of the General Staff under *Oberstleutnant* Thilo to oversee the construction.[11]

Alongside the repair and renewal of the existing fortifications along the western and eastern borders being carried out by trained personnel – which by the sixth year of the war naturally moved along at a very slow pace, and whose armament could only be regarded as inadequate – the land lying between the permanent fortifications where no kinds of defensive positions existed had to be prepared for defence. To oversee the construction of such defensive measures – in the East the construction of the so-called East Wall – Hitler nominated the Party *Gauleiters*, who at the same time became 'Reich Defence Commissioners', responsible for the area of a *Gau*. The

Gauleiters, who were entrusted with making defensive measures, and accordingly could call up personnel to support their work, had received an order to "give the necessary instructions" from the leader of the Party Chancellery, Martin Bormann, acting on a directive from Hitler of 1 September 1944 (see Appendix I).

The workforce that the homeland could still provide consisted of women, children and old men, equipped with shovels, spades and pickaxes to fortify the borders.

> The Hitler Youth hereby provided the greatest service. All of these valiant German men worked with the greatest zeal and understanding, despite the weather soon changing for the worse, in the belief that their homeland, for which they had the greatest love, would provide some protection for their soldiers, some support in their bitter defensive battles.[12]

With the repair and garrisoning of those positions already constructed, and the continuing construction of additional fortifications, in an Order of the Party Chancellery of 27 September 1944, sent from Bormann "on the orders of the *Führer*", the *Gauleiters* were entrusted with the continuation of the construction plans. (Appendix I). Following the same order of 27 September, thus four weeks before the creation of the *Volkssturm* was officially authorised, Bormann ordered the creation of security detachments in the manner of the *Volkssturm*, who were to occupy these defensive positions on the approach of the enemy, and to defend them until a coherent defence line could be established by regular forces. All these measures were carried out in concordance with the relevant military authorities.

During the consideration of measures to be taken for the defence of Fortress Germany, the question of which troops should occupy these positions arose, in addition to the problems of the fortifications themselves. Defensive positions without the provision of defenders are useless. That is why even before the decision had been made to fortify the borders – the precise date cannot be determined due to the unavailability the relevant documents – the decision was taken to provide fortress troops from sources other than regular combat troops. The then acting Chief of Operations Staff in the OKW, General Warlimont, who at the beginning of September 1944 had been removed from his post, could not remember any more particulars. His replacement, General a. D. Freiherr Horst von Buttlar, whose similarly could not supply any further details from his few personal notes, wrote the following in a letter of 20 November 1959:

> The fact is that during the initial phase of thinking regarding the defence of 'Fortress Germany', fortress troops were to lend support to the defence of larger locations and junctions on the transport network in support of regular Army forces. It was envisaged that these units were to be deployed in defensive positions – thus in a similar fashion to those peacetime fortress troops in the West – and would be confined to such a role after training and equipping. Initially, these measures were particularly envisaged taking place in the East, to be followed later in the West – the reconstructed West Wall.

Generaloberst Guderian wrote regarding the problem of 'fortress troops' in his book:

> Initially 100 fortress infantry battalions and 100 batteries were created. Fortress machine gun, *Panzerjäger*, engineer and signals units were to follow. However, before the first of these units was fit for service, 80% of them were sent to the Western Front.[13]

These remarks certainly conflict with the views of General von Buttlar, who wrote in the above-mentioned letter:

> Because of the fluent development of events in the East, these fortress troops were, as far as I can recall, not left at the disposal of the Army General Staff, but were supplied with their agreement to plug gaps in the frontlines, despite the fact that their unsuitability in a war of movement was clear. It was an undesirable event, but the situation on the Eastern Front made it unavoidable.

Nevertheless, the fact was that shortly before the newly-created fortress troops were to occupy the 'fortifications' and take up duties on the borders, they had been used elsewhere, and the problem was now a pressing one.

Generaloberst Guderian had the following to say regarding the problem of replacing these fortress troops:

> When the supply of fortress troops to me was, for the most part, taken away, I recalled that a time ago proposals had been made by the Operations Department of the OKH under General Heusinger, which at the time had been dismissed by Hitler, for the creation of a *Landsturm* in the threatened Eastern provinces. I envisaged that it could draw on personnel fit for service, who were however prevented from fulfilling their military duties by their wartime occupations,

and commanded by *Landsturm* officers. It would be something that was only called-up when a Soviet breakthrough threatened. I went to Hitler with this proposal and asked for the task to be entrusted to the SA, insofar as it was composed of dependable people. I had already obtained the cooperation in principle of the Chief of Staff of the SA, the understanding and pro-military Schepmann. Initially, Hitler agreed to my proposal, however the next day he contacted me to tell me that he decided he did not wish the SA to be responsible for this levy, but intended to use the Party, with *Reichsleiter* Martin Bormann in charge, and that he had given the organisation the name of the *Volkssturm*.[14]

In relation to the above comments made by Guderian regarding General Heusinger, the latter responded to me in a letter of 2 October 1956 that in June 1944 he had merely made the suggestion to Hitler that they could:

> begin by evacuating the civilian population from East Prussia. I did not make a proposal for the creation of a *Volkssturm* in East Prussia in connection with this, as I was convinced that a proposal of this sort in modern warfare could only lead to unnecessary casualties. Guderian has cited my proposal for the evacuation of East Prussia in a false light.

Regarding the question of the replacement of the fortress troops General *Freiherr* von Buttlar wrote in his letter of 20 November 1959:

> As far as I can remember, a wide variety of possibilities were aired regarding the replacement of the fortress troops. The Replacement Army, SS, SA and Party were all mentioned in connection with this, particularly who would prove the most effective in not only organising localised evacuations but also in taking the necessary defensive measures. If my memory serves me correctly, it was concluded that the prevailing situation admitted only one organisation to be involved, as the state of the economy would allow only one group the necessary means to support the requisite number of men, and sufficient materials for clothing and equipping a new organisation were no longer available.
>
> Hitler believed that the Party occupied first place in such considerations, as it possessed the necessary administrative and economic powers, accompanied by additional responsibilities for short-term training programmes, and abilities to provide localised defences in the event of emergency, in order to take on the main duties of organising such a force, supported by the *Wehrmacht*, SS and SA. The decision in favour of the Party was, in my opinion – without considering Hitler's personal reasons – probably the correct one, because it was felt that only the Party, due to its influence, could effectively cope with the administration and organisation of such a force, compared to the SA, and that because of this influence it should stand to the fore, coping with the difficulties expected from all sides.

The idea of a *Landsturm* again arose in the discussion mentioned above. According to the Defence Statutes of 21 May 1935, Section 6, the Reich Minister for War could "in time of war and during particular emergencies" empower "the *Kreis* to consider expanding the criteria for the fulfilment of compulsory military service amongst German men." The statutes stated that those men called up as a result of Section 6, above the ages of 45, would form a *Landsturm*.

Although these empowerments were designed to allow timely measures, the fact was that countless members of the younger age groups from all parts of the armed forces had been sent to the front with the Army, and particularly in the infantry, so that since the winter of 1941/42 a rapidly increasing weakness in battle strength was discernible. This shortage could not entirely be ascribed to the catastrophically worsening military situation. The knowledge that throughout military history numerical inferiority was the most frequent cause of defeat was familiar to the greatest soldiers all epochs and nations. Not for nothing did Napoleon hold that victory smiled on the side with the biggest battalions; and not for nothing did Clausewitz state that "the best strategy is: always be very strong."[15]

Why no use was made of the above-mentioned law is not up for discussion here. Anyway, in the summer of 1944, for a variety of reasons, it was too late to enforce it, especially when one considers the task involved in creating, mustering, training and meaningfully organising the draftees. Additionally, if *Landsturm* units had been created purely in the Eastern provinces, they would have been but a drop in the ocean of manpower on that front.

In order to stem the entry of the enemy into the Reich, considerably more than the relatively few men who fell within the *Landsturm* age groups would be required. An indication of the numbers required is provided by examining the number of young men liable for military service – even allowing for people in reserved occupations, the number far exceeded the men falling within the age groups of the *Landsturm*. For instance, in 1944, "the number of men falling within the age groups born between 1895 and 1925 exceeded 5 million".[16] The strength of the entire field army in the same year amounted to only 4.4 million men. Of those men falling within the given age ranges, many received military training, and of these, a proportion was sent to the frontline.

Militia units from these young men and from older men unfit for frontline service could, in times of crisis, be organised and employed under the direction of the *Wehrmacht* in active defence of the land. It was hoped that the situation would provide sufficient time to employ these units to stem the enemy's advance in order to allow the deployment of the "new" weapons or for a political solution to be found. That the creation of such an organisation required the provision of training and equipment to occur in a very short period of time, must be borne in mind.

The final decision to create the *Volkssturm* came about on 6 September 1944, presumably emanating from Hitler's closest circle. The date of 6 September 1944 is given in a letter written by the *Chef der SS-Hauptamtes* on 7 October 1944 to *Reichsminister* Dr Lammers, and which can be found in the *Reichskanzlei* papers in Koblenz.

From the documents in the *Reichskanzlei* papers one can further discover that on 14 September 1944 the drafts of two documents, "Directions for the Creation of the German *Volkswehr*" as well as "Regulations for Leaders of the Party Chancellery", were prepared. These two draft proposals were cleared with the Chief of the OKW on 20 September 1944 on the understanding that the creation of the *Volkswehr* would not hinder the ongoing provision of equipment to the *Wehrmacht* in any way.

On 22 September 1944, in the Berlin offices of the Party Chancellery, the two draft proposals – the designation *Volkswehr* had in the meantime been changed to *Volkssturm* – were handed out to the *Organisationsleiter der NSDAP* Dr Ley, the SA's Chief of Staff Schepmann, *NSKK-Korpsführer* Kraus, *Stabsführer der Reichsjugendführung* Moekel and a *SS-Obersturmbannführer* as representative of the *SS-Hauptamtes*. In the corresponding conversations, *Oberbefehlsleiter* Friedrichs, as spokesman for *Reichsleiter* Bormann, clarified the viewpoint of the Party Chancellery: the creation of the *Volkssturm* was not only to be seen as a task for the political organisation of the Party, but as a task for the entire Nazi movement, because only this approach could ensure that the necessary strengths of leadership and materiél were provided. In addition, because of its personnel situation, the SA was "not in a position to address the creation of the *Volkssturm*."[17]

On 25 September 1944 Hitler signed the "Decree of the *Führer* regarding the creation of the German *Volkssturm*" (Appendix II). On 27 September this decree, accompanied by a letter and the first "Regulations" (Appendix III) were sent to all *Gauleiter* by telex. On the same day, at the Party Chancellery in München, *Staatssekretär* Dr Klopfer received the Decree with a request to bring it the attention of *Reichsminister* Dr Lammers, in the Reichs Chancellery. In the accompanying letter it was stated that publication of these measures was not intended.

At the same time, on 27 September, on the basis of a telephone call from *Reichsleiter* Bormann to *Oberbefehlsleiter* Friedrichs, *Arbeitsstab* V was established at the Party Chancellery's main offices in Berlin (W 8, Wilhelmstr. 63), as a permanent working staff to handle all matters relating to the *Volkssturm*, headed by *Gaustabsamtsleiter* Bofinger. On 6 October an Army *Generalmajor* was attached to this working staff as an "adviser" to deal with all military questions that would arise during the creation of the *Volkssturm*. *Generalfeldmarschall* Keitel "placed great store on the OKW being intimately involved with the formulation of the regulations."[18]

On the basis of the *Führer* Decree of 25 September, *Reichsführer-SS* Himmler, "in agreement with the Leader of the Party Chancellery, *Reichsleiter* Bormann", also nominated *SS-Obergruppenführer und General der Waffen-SS* Gottlob Berger as *Stabsführer des deutschen Volkssturms*,[19] "with responsibility for the tasks, assigned in the first instance to me, of military organisation, training, armament, equipment, and combat deployment of the German *Volkssturm*". To deal with this additional area of responsibility now assigned to him, Berger sets up a permanent working staff under an Army staff officer (later *Generalmajor* Kissel), which included a round dozen Army and *Waffen-SS* officers as specialist advisors. An Army Staff major was appointed as head of the organisation section. At no time did the strength of this working staff, including subordinate and clerical staff, ever exceed about 40 personnel. It was assigned the name (in actual fact, not entirely accurate) of "*Führungsstab Deutscher Volkssturm*" (*Volkssturm* Command Staff), and a headquarters in Douglassstrasse, Berlin-Grünewald.

While consideration was being given at the highest levels to the formation of the *Volkssturm*, and the first organisational measures were already being taken, elements of the *Wehrmacht*, which knew nothing of the *Volkssturm* project, were turning their attention to the current problem of reinforcing resistance forces on the soil of the German homeland. Thus, based on an instruction issued by the *Wehrmacht* Command Staff, the *Oberbefehlshaber West* issued the following order on 30 September 1944:

"In every place on German soil which becomes involved in combat operations, all men capable of bearing arms, irrespective of their age, will be subject to the command of the local military commander for the purpose of reinforcing the defensive forces. If it is not possible to provide them with *Wehrmacht* uniform, they will be provided with a yellow armband bearing the inscription '*Deutsche Wehrmacht*' and a military pass."[20] Only if orders were given to evacuate the population of a district would the men capable of bearing arms not be retained. The formation of the *Volkssturm* brought to an end all measures of this kind and superseded the orders issued by the *Wehrmacht* authorities.

On 7 October, Dr Klopfer requested *Staatsekretär* Kritzinger in the office of *Reichsminister* Dr Lammers to bring the *Führer's* decree of 25 September to the attention of the highest Reich authorities. But *Reichsminister* Lammers suggested to *Reichsleiter* Bormann that he should delay notification of the decree on account of the clumsy formulation of section two of the preamble, because the comparison made there of the present situation with that of August 1939 "would not be taken quite seriously enough by the people".[21]

The same day, 20 October 1944, on which *Reichsminister* Dr Lammers received approval to his suggested revision to the preamble, an instruction was issued from the Reich Chancellery to the office of the *Reichsgesetzblatt* to publish the *Führer* Decree "today". With the official announcement in the *Reichsgesetzblatt* for 1944, Part I, page 253, the "*Führer* Decree of 25 September 1944 regarding the formation of the German *Volkssturm*" (see Appendix II) came into force as law.

Two days previously, on 18 October, the anniversary of the Napoleonic Battle of the Nations at Leipzig, in Königsberg, *Reichsführer-SS* Himmler had already issued the first appeal to the *Volkssturm*, and had taken this opportunity to announce the "*Führer* Decree concerning the formation of the *Volkssturm*". In his speech, which was reported *verbatim* in the *Völkischer Beobachter* of 19 October, 1944, he shamelessly accused the officers of the *Wehrmacht*, and particularly the officers of the Army, of dereliction of duty and of living a life of debauchery away from the front, and blamed them for the reverses on the Eastern Front.

The NSDAP *Gauleiters* and *Reichsleiters* had already, on 12 October, been issued, in the form of Party Chancellery "Order 318/44" (see Appendix IV), with "Schedule 2 of instructions for the implementation of the *Führer* Decree concerning the formation of the *Volkssturm*". But in order to put these instructions into force in an integrated and definite form, supplementary instructions were required, which were only issued on 3 November 1944 as "Order 379/44" (see Appendix V).

Since, in his book *Erinnerungen eines Soldaten*, *Generaloberst* Guderian accuses *Reichsleiter* Bormann of having delayed the formation of the *Volkssturm*, it seems appropriate to conclude this chapter with a review of the sequence of events:

After his fortress troops had been lost, it was only at the end of August/beginning of September 1944 at the earliest that *Generaloberst* Guderian could have recommended to Hitler that *Landsturm* units should be formed. And after that, it was only on 6 September that Hitler had made his final decision regarding the formation of a "German *Volkswehr*".

On 14 September, the first drafts for discussion of an "Order of the *Führer* concerning the formation of the German *Volkswehr*" and the first "Schedule of instructions for implementation" prepared by the Leader of the Party Chancellery were available. Both drafts were immediately submitted for comment to the senior authorities of the *Wehrmacht* and the Party.

On 25 September, Hitler signed the "Decree of the *Führer* concerning the formation of the German *Volkssturm*", which, together with the first "Schedule of instructions for implementation", were already in the hands of the *Gauleiters* by the early morning of 27 September. Work could thus then begin on organisation and registration, and soon afterwards it was possible to begin the first registration of men liable for service in the *Volkssturm*.

If, as is evident from the telegram sent by Bormann to his representative Friedrich on 1 October, 1944 (Appendix VI) and later comments, we take into account the many difficulties which mounted up from the outset, then it is amazing that by the second half of October, all *Gaue* were able to report positively on the state of preparation of their *Volkssturm* forces.

For example, as early as 18 October, in Königsberg, many thousands of *Volkssturm* men had turned up to Himmler's speech and in response to the "First Appeal", and as early as 20 October, seven East Prussian *Volkssturm* battalions were fighting at the front, with their combat readiness being mentioned "in glowing terms" by the 170th Infantry Division. On 20 October, in Upper Silesia, some 60 *Volkssturm* battalions were in the process of being formed. In Danzig-West Prussia, on 24 October, "432 companies with 7,344 NCOs and 70,474 other ranks" had been called up to registration parades.

Thus, when *Generaloberst* Guderian speaks of "procrastination of the *Volkssturm* plan", in this instance he is without doubt suffering from a lapse of memory. But even Bormann, as is evident from his telegram of 1 October to his representative Friedrich, was initially inclined to ask for more than the situation would permit at the time.

Erlass des Führers
über die Bildung des deutschen Volkssturms

Nach 5jährigen schwersten Kampf steht infolge des Versagens aller unserer europäischen Verbündeten der Feind an einigen Fronten in der Nähe oder an den deutschen Grenzen. Er strengt seine Kräfte an, um unser Reich zu zerschlagen, das deutsche Volk und seine soziale Ordnung zu vernichten, sein letztes Ziel ist die Ausrottung des deutschen Menschen.

Wie im Herbst 1939 stehen wir nun wieder ganz allein der Front unserer Feinde gegenüber. In wenigen Jahren war es uns damals gelungen, durch den ersten Großeinsatz unserer deutschen Volkskraft die wichtigsten militärischen Probleme zu lösen, den Bestand des Reiches und damit Europas für Jahre hindurch zu sichern. Während nun der Gegner glaubte, zum letzten Schlag ausholen zu können, sind wir entschlossen, den zweiten Großeinsatz unseres Volkes zu vollziehen. Es muß und wird uns gelingen, wie in den Jahren 1939 – 41 ausschließlich auf unsere eigene Kraft bauend, nicht nur den Vernichtungswillen der Feinde zu brechen, sondern sie wieder zurückzuwerfen und so lange vom Reich abzuhalten, bis ein die Zukunft Deutschlands, seiner Verbündeten und damit Europas sichernder Friede gewährleistet ist.

Den uns bekannten totalen Vernichtungswillen unserer jüdisch-internationalen Feinde ....

The *Führer's* decree for the creation of the *Volkssturm*.
Alexandr Grinev

This image was one of the first taken of members of the then newly-formed *Volkssturm* – Potsdam, autumn 1944. It appears that at the time this photograph was taken the men (and boys) had only been issued plain white armbands.
Hilmar Pabel/ Bildarchiv Preußischer Kulturbesitz, Berlin

Above: Two members of the *Volkssturm* in a slit trench, Potsdam, autumn 1944 – a propaganda shot taken during the very early days of the organisation's existence. The weapons are, from left to right: Erma machine-pistol, *Panzerfaust* 60, standard K98 rifle. The Erma is a very interesting weapon to see carried at this stage of the war. Designed in the late 1920s, it was replaced in regular units by the MP38 in 1938. Apart from *Wehrmacht* and SS use, the Erma also saw use in the Spanish Civil War, and with the French Foreign Legion. Heinrich Vollmer, the designer of this weapon, later designed the MP38 and MP40 machine-pistols.
Hilmar Pabel/Bildarchiv Preußischer Kulturbesitz, Berlin

Right: One of the first members of the *Volkssturm* to be called-up, 55-year old textiles salesman 'D' sporting nothing more than the first white armband, autumn 1944.
Bundesarchiv 146/74/33/9

11

Left: Some of the earliest *Volkssturmmänner* to take to the field were in East Prussia, October 1944. Here they are receiving training on an anti-tank gun. The original official caption to this image states 'With great enthusiasm, men of the *Volkssturm*, most of whom served in the Great War, bring a gun into position'.
Museum of Modern History, Ljubljana, Slovenia

Below: Weapons are handed out to one of the first *Volkssturm* units in East Prussia, October 1944. A high proportion of the men would have had experience handling weapons during the First World War, although their combat capability varied greatly.
Museum of Modern History, Ljubljana, Slovenia

Right: Interesting photo of a collection point for a newly-forming *Volkssturm Bataillon* in an unidentified town somewhere in the East, October 1944. The man holding the sign is wearing a SA uniform.
Museum of Modern History, Ljubljana, Slovenia

Below: Another view of the *Volkssturm Bataillon*'s collection point. The presence of *Kriegsmarine* ratings may suggest that the town was one of the Baltic seaports, such as Danzig or Kolberg.
Museum of Modern History, Ljubljana, Slovenia

The swearing-in of the Munich Volkssturm, 9 November 1944

Himmler salutes a honour guard provided by the *Waffen-SS* on his way to the Munich *Volkssturm*'s swearing-in ceremony, 9 November 1944. **Museum of Modern History, Ljubljana, Slovenia**

The Munich *Volkssturm* is sworn-in, 9 November 1944. Himmler, along with other Party dignitaries, can be seen in the background. **Museum of Modern History, Ljubljana, Slovenia**

The swearing-in of the Munich Volkssturm, 9 November 1944

Members of the Munich *Volkssturm* listen to Himmler's speech, 9 November 1944.
Museum of Modern History, Ljubljana, Slovenia

With all the pomp and ceremony the Nazi Party could muster by this time in the war, the Munich *Volkssturmmänner* take their oath, 9 November 1944. **Museum of Modern History, Ljubljana, Slovenia**

The swearing-in of the Munich Volkssturm, 9 November 1944

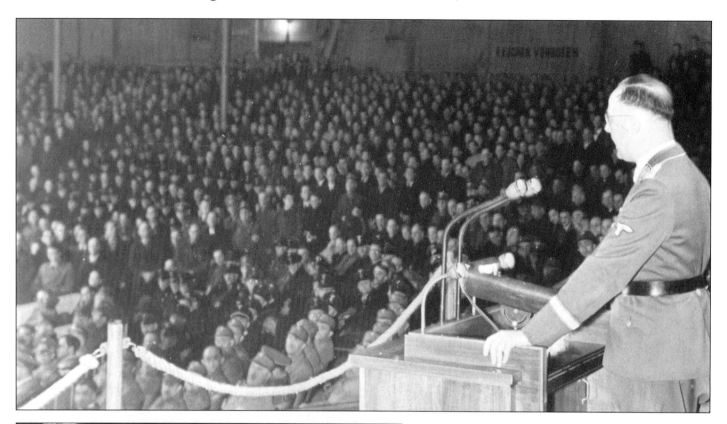

Above: Himmler delivers his speech, Munich, 9 November 1944.
Museum of Modern History, Ljubljana, Slovenia

Left: Another view of the swearing-in of the Munich *Volkssturm*, 9 November 1944, with the Nazi *Blutfahne* highly prominent. The standard bearer is *SS-Standartenführer* Grimminger, and interestingly, both he and his comrade are wearing old SA uniforms (actually windjackets, probably grey in colour) recalling the *Putsch* of 9 November 1923. Grimminger, a First World War veteran, had taken an active part in the 1923 *Putsch*, and from 1925 was the official bearer of the *Blutfahne* or 'Blood Banner', a flag carried during the *Putsch* itself by a man named Heinrich Traumbauer. The 'Blood Banner' tag came about because during the *Putsch*, Nazi Andreas Bauriedl, standing next to Traumbauer, was shot and killed, his blood staining the banner. His blood remained on the flag as a reminder of the deaths suffered that day by the Nazis. A member of the Munich city council, Grimminger was also a close friend of Hitler. He died in poverty and obscurity in 1969.
Museum of Modern History, Ljubljana, Slovenia

CHAPTER THREE

Leadership

The "Decree of the *Führer* of 25 September, 1944 concerning the formation of the German *Volkssturm*" (Appendix II) made all German men between the ages of 16 and 60 capable of bearing arms liable for service in the *Volkssturm*. This decree assigned to the *Volkssturm* the task of reinforcing the active forces of the *Wehrmacht* and in particular of fighting doggedly where there was any threat of the enemy entering upon German soil.

The people affected by this decree were almost all men in the age groups mentioned who were capable of bearing arms, insofar as they were not already soldiers of the *Wehrmacht*. The second "Schedule of instructions for implementation to the Decree of the *Führer* concerning the formation of the German *Volkssturm* of 12 October, 1944" (Appendix IV) clearly established that the *Wehrmacht* had primacy over the *Volkssturm*. Figure II 5 of these instructions for implementation said that membership of the *Volkssturm* lapsed when an individual was called up into the *Wehrmacht*, and that the fact that individuals were members of the *Volkssturm* should not be allowed to delay them being called up for normal military service.

With regard to the overall number of German men born between 1884 and 1928 who became liable for service in the *Volkssturm*, it has already been mentioned that in 1944 alone there were over 5 million men with dates of birth between 1895 and 1925 who were registered as exempt from military service. The following figures give more indications. On 30 September 1944 there were, not taking into account women and foreign workers, a total of 13.5 million German men registered as civilian workers.[22] One "Statement of Weapons Requirements"[23] prepared by the Chief of Staff in the office of the *Reichsführer-SS* on 30 November 1944 and available among the documents (Appendix X), estimates, on the basis of the reports made by the *Gaue* and an extremely careful enquiry into the number of men potentially available in the various age groups, that around 6 million men were available for service in the *Volkssturm*. Of these 6 million men, 4 million were in the first and second levies, from which no fewer than 6,710 *Volkssturm* battalions could have been formed. And one final figure: in the city of Stuttgart, more than 35,000 men were registered as liable for service in the *Volkssturm*.

The decree and the other instructions which were issued provided that the registration of men liable for service in the *Volkssturm* and also the development and command of the *Volkssturm* units which were to be formed were the responsibility of each *Gauleiter* in his respective *Gau*. The formation of *Volkssturm* units was to be carried out by "senior personnel" of the NSDAP on a district and local basis and these units were to be organised into companies and battalions. But the units were to be formed without taking account of any membership of the party or its subsidiary organisations among the men liable for service. In addition, there was a basic principle that such subsidiary organisations were not to be drafted *en bloc* into the *Volkssturm*.

The two schedules of instructions for implementation, dated 27 September and 12 October respectively (Appendices III and IV), did not envisage any plans for combining several *Volkssturm* battalions under more senior *Volkssturm* command staffs either during the formation and training of the units or when units were deployed in combat. If, despite this, in individual instances such as in East Prussia, several *Volkssturm* battalions were combined under senior *Volkssturm* commanders and even attempted to fight as autonomous units, this was the responsibility and fault of the excessively headstrong *Gauleiter* of East Prussia, Koch. There are many other instances when Koch did not adhere to the general instructions.

The two schedules of instructions for implementation specified that the *Gauleiters* were responsible for dealing with all questions relating to the formation and leadership of the *Volkssturm*, "even if they had to carry out the appropriate tasks in person", and the second schedule of instructions for implementation specified that the *Kreisleiter* similarly had to appoint assistants who were designated as *Gau-Stabsführer* (Chief of Staff, *Gau*) and *Kreis-Stabsführer* (Chief of Staff, *Kreis*).

All Chiefs of Staff were, "as committed, fanatical, and thus determined National Socialists, unit commanders with experience at the front and good organisers", to set up the *Volkssturm* units and select individuals for leadership in accordance with the instructions of their respective *Gauleiters* or *Kreisleiters*. But the *Gauleiters* and *Kreisleiters* were personally responsible for the selection of suitable battalion, company, platoon and section commanders. The *Gauleiter* was responsible for appointing the battalion commanders, the *Kreisleiter* was responsible for appointing the company commanders, the battalion commander was responsible for appointing the platoon commanders, and the company commander was responsible for appointing the section commanders. All appointments were to be regarded as 'temporary' until properly approved

All commanders in the *Volkssturm* were to be selected on the basis that they were "reliable and steadfast National Socialists, who, if at all possible, had gained military experience in frontline actions in the present war", and had proved themselves in a position of command.

The distinct emphasis on the 'committed' and 'reliable' National Socialist indicates the increasing mistrust the Party leaders had of the soldiers of the *Wehrmacht*. This had the consequence that initially it was often inexperienced young party functionaries who were placed in command positions within the *Volkssturm*, while older NCOs and officers with greater combat experience – up to the rank of *Oberst* and even of *General* – had to enlist in the ranks as ordinary *Volkssturmänner*. The problems which inevitably resulted from this procedure, however, soon made it necessary to make the principal criterion for selecting *Volkssturm* commanders their military suitability for the post. Even *Reichsleiter* Bormann, who was certainly by no means inclined to be kindly disposed to the *Wehrmacht*, and even if it was only in mid-February 1945, felt obliged to send a telegram (Appendix VII) to his *Gauleiters*, in which he stated that the prime consideration for selecting all unit commanders and the *Kreisstabsfuhrer* of the German *Volkssturm* was evidence that they possessed "the necessary military knowledge, and, if at all possible, frontline combat experience in the present war, but in any event that they have proved and distinguished themselves as military commanders in one of the two World Wars ... They are then to be selected, without taking any account of any position they may hold in the Party, within the State or within the economy, solely on the basis of their military suitability".

It may therefore be assumed that at least all those *Volkssturm* battalions which came to be deployed in combat were commanded by officers and NCOs who, because of their previous military career, possessed the military knowledge and experience required to carry out their duties.

Bormann had set 30 September 1944 as the deadline for the appointment of assistants to the *Gauleiters*. Because the *Volkssturm* was "to serve to reinforce the active forces of the *Wehrmacht*", and because Bormann assumed that every *Gau* "had at its disposal a suitable number of National Socialists who had proved their worth in frontline action", he had ordered that officers of the field army fit for frontline service should not be withdrawn in order to be reassigned to the *Volkssturm*. The available documents indicate that in several cases he turned down fellow-members of the Party who had been proposed to him as *Gaustabsführer*, because the proper place of such individuals was in the army in the field. The same standard principle applied to the selection of the *Kreisstabsführer* and all *Volkssturm* commanders.

In order to give officers discharged from the field army, insofar as these were fit for military service and "possessed the required political momentum", the opportunity "to assist in the formation of the German *Volkssturm*", on the instigation of Bormann, the chief of the *Heerespersonalamt* issued the following order at the beginning of October 1944:

> The *Heerespersonalamt* is at the present time in the process of discharging officers of all ranks who are no longer suitable to serve as unit commanders in the field army.
>
> Some of these officers, however, after their discharge, and appropriate labour service, may be able to provide useful service in the *Volkssturm*.
>
> The selection of these commanders will be carried out in accordance with the following guidelines:
>
> 1. The officers must be familiar with the new weapons being used in the present war.
>
> 2. They must have held unit command in the present war.
>
> 3. They must be physically fit enough to be able to serve in the field in the area near their place of residence.
>
> After their discharge from active military service, the names of these officers must be notified by the *Heerespersonalamt* to the appropriate *Gau* administration, giving details of the officers' names, the rank they have held, their date of birth, their civilian occupation, the highest gallantry award they hold, and in what specific military capacity they have served in the present war.

The *Gauleiters* were responsible for deciding what use to make, within the *Volkssturm* command structure, of retired generals who themselves were members of the *Volkssturm*. All cases in which it was decided that such individuals should not be assigned a command position had to be reported to *Reichsleiter* Bormann, giving details for the decision. All other retired officers were to be employed in the *Volkssturm* in a suitable capacity. It was the responsibility of the *Gauleiters* to decide what use to make of retired officers who were unsuitable for being appointed to command positions.

Consequently, while registration, staffing and command of the *Volkssturm* (which themselves were to a certain extent organised along peacetime lines) were the responsibility of the political organisation of the NSDAP, in his capacity as Commander of the Reserve Army, the *Reichsführer-SS* was responsible "for military organisation, training, armament and equipment", and also – on the instructions of Hitler – for all questions connected with "combat deployment".

But the detailed responsibilities of the *Reichsführer-SS*, and hence of his Chief of Staff and the Chief of Staff 's *Führungsstab Deutscher Volkssturm*, included the determination of appropriate strengths and levels of equipment for *Volkssturm* units, the preparation and issue of guidelines and appropriate instructions for training, the integrated management of the training process, the procurement, allocation and distributions of weapons, equipment and uniforms, and the procurement and distribution of pay books and armbands of standard pattern. In addition, the *Reichsführer-SS*, in his capacity as the Supreme Commander of the Reserve Army, had been assigned the right to call up *Volkssturm* units for "combat deployment". Responsibility for maintaining the continuous links which were necessary between the authorities responsible for the *Volkssturm* and the authorities of the field and reserve army similarly fell within the purview of the work of the *Fuhrungsstab Deutscher Volkssturm*.

The dualism in the development and the command of the German *Volkssturm* was without doubt intentional on the part of Hitler, because he did not want either Bormann or Himmler alone to benefit from the resultant influence and increase in personal power. Of course this dualism often led to friction and even to contradictory orders, although both authorities, Bormann and Himmler, had been instructed to issue all orders directed to the *Gauleiters*, and all other orders and instructions only "after reaching mutual agreement between themselves". By making the *Volkssturm* strongly dependent on the *Reichsführer-SS* in his capacity as Commander of the Reserve Army, Hitler doubtless hoped to make the process of arming and equipping, and also training the *Volkssturm* battalions, both easier and quicker.

The authorities responsible for the German *Volkssturm* were: the Leader of the Party Chancellery; the *Reichsführer-SS* as Commander of the Reserve Army; the *Gauleiters*; the *Kreisleiters*; the battalion commanders and the company commanders.

The Leader of the Party Chancellery, the *Reichsführer-SS* and also the *Gauleiters* and *Kreisleiters*, as has already been explained, exploited the range of tasks which had been assigned to their Chiefs of Staff to develop and to provide leadership for the *Volkssturm*. Their official titles were as follows: the Leader of the Party Chancellery, *Stabsführer* (Chief of Staff); the *Reichsfuhrer-SS* in his capacity as Commander of the Reserve Army, *Stabsführer* (Chief of Staff); the *Gauleiter, Gaustabsführer* (Chief of Staff, *Gau*); the *Kreisleiter, Kreisstabsführer* (Chief of Staff, *Kreis*).

All authorities responsible for the German *Volkssturm* carried notepaper and official seals of a standard pattern. The use of notepaper of other organisations in all circumstances related to the German *Volkssturm* was forbidden.

With the exception of that for individual units, the notepaper was pre-printed. The designation of the individual authorities was shown on the notepaper at the top left-hand corner in Latin script and Arabic numerals. Examples are:

a)   *die Oberste Führung* [The Supreme Command] (in the case of all documents to be signed jointly by the *Reichsfuhrer-SS* and the Leader of the Party Chancellery)

b)   *der Reichsführer-SS als BdE* (The *Reichsfuhrer-SS* in his capacity as Commander of the Reserve Army), *Stabsführer;*

c)   *Gau 29, der Gauleiter;*

d)   *Gau 19, Kreis Weilheim* (Weilheim District), *der Kreisleiter, Kreisstabsführer*

The official seals bore the national emblem, with the eagle facing to the left, and around this, in Latin script and Arabic numerals, the designation of the authority in question.

The 'Basic Principles of Command within the German *Volkssturm*' had been set out in a circular issued by the Supreme Command on 26 October 1944. There they were circulated to all *Volkssturm* commanders, and it is worth citing some extracts from them:

> The most precious asset belonging to our *Volk* has been entrusted into your hands. Always remember that. You will need all your strength of purpose to lead your men in the manner in which they should be led.

> Diligence can save lives. Therefore, above all else, work on improving your military skills. Bravery alone will not be enough.

> The responsibility which you have been given obliges you to provide truthful reports. Do not underplay anything, do not conceal anything, do not exaggerate anything.

> Never rest yourself until the last of your men has been found a billet. Never eat and drink anything which your men do not eat and drink too.

> Old people who have had a wide experience of life must be spoken to in a different way to young people. One encouraging word, and you will see for yourself how every man will make greater efforts to improve his performance.

> Encourage always and everywhere a healthy sense of responsibility. Every weapon, every object must be handled carefully, and this applies to captured weapons just as much as it does to your own weapons.

> Make use of every opportunity to increase love for our *Volk* and for our Fatherland. School your men in a passionate hatred for the enemy!

With regard to the costs arising in connection with the formation and running of the *Volkssturm*, in a telegram of 16 October 1944, the Reich Treasurer authorised the *Gau* Treasurers to meet these costs from the liquid assets available to their respective *Gaue*. The details of this arrangement were clarified in a telegram dated 27 October 1944, which (in somewhat abbreviated form) read:

> In accordance with the task assigned to the *Gauleiters* by authority of the decree of the *Führer* dated 25 September 1944, of forming and running the German *Volkssturm*, the costs associated with this management role of the party are to be met by the *Gau* Treasurers. These costs include:

> a)   The propaganda costs for the respective propaganda actions ordered by the Reich Propaganda Ministry, insofar as these costs are not centrally administered by the Propaganda Ministry and directly financed by myself;

> b)   Overheads arising from appeals and events in connection with the formation of the *Volkssturm*;

> c)   Costs for the cultural and political education of leaders and other members of the *Volkssturm* (pamphlets, booklets etc);

> d)   Overheads for running courses for officers and NCOs, including travel costs, expenses and subsistence;

> e)   Other overheads for rental of vehicles for transport etc.

> All other expenditure outside the above parameters connected with the deployment and the armament, equipment and clothing of the *Volkssturm* cannot be accepted by the NSDAP. Demands for payments of this kind passed on to the *Gau* Treasurers are to be declined, giving reference to Figure 6 of the *Führer* decree concerning the formation of the German *Volkssturm* dated 25 September 1944, in accordance with which the *Reichsführer-SS* as Commander of the Reserve Army is responsible for the provision of armament and equipment for the *Volkssturm*.

> In the same way any payments and obligations resulting from accidents which take place during service with the *Volkssturm* or during combat actions cannot be accepted as being the responsibility of the Party. Obligations regarding welfare and discipline are defined under Figure 4 of the same decree, in accordance with which the members of the German *Volkssturm* are, during the period of their service, classed as soldiers as defined under military law.[24]

It will be seen from the telegrams sent by the Reich Treasurer of the NSDAP, and quoted above, that the costs resulting from the tasks assigned to the *Reichsführer-SS* in his capacity as Commander of the Reserve Army, and in particular those costs associated with provision of armament or equipment or with combat deployment of the *Volkssturm*, were many times higher than the costs for which the Party itself was responsible.

Above: *Reichsleiter der Deutschen Arbeitsfront*, Robert Ley, visiting a *Volkssturm* unit in the late autumn of 1944. The unit's commander (on the left, with his back to the camera), is wearing a HJ fatigue jacket, woollen breeches with leather reinforcement, and a HJ leaders' peaked cap.
Bildarchiv Preußischer Kulturbesitz, Berlin

Right: Members of the Lower Silesian *Volkssturm* at a Party rally, 30 October 1944. Although all appear to be armed (quite possibly only for the duration of the rally!) there is no standardisation of dress. Some wear civilian clothes; Hitler Youth, Party and SA uniforms and headgear can also be seen.
Museum of Modern History, Ljubljana, Slovenia

CHAPTER FOUR

Military Organisation

As will be evident from what has been outlined above, and particularly from Appendix IV, Part IV, it was originally only intended to form *Volkssturm* (infantry) battalions, because the most urgent need seemed to be to reinforce the infantry strength of the Army in the field. For this reason, the organisation of the normal *Volkssturm* Battalion with staff, signals and pioneer sections, medical and dispatch rider sections, three companies of infantry and one heavy weapons company largely resembled the organisation of an Army infantry battalion.

But since the military organisation of units was to be directed in accordance with the District Organisation of the NSDAP – the integrity of the local organisation and, as far as possible, cell and block organisation were to be maintained – often it was necessary to take into account departures from these norms. As a result, there were *Volkssturm* battalions with only two, and some with four, rifle companies and also companies with three and four platoons, the platoons consisting of three or four sections. The sections had an average strength of one *Gruppenführer* and nine men.

All members of the *Volkssturm* were *Volkssturmsoldaten*. Corresponding to the organisation of individual units, the following ranks had been introduced:

a) *Volksturmmann*

b) *Gruppenführer*

c) *Zugführer*

d) *Kompanieführer*

e) *Battalionsführer*

As insignia of rank, the *Gruppenführer* wore a silver star, the *Zugführer* two stars, the *Kompanieführer* three stars and the *Battalionsführer* four stars of the same kind on two triangular collar patches which were to be produced in a makeshift fashion from black material measuring five by six centimetres.

The *Kreisstabsführer* wore the service insignia of a *Battalionsführer*. *Gaustabsführer* only had to wear the armband of the German *Volkssturm*. The same regulation applied to *Gauleiters* and *Kreisleiter*s in their capacity as *Volkssturm* commanders.

All *Volkssturmsoldaten*, serving in whatever capacity, had to put on the black white and red armband issued by the *Reichsführer-SS* in his capacity as Commander of the Reserve Army, bearing the inscription 'Deutscher *Volkssturm – Wehrmacht*'.

Units of the *Volkssturm* were assigned numbers in Arabic numerals corresponding to the appropriate Party identification number for the individual *Gau* (see Appendix VIII), the battalion number and the company number. Battalions were then sequentially numbered within each *Gau* and the companies within each battalion. The two or three figures were written together and separated by diagonal slashes. For example, the numerals 21/43/1 designated the first company of *Volkssturm* Battalion No. 43 of the *Gau* of Lower Silesia.

On documents, the designation of battalions and companies was shown at the top left-hand corner under the heading 'Deutscher *Volkssturm*', e.g.:

Deutscher *Volkssturm*
2/31/2

It very soon proved to be necessary to provide lorry companies for transport purposes for the *Stabsführer* in the office of the *Reichsführer-SS*, for the *Gaue* and also for the *Kreise*. Thus, as early as 14 October 1944, the *Stabsführer* in the office of the *Reichsführer-SS* ordered the formation of motorised *Volkssturm* transport squadrons within the respective *Gaue*, together with the repair and maintenance services required to support them. Generally the leaders of the motorised groups of the NSKK[25] within the individual *Gaue* were responsible for the formation and organisation of these motorised transport squadrons. The NSKK provided its own mechanical specialists as officers, NCOs and other ranks for these transport sections. To serve as vehicles, civilian vehicles were selected and temporarily commandeered to carry out transport duties for the *Volkssturm*. The number and the strength of the transport sections depended on local circumstances.

The NSKK was also responsible for selecting and forming the dispatch rider section within each *Volkssturm* Battalion, consisting of one leader and four men.

The medical service within the *Volkssturm* was regulated by the Party Chancellery Directive 393/44 issued on 9 November 1944 in agreement with the *Reichsfuhrer-SS*. Its tasks included carrying out medical examinations on enlistment and the general medical care of the *Volkssturmsoldaten*, and also the management and deployment of medical personnel, medical materials and ambulance transport.

In agreement with the *Reichgesundheitsführer für Volksgesundheit* (Reich Director of Public Health), a *leitender Arzt des Deutschen Volkssturms* (Medical Director for the German *Volkssturm*) joined the staff of the *Stabsführer* in the office of the *Reichsfuhrer-SS*. The *Gauleiters* used the services of the *Gauamtsleiter für Volksgesundheit* (*Gau* Directors of Public Health) who were responsible for meeting the provisions of the tasks assigned to them in accordance with the directives of the Party and of the German Red Cross. The German Red Cross was responsible for providing the equipment for the medical services within the German *Volkssturm*. The *Wehrmacht* was to supply any additional materials etc which could not be provided from within the stocks of the German Red Cross or of the Party.

If possible, a Medical Officer was to be assigned to every *Volkssturm* Battalion. This officer, or a local doctor appointed for the purpose, was responsible for providing the medical service. On registration, medical examinations were only carried out on those men who did not feel fit to carry out the duties required for the draft to which they were assigned. For the first and second levies, everyone was considered fit who was able to carry and use weapons and carry out short marches. The general principle was that a man who was capable of working was also capable of bearing arms.

At least one ranking medical officer was to be assigned to every battalion and every company. To carry out transport of the sick and wounded, the medical officers had to use the arrangements provided by the German Red Cross, the *Volkssturm* transport squadrons and, in actual combat situations, the transport services of the *Wehrmacht*. The *Volkssturm* had no medical services of its own within the lines of communications.

All personnel serving in the medical services of the *Volkssturm* had to wear the Red Cross armband on their upper left arm. In addition to this, the battalion medical officer wore three stars and an Aesculapian staff, and the subordinate medical personnel wore one star.

One curious fact should be mentioned, namely that the *Gauleiter* of East Prussia, Koch, formed a *Volkssturm* night fighter squadron from men from the NSFK[26] who were liable for service in the *Volkssturm*, and using available training and sports aircraft. 2/*Nahaufklärungsgruppe 4* of the *Luftwaffe* stationed in East Prussia provided assistance in setting up and training this squadron. Whether this *Volkssturm* nightfighter squadron ever actually saw action of the kind seen by similar Russian nightfighter units is not known, but it cannot be regarded as likely due to the catastrophic shortage of fuel.

Above: Led by two members of the SA, men called up for service in the *Volkssturm* march to their barracks somewhere in 'the East' of Germany, October 1944.
Museum of Modern History, Ljubljana, Slovenia

Left: *Volkssturm* members report for duty somewhere in the Rhineland, October 1944. The NCO issuing uniforms is a *Feuerwerker* or ordnance technician, as denoted by his specialist badge worn on the lower right sleeve (a yellow 'F' in gothic script on a dark blue-green field).
Museum of Modern History, Ljubljana, Slovenia

Members of the East Prussian *Volkssturm* receive training in the field, October 1944.
Museum of Modern History, Ljubljana, Slovenia

Members of the *Volkssturm* undertake target practise in an unknown location, 1945. Interestingly, they have been issued with the black *Schutzmannschaft* uniform, normally issued to security police units in the East. This was originally the black uniform of the *Allgemeine SS*, with SS insignia removed and alterations made to the collar and tunic. They are armed with Italian Mannlicher Carcano M1891 rifles and wear Italian carbine ammunition bandoliers. **Bildarchiv Preußischer Kulturbesitz, Berlin**

CHAPTER FIVE

Registration and Recruitment

Registration and recruitment for the *Volkssturm* were regulated by the instructions for implementation issued by the Party Chancellery on 27 September, 12 October, and 3 November 1944 (Appendices III, IV and V).

By means of registration, all men of the relevant age groups from 16 to 60 years old who were fit for military service and not currently serving in the military were assigned for service in the *Volkssturm*. Voluntary enlistment below and above the prescribed age groups was allowed. Recruitment had to take account of the men's duties associated with armaments, food, transport and communications services, and also administrative services, which would have the greatest effect on the war effort.

The registration of men called up for service was first carried out by the local NSDAP authorities on the basis of lists drawn up in their places of residence. The registration process was to make use of all available documentation such as the NSDAP membership index and the indexes of local registry offices, food agencies, and other resources.

The registration lists had to provide details of name, Christian name, date of birth, place of residence, telephone number, place of work, current profession and any special professional qualifications, membership and/or association with the NSDAP, its subsidiary organisations and linked associations, membership of other organisations (German Red Cross, *Technische Nothilfe*, and others), military service, weapons experience, war experience, decorations, and military rank last held.

On registration parades the men being called up were assigned to different levies corresponding to their readiness for deployment and their civilian occupation. Men who were physically unfit were exempted.

The *Volkssturm* units were formed without taking any account of whether those liable for service in the *Volkssturm* were members of the NSDAP, its subsidiary sections or other organisations. Specialist and professional qualifications were to be taken into account in assigning men to specific duties. As a basic principle, units of the Party or associated organisations were not to be transferred *en bloc* into the *Volkssturm*. Only special units of Party or other organisations could be transferred *en bloc* into the German *Volkssturm* in accordance with the requirements of the military instructions issued by the *Reichsfuhrer-SS* with regard to carrying out special duties. Thus, for example, members of the general emergency services often formed the pioneer detachments of *Volkssturm* battalions.

When the men had been registered and assigned, they were drafted to serve in the individual *Volkssturm* units by their company and battalion commanders. They were issued by the companies with a paybook, with the issue of the paybook formally designating them as *Volkssturmsoldaten*.

As has already been mentioned, membership of the *Volkssturm* lapsed when an individual was called up for service in the *Wehrmacht*. Membership of the *Volkssturm* was not permitted to interfere with or delay the drafting of an individual into the *Wehrmacht*.

Each *Volkssturmsoldat* swore an oath which ran as follows:

I swear before God this sacred oath, to give absolute loyalty and obedience to the *Führer* of the Greater German Reich, Adolf Hitler.

I swear that I shall fight bravely for my homeland, and rather die than surrender the freedom and thus the social future of my *Volk*.

The *Volkssturm* was composed of four levies:

The first levy included all men with dates of birth between the years 1924 and 1884 who were fit for combat. These could be liable for *Volkssturm* service for an unlimited or for a near limited period, to the extent that this service did not endanger essential services on the home front.

The average age of the men in this levy was 52.

Most of them had served in the First World War. *Volkssturm* battalions from this levy could be used within the whole area of their home *Gau* and, if required, also outside their home *Gau*. For example, guard duties on frontier posts were only provided by *Volkssturm* battalions from the first levy.

The second levy included all men born between the years 1924 and 1884 who were fit for combat, but who, because of their civilian employment in essential services, were to remain in their posts on the home front until the enemy actually approached, and for this reason could not be called up in the first levy.

The men called up in this levy were predominantly men exempted from military service. Because they were aged between 25 and 50 years old, they were physically fitter than the men called up in the first levy. The majority of these men had not yet served in the military, and a minority had only seen military service after 1935 or during the war. By far the largest number of all men liable for service in the *Volkssturm* belonged to the second levy. *Volkssturm* battalions from the second levy could only be deployed in combat if the enemy was actually standing 'at the gates', and therefore could only be deployed on a local basis. Generally, deployment on a local basis meant deployment within an individual district or *Kreis*.

Men were called up into the first and second levies of the *Volkssturm* by the *Gauleiters*, who charged the *Kreisleiters* and the *Ortsgruppenleiters* with the responsibility for implementing the actual procedures.

Men were assigned to the second levy by means of a standard *Zuteilungskarte* (assignment card). This *Z-Karte* had to provide the following information: name, Christian name, date of birth, place of residence, place of work, current profession and any special professional qualifications, as well as the responsible NSDAP *Ortsgruppe*. The individual civilian services, i.e. the sectors of the economy, transport, and local administrative and Party authorities which were considered to be essential to the war effort had to present these *Z-Karten* to the *Kreiskommission* responsible for their individual district, the *Kreiskommission* having been set up in August 1944 to ensure that all services were mobilised for total war. Once the *Z-Karten* were approved, the respective *Kreiskommission* passed them to the local *Ortsgruppenleiter*, or district party officials, responsible for recruitment to the *Volkssturm*, who then included the individuals in question in the second levy.

Men within the second levy whose professional or local obligations did not allow them to take regular part in the training exercises for their local *Volkssturm* unit were assembled into *betriebsgebundene*, or employment-related, units (platoons, companies, battalions) within the framework of their local units. Men from outside the industries and economic sectors in question could also be assigned to such units. For instance, the members of the Reich chancellery in Berlin were brought together into a *betriebsgebundene Volkssturm* unit.

Men within the second levy whose employment involved them regularly travelling outside their place of residence, such as, for example, the railway police, were recruited into *betriebseigene*, or employment-based, units.

Agreements, often only reached after lengthy negotiations with the numerous individual civilian services within the economy and the responsible administrative authorities, determined which groups within their particular organisations should be included in the first levy, and which in the second levy. The civilian authorities with which such agreements were reached and which were recorded in *Anordnungen* (Directives: prefixed 'A.') of the Party Chancellery were:

a) the Research Department of the Reich Aviation Ministry and its subordinate authorities (A. 390/44 dated 7.11.44);

b) the transport carriers (railways/*Reichsbahn*, tramways, internal waterways, waterways administration) (A. 387/44 dated 8.11.44);

c) the industrial sectors of the economy under the control of the Reich Minister for Armaments and War Production (A. 408/44 dated 20.11.44);

d) the *Reichspost* (postal and communications services) (A. 407/44 dated 20.11.44);

e) the Head of the *Oberkommando der Wehrmacht* (*Wehrmacht* Supreme Command) in connection with the civilian employees of the *Wehrmacht* (A. 428/44 dated 28.11.44);

f) the *Reichsfinanzverwaltung* (Reich financial administrative authorities) (A. 428/44 dated 2.12.44);

g) the civil service and local government administration (A. 429/44 dated 2.12.44);

h) the *Reichversicherungsverwaltung* (Reich Insurance authorities), *Reichsversorgungsverwaltung* (Reich Food and Supply Administration), and *Gewerbeaufsichtsverwaltung* (commercial supervisory authorities) (A. 430/44 dated 2.12.44);

i)   the *Reichsjustizverwaltung* (Reich judicial authorities) (A. 431/44 dated 2.12.44);

j)   the *Reichforstverwaltung* (Reich Forestry Authority) (A. 432/44 dated 2.12.44);

k)   the agricultural and food industries and agricultural administration (A. 424/44 dated 4.12.44);

l)   the NSDAP (A. 427/44 dated 4.12.44);

m)   special cases (stateless persons, ethnic lists, etc.) (A. 443/44 dated 9.12.44);

n)   the civilian police (A. 3/45 dated 26.1.45);

o)   the *Deutsche Reichsbank* (A. 21/45 dated 6.2.45);

p)   the highways authorities and the *Reichsautobahn* (A. 19/45 dated 6.2.45);

q)   *Deutsche Lufthansa A. G.* [civilian airline] (A. 24/45 dated 13.2.45);

r)   the news services (A. 25/45 dated 13.2.45);

s)   skilled orthopaedic personnel (A. 27/45 dated 20.2.45);

t)   industrial plant protection and air raid protection services and auxiliary services associated with guarding prisoners of war (A. 35/45 dated 2.3.45);

u)   hospitals and clinics (A. 38/45 dated 9.3.45).

Appendix IX contains examples of the content of such agreements in the form of the agreements which were reached with the *Deutsche Reichspost*, the operational sectors of the economy under the control of the *Reichsminister* for Armaments and War Production, with the *Reichsführer-SS* in his capacity as head of the civilian police, and with the agricultural and food industries.

The negotiations with the many civilian authorities lasted from the beginning of November 1944 until the beginning of March 1945. It was therefore not possible before the war ended to enlist all those liable for service in the *Volkssturm* into formations formed within the framework of the first and second levies. All recruitment parades and also training, insofar as it was actually possible to carry it out (of which more will be said later), were therefore carried out jointly. If battalions were to be called up for some kind of service which would last for a longer period, then such battalions had to be specifically formed for that purpose. It goes without saying that in such units at first there was little cohesion and *esprit de corps*, a shortcoming which often led to disasters in individual cases. The planned designation of the *Volkssturm* battalions in accordance with the guidelines issued also encountered problems for the same reasons, something which today makes it difficult for historians and for those interested in finding out what became of many individual units and their members to obtain information.

The third levy of the German *Volkssturm* included men with dates of birth between 1928 and 1925, insofar as these young men were not already on active military service.

In accordance with the third schedule of instructions on the Decree of the *Führer* concerning the formation of the German *Volkssturm* dated 27 October, 1944, men with dates of birth in 1928 were to receive military training until 31 March, 1945 in the defence training camps of the Hitler Youth and in the *Reichsarbeitsdienst*.[27] The training was carried out in accordance with instructions issued by the *Reichsführer-SS* in his capacity as Commander of the Reserve Army.

Individuals with dates of birth in 1928 were immediately registered from the Hitler Youth and assigned to special training. In association with this training, they were placed at the disposal of the *Reichsarbeitsdienst*, which, for its part, on 20 November, 1944 had to begin to transfer to the *Wehrmacht* the first individuals with dates of birth in 1928.

Those individuals with dates of birth between 1925 and 1928 who were found to be unfit similarly received their training at the same time as the registration of those with dates of birth in 1928, in the defence training camps of the Hitler Youth and the *Reichsarbeitsdienst*. It was intended that the procedure should operate in such a way as to avoid gaps in the training process and to ensure that individuals were directly transferred from the *Reichsarbeitsdienst* to the *Wehrmacht*.

Those with dates of birth between 1925 and 1928 who were exempted from service in the *Wehrmacht* were enlisted in the local units of the *Volkssturm*.

With the issue of Party Chancellery Directive 29/45 on 27 February 1945, all those men with dates of birth in 1929 were also enlisted into the German *Volkssturm*. Registration and training had to be carried out according to the provisions of the implementation instructions associated with the Fuhrer decree of 27 October 1944.[28]

The senior command of the *Volkssturm* had not contemplated deploying any units of the Hitler Youth in actual combat. Even Directive 36/45, issued by the Party Chancellery as late as 7 March 1945, stated that men with dates of birth in 1928 and earlier and serving in the *Volkssturm* were not to be deployed in combat situations, even on a voluntary basis. The only exceptions to this were 'special missions' which the *Führer* himself had ordered.

Thus, when, in the inferno of the last weeks of the war, units of the Hitler Youth came to be used in combat, it must have been on the basis of such 'special missions', or have been as the result of measures agreed in situations of extreme urgency between subordinate authorities of the *Wehrmacht* and the Party. Here, we should remember with special gratitude the gallant actions of these young German men.

An individual's membership of the *Volkssturm* lapsed when they were called up for service with the *Reichsarbeitsdienst*. If circumstances required units of the *Reichsarbeitsdienst* to be deployed with the *Wehrmacht*, this took place "within the framework of the German *Volkssturm* on the orders of the *Reichsfuhrer-SS* in his capacity as Commander of the Reserve Army and in agreement with the Reich Labour leader".

The fourth levy of the German *Volkssturm* included all those men liable for service with the *Volkssturm* who were not fit for armed combat, but could still be used for guard and security duties. In cases where there was doubt about the degree of fitness of men liable for service in the *Volkssturm*, doctors appointed by the *Kreisleiters* had to decide – without taking any account of other medical evidence.

As will be clear from what has been outlined above, the units of the German *Volkssturm* were formed in battalions corresponding to the 1st, the 2nd, the 3rd, and the 4th levies. After units had been formed, *Volkssturmsoldaten* from different levies could no longer belong to one and the same battalion.

The *Landwacht* and the *Stadtwacht* (organisations which assisted the *Gendarmerie* and the *Schutzpolizei*), the reorganisation of which had already been announced in the "Second schedule of instructions for implementation in association with the *Führer* Decree concerning the formation of the German *Volkssturm* of 12 October 1944", were dissolved in January 1945. Their members thereby became unrestrictedly available for service in the German *Volkssturm*. In accordance with the directives of 26 January 1945 concerning the "Recruitment of members of the civilian police into the German *Volkssturm*" (Appendix VI), members of the *Volkssturm*, especially those who had previously been members of the *Landwacht*, could carry out tasks which had previously been carried out by the *Landwacht*. The previous *Landwacht* posts were taken over by the *Volkssturm* as *Volkssturmposten*. To carry out the duties previously undertaken by the *Stadtwacht*, the required units were to be provided by the *Volkssturm* to the local commanders of the *Schutzpolizei* when required, and if requested to the *Kreisstabsführer*, or in the cases of urban *Gaue*, to the *Gaustabsführer*.

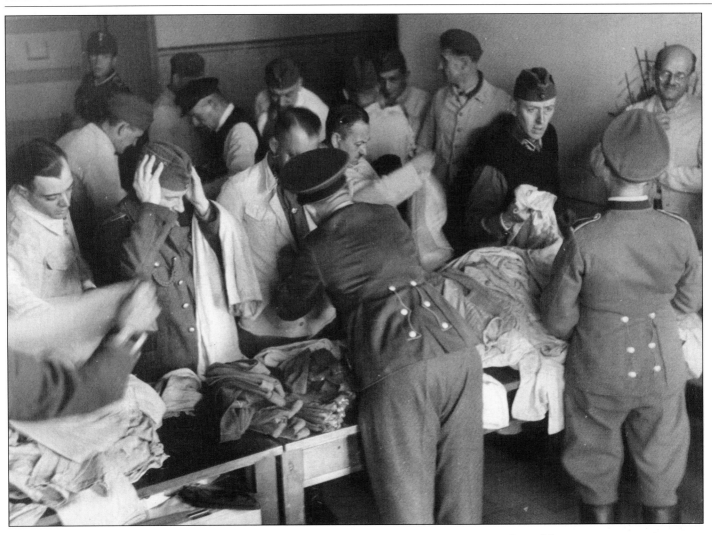

New members of the *Volkssturm* are issued with clothing at a barracks, 23 October 1944. **Bundesarchiv 146/74/120-21A**

Members of the *Volkssturm* are sworn-in, East Prussia, 12 November 1944. Similar ceremonies took place all across Germany on this day. **Bundesarchiv 146/78/87/24**

Providing an excellent opportunity for propaganda photos to be taken, units of the Berlin *Volkssturm* march past Goebbels during the day of oath-taking ceremonies, 12 November 1944. This date was deliberately chosen as the Sunday following the anniversary of the 'Beer Hall *Putsch*' of 9 November 1923. The image of such a well-armed body of men was an illusion, however, as following the parades the *Volkssturm* had to hand these weapons back! **Bundesarchiv 146/71/33/15**

Some of the newly-formed Berlin *Volkssturm* listen to a speech by Goebbels during the nationwide day of oath-taking, Sunday 12 November 1944. The banner hung upon the building proclaims 'The *Volkssturm* fights for the life and freedom of Greater Germany!' **Museum of Modern History, Ljubljana, Slovenia**

Another shot of the same Berlin rally, 12 November 1944. The men in the foreground may well be members of the RLB (*Reichsluftschutzbund* or Reich Air Protection League) drafted into the *Volkssturm*; they wear the distinctive M1944 RLB helmet and have been issued with gasmasks **Museum of Modern History, Ljubljana, Slovenia**

CHAPTER SIX

Armament and Equipment

Responsibility for arming and equipping the *Volkssturm* had been transferred to the *Reichsführer-SS*, in his capacity as Supreme Commander of the Reserve Army, by the *Führer* decree of 25 September 1944. Both when this decree was announced and also later when other announcements and appeals were made in the press and on the radio, leading and less prominent Party senior officials had always stressed that the *Volkssturm* would only be equipped with the best and newest weapons.

The list compiled by the Chief of Staff in the office of the *Reichsführer-SS*, which is attached as Appendix X, gives an overall outline of the quantity of weapons which were available for the German men who were liable for service in the *Volkssturm*, at least 6 million of them, and for the approximately 6,700 battalions of the first and second levies. This list indicates the increasingly smaller numbers of German weapons – rifles, machine guns, machine pistols and pistols – which at the end of 1944 were in the possession of the Party and its subsidiary organisations and which could be drawn upon to arm the *Volkssturm* units.

During the negotiations which were initiated immediately after 25 September 1944 between the Chief of Staff at in the office of the *Reichsführer*-SS and the responsible authorities within the *Wehrmacht* (the *Generalstab des Heeres* and the *Allgemeines Heeresamt*) and within the department of the *Reichsminister* for Armaments and War Production, it became clear that that the shortage of weapons and war equipment of all kinds was extraordinarily large and that the production figures for weapons were unusually worrying. Thus, for example, in the autumn of 1944 a total of only 200,000 rifles of the 98 K variety was being produced, while the *Wehrmacht*, as a result of the unusual increase in losses of weapons, required over 300,000 new rifles per month. From 1 June 1944 to 1 March 1945, that is, within a period of nine months, no fewer than 3½ million rifles were lost, according to a summary in the *Wehrmacht* General Staff war diary.

As a result of these negotiations it became clear that it was no longer possible to increase rifle production to over 200,000 rifles per month, and therefore that any divergence into producing rifles for the *Volkssturm* was unsustainable. The only solution was to design and manufacture a simplified rifle which would save on materials and would largely consist of pressed metal components, the production of which would also not have to hinder production capacity for the 98 K rifle.

As early as 5 November, 1944, seven firms made to Hitler presentations of nine different models of the *Volksgewehr* (People's Rifle), comprising single loading, multiple loading, and self-loading versions. Since none of these models was completely satisfactory, a new model was constructed by the firm of Carl Walther in Zella-Mehlis, and put into production at the same time as a simplified *Volksmaschinenpistole* (People's Machine Pistol), which was based on the design of the English Sten machine pistol. The letter written on 8 December 1944 by the "Main Committee on Weapons" in the Ministry of Armaments and War Production, which initiated the production of these two weapons under the direction of a managing firm and on a decentralised basis throughout the Reich, is so interesting that it is included among the appendices as Appendix XI.[29]

It was planned that these weapons should be produced at the rate of up to 150,000 per month. Since the most difficult problem was the production of the gun barrels, to ensure that production achieved a high rate as soon as possible, the Chief of Supplies in the *Wehrmacht* General Staff authorised the release of 245,000 gun barrels from the Luftwaffe machine guns models 15, 17 and 18, "because the current stock of reserve gun barrels for these weapons appeared to be too high". To fit the *Volksgewehr*, these gun barrels only had to be machine-turned on the outside. A little later another 180,000 reserve gun barrels for other models of machine gun were released, which with relatively minor modifications could similarly be used for the *Volksgewehr*.

On the basis of local circumstances and on the initiative of individual *Gauleiters*, a few more other types of *Volksgewehr* were produced in smaller quantities, for example Steyr, Spreewerk and Rheinmetall models.

On 27 November 1944 *Reichsleiter* Bormann asked all *Gauleiters* to support *Reichsminister* Speer in the implementation of the programme for production of a *Volksgewehr* for the *Volkssturm* with all means at their disposal. "In the *Gaue*", he urged, "all possibilities for rapid production of the *Volksgewehr* must be fully investigated".[30]

On 10 February 1945, the first 500 Walther models of the *Volksgewehr* were ready for collection in Zella-Mehlis. In accordance with a note from *Gauleiter* Eigruber to the Reichsminister for Armaments and War Production dated 25 January 1945, with effect from 26 January, 650 Steyr *Volkskarabiner* were being completed daily, and in February it was expected that 15,000 of these weapons would be produced. "*Gauleiter* Bracht", the letter stated, "will receive the first of these weapons" for Breslau. But the total number of the *Volksgewehr* which were eventually produced by the end of the war is no easier to determine than the local *Gaue* of the individual *Volkssturm* units which were equipped with such weapons.

Other war material which was ordered for the *Volkssturm* included splinter grenades, glass mines, disposable flamethrowers, and, last but not least, great quantities of the *Panzerfaust* anti-tank projectile.

With regard to the organisation of this process, on 30 November 1944, in a meeting at the offices of the Chief of the Armaments Staff, *Hauptdienstleiter* Saur, it had been established that *SS-Obergruppenführer* Berger, as Chief of Staff for the *Reichsführer-SS*, was to place all weapons orders for the *Volkssturm* directly with the Main Committee on Weapons, and that he alone would be responsible for the management of all weapons and equipment destined for the *Volkssturm*. Even weapons which were to be produced on the initiative of the *Gauleiters* in individual *Gaue* were to be reported to him for record purposes. In his capacity as Chief of Staff for the *Volkssturm*, on 2 December 1944, Berger appointed *Generaldirektor* Purucker of Deutsche Werke A. G. as his representative responsible for the armament and equipment of the *Volkssturm*. At the same time, Purucker was appointed as a member of the Armaments Staff by *Hauptdienstleiter* Saur, to enable him to carry out this responsibility.

Because of the difficult weapons situation, and because the most urgent priority seemed to be to prevent the Russians from advancing into the interior of Germany, *SS-Obergruppenführer* Berger, in his capacity as Chief of Staff of the *Volkssturm*, had expressly urged all weapons which were currently in the hands of the Party and its subsidiary organisations, and all weapons for which deliveries were expected, to be passed over to the *Gaue* located along the borders of Germany, with special emphasis on those in the East. In this way, he said, there would, for the foreseeable future, be at least a certain number of *Volkssturm* battalions ready for combat in the *Gaue* along Germany's eastern borders.

But the Party Chancellery, and probably also Hitler himself, did not agree with this proposal. Rather, it was decided that in planning the allocation of weapons, equal account had to be taken of the needs of all *Gaue*, including those within the interior of Germany. But the reasons given for rejecting Berger's proposal were that in all *Gaue* weapons needed to be available for training purposes. In addition, evidently misjudging the actual circumstances then prevailing, it was expected that the appeals made to the male civilian population would have a good psychological effect on the fighting spirit of the entire population. The possibility or necessity of any engagement of the *Volkssturm* in actual combat had apparently not been considered.

In order to be able to make at least some attempt at meeting the extensive demands for weapons made by the *Gaue* as a result of this decision, and to bridge the time interval before rifles and machine pistols became available through the *Volkssturm* weapons production programme, requests for weapons were submitted to the *Allgemeine Heeresamt, Stab Ib*, and to the Quartermaster-General's Department. But in all the discussions which took place it became abundantly clear that there was no question of it being initially possible to equip the *Volkssturm* from *Wehrmacht* weapons stocks. At best, consideration might be given to equipping those *Volkssturm* battalions which were to be deployed in combat. On the other hand, responsibility for supplying units of the *Volkssturm* called up for combat duties fell to the Field Army.

These negotiations resulted in the issue of the "Directives for Supply of the *Volkssturm*" by the Quartermaster-General on 12 December 1944 under Abt. I No. I/30630/44 geh. Extracts from these directives read as follows:

> The equipment and supply of the *Volkssturm* is essentially the responsibility of the Party. In this connection, as a result of shortages in this sixth year of the war, considerable difficulties will arise which must be resolved with all available means. It is the responsibility of all Army authorities to provide support without any petty-minded bureaucratic considerations. Questions of precise responsibility should play no part in this. In the final analysis, it is in the interest of the Field Army that the *Volkssturm* is well equipped.
>
> In combat situations, the *Volkssturm* will be supplied by the *Wehrmacht* in the field. The overriding principle in this is that in particularly unfavourable combat circumstances, National Socialist energy and comradeship must ensure that preference is given to providing appropriate supplies to the men of the *Volkssturm* who are actually engaged in combat.
>
> Once they are ordered into action with the *Wehrmacht* in the field, responsibility for supplying the *Volkssturm*

battalions shall fall to the appropriate the *Wehrmacht* command authorities, and *Volkssturm* units will be supplied in the same way as units of the *Wehrmacht* in all areas.[31]

Certainly, if the Quartermaster-General was under the impression that it was the responsibility of the Party in the first instance for equipping the *Volkssturm*, then he was mistaken. Under the provisions of the *Führer* decree of 25 September 1944, the *Reichsführer-SS*, in his capacity as Commander of the Reserve Army, was responsible for arming and equipping the *Volkssturm*, and in accordance with the first directives for implementation associated with this *Führer* decree, armament for the *Volkssturm* was to be provided through the subordinate authorities of the *Reichsführer-SS* in his capacity as Commander of the Reserve Army, that is, in the final analysis, by the Army itself.

Thus, the *Allgemeine Heeresamt*, as the authority directly subordinate to the Commander of the Reserve Army, could not entirely ignore the urgent request for weapons for the *Volkssturm*. He agreed to assign a certain quantity of weapons to the *Volkssturm* from current weapons production for the months of December 1944 and January 1945. As a result of this, by the end of January the following numbers of weapons were delivered: 13,000 models of the 98K carbine, 1,000 models of the MG 42 machine gun, 1,243 medium mortars, 2,000 grenade launchers and 100,000 *Panzerfäuste*.

On 23 November 1944, the Reich Treasurer of the NSDAP had authorised the release of of items of equipment from the stocks of the Party, the SA and the NSKK for use by the *Volkssturm*. Appendix X contains numerous items of reference material relating to this. In addition, the Chief of Staff of the *Reichsführer-SS* was able to release approximately 25,000 additional models of the 98 rifle and the 98 K carbine from the stocks of the police, the former border security service and other organisations such as the postal security service, and from secondary stocks held by industry, and to allocate them to the *Gaue* by the end of the year.

Thus, when on 12 January 1945 the large-scale Soviet attacks began and on 14 January the entire *Volkssturm* within Eastern Germany was called up for deployment alongside the *Wehrmacht* on the request of the Army Chief of General Staff, the relatively few German weapons which were actually in the hands of the *Volkssturm* were distributed throughout all 42 *Gaue* within the Reich and the General Government of Poland. The result of this was that the majority of the countless *Volkssturm* battalions which had been called up for service had to go into action armed with weapons from captured stocks which were already available to the *Gauleiters* or which had been assigned expressly for this purpose by *Stab Ib* of the *Allgemeine Heeresamt*. Overall, the stocks of ammunition for these weapons were so small, that often only 10 rounds per rifle could be issued. These captured foreign weapons mostly consisted of Italian carbines which were difficult to use in the field, and for which, in any event, there was little ammunition available. The original plan to adapt the available 800,000 Italian carbines to take standard cartridges had to be abandoned.[32]

Since there was an even greater shortage of weapons suitable for the heavy weapons companies within the *Volkssturm* battalions, and since there were no anti-tank weapons at all apart from the *Panzerfaust*, a number of these companies were equipped each with four captured guns of Soviet manufacture. It was intended that these weapons would, as the *Führer* decree put it, be "adequate to set up to provide anti-tank defences on the approaches to towns and villages". But even for these guns, the available stocks of ammunition were too small.

The rate of supply of the *Panzerfaust* was relatively good. But these weapons could nevertheless not be used to the greatest effect, because generally there was not sufficient time and opportunity to provide suitable specialist training. In addition to this, the older members of the *Volkssturm* – unlike the Hitler Youth – proved not to be particularly suitable for close combat with armour.

When, at the beginning of March 1945, it was reported to Hitler that in the past nine months almost 400,000 rifles per month had been lost, and that units of the Field Army were suffering shortages of rifles and other weapons, he gave orders for all weapons of the *Volkssturm* suitable for use in the field, plus the associated stocks of ammunition, to be handed over to the *Wehrmacht*. The introduction to the directives which Bormann issued (under the top-secret rubric of "*Geheime Reichssache*") on 11 March 1945, to implement this decision by Hitler, reads: "So long as *Wehrmacht* units in the field and currently under formation are suffering shortages of necessary armament, units of the *Volkssturm* must not under any circumstances be supplied with weapons which are suitable for use in the field. The procedure which has been followed hitherto has resulted in some of the weapons which are urgently required being removed from the front line". The only exceptions to this directive for the surrender of weapons were those units of the *Volkssturm* which were deployed under the command of the *Wehrmacht*, and the weapons specifically required for the defence of NSDAP installations and authorities.[33]

Because, "on the basis of the procedure which had been followed hitherto", the Chief of Staff of the *Reichsführer-SS* had intended urgently required weapons to be withdrawn from the front, he had planned to make the few German weapons which could be obtained available to the *Gaue* along the eastern borders of Germany and not to those in the interior of Germany. From this point, the failure of this intention made itself felt. For the rest, after the Soviet offensive had begun on 12 January 1945, weapons suitable for use in the field had only been delivered to *Volkssturm* units whose home districts were in the East and which were to be deployed there in support of the *Wehrmacht*.

If the *Führer* decree had resulted in all the men of the *Volkssturm* being released from their service after surrendering their German weapons to the *Wehrmacht* and all *Volkssturm* battalions equipped with weapons suitable for use in the field being relieved from their service on the front, then it would have served a good purpose. The *Volkssturm* leadership, in both East and West, had already for a long time been making unremitting, if vain, efforts to get their battalions out of the long term active service which was evidently failing by allowing *Wehrmacht* units to take over front line positions.

But the *Führer's* order was based on the completely mistaken assumption that the *Volkssturm* based in the interior of Germany still had stocks of weapons which would weigh favourably in the balance. In actual fact, all the weapons which the *Volkssturm* did possess and which were suitable for use in the field were in the hands of those units which were already deployed within the framework of the *Wehrmacht* or had been requested by the *Wehrmacht* command authorities to provide support for the *Wehrmacht*. The deployment of the *Volkssturm* in Austrian border positions described elsewhere in this book is just one example of many of this fact.

Accordingly, this *Führer* decree did not produce any significant results. Neither the old *Volkssturmsoldaten* nor the *Volkssturm* battalions which were equipped with weapons suitable for use in the field were released from their long-term deployment within the *Wehrmacht*. The front required men just as much as it required weapons.

There were also no longer any field kitchens to supply the *Volkssturm* battalions. Therefore the units called up in support of the *Wehrmacht* had to make do with makeshift boilers mounted on agricultural vehicles or with locally-based cooking facilities behind the front lines. Instead of normal military baggage train vehicles, which of course were also no longer being delivered, vehicles and horses were commandeered from the agricultural sector of the economy to serve the needs of the *Volkssturm*.

Because, in this the sixth year of the war, it was no longer possible to supply uniform clothing and equipment, in accordance with the instructions for implementation associated with the *Führer* decree of 12 October, 1944, "all *Volkssturmsoldaten*, irrespective of rank, were to supply their own uniforms and equipment. Any kind of uniform or weatherproof sports and work closing is suitable for use as clothing in this regard. Stout footwear and overcoats are particularly important. Equipment must be restricted to absolute essentials. It should include, even if only on a makeshift basis, a back pack, cooking utensils, haversack, water bottle, drinking cup and cutlery". (Appendix IV).

Because civilian clothing and makeshift equipment, though they were perhaps just about suitable for training purposes, were completely unsuitable for use in combat, the Party and its subsidiary organisations were expected to place at the disposal of the *Volkssturm* any available stocks of uniforms and items of equipment. Where these stocks were not sufficient, it was necessary to have recourse to the stocks of uniforms and items of equipment which had been collected as a result of the *Nachbarschaftshilfe* and *Volksopfer* voluntary civilian collection schemes. All Party uniforms were to be dyed field grey before being used in any combat situations. There were sufficient stocks of M44 dye to achieve this, and the necessary production capacity.

In this way it was possible to provide all battalions called up for service in support of the *Wehrmacht* with uniforms, even if the uniforms were those of the Party, the SA, the SS, and the NSKK. In actual deployment in the field, the supply system of the Field Army could then, more or less quickly, replace these with field grey uniforms where these were in fact lacking. Footwear presented the biggest problem. For this reason, many *Volkssturmsoldaten* had initially to go into action in boots which were in poor condition or unwearable and often even only in ordinary shoes. Even with the support of the Field Army supply services, it generally took a long time to relieve this supply bottleneck.

Volkssturmmänner in Berlin are issued with Mannlicher M95 rifles, Berlin, October 1944. They wear the early issue armband, white with black printing. **Bundesarchiv 146/74/120/23A**

The Berlin *Volkssturm* are issued with weapons, 2 November 1944. A posed shot for propaganda, the weapons would have been taken away from the men again once the photographer left! The weapons appear to be Italian 7.35mm M38 cavalry carbines. During the last months of the war quantities of them were modified to accept standard German 7.92mm Mauser cartridges – the modified weapon was fairly dangerous to its user due to the resultant high chamber pressure.
Museum of Modern History, Ljubljana, Slovenia

Volkssturmmänner are inspected during target practise by *Stabschef* der SA Wilhelm Schepmann, nominally entitled *Inspekteur für die Schiessausbildung des deutschen Volkssturms*, 20 November 1944. **Bundesarchiv 146/79/107/12**

Stabschef der SA Schepmann demonstrates his own prowess at shooting whilst visiting members of the *Volkssturm* during target practise, 20 November 1944. **Museum of Modern History, Ljubljana, Slovenia**

Rifle practise for a *Volkssturmmann*, 20 November 1944. **Museum of Modern History, Ljubljana, Slovenia**

A *Volkssturm* company on parade. They are wearing the black *Schutzmanns*chaft uniform normally issued to eastern security police. A few of the men have *Organisation Todt* M42 field caps, whilst their *Zugführer* wears the standard M43 field cap. Note the bicycles, and Italian carbine ammo bandoliers being worn. Many of the men are issued with Italian M91 Carcano rifles, a weapon which was distributed in some quantity to the *Volkssturm*. Other weapons to be seen include a MP44, MG34 and *Panzerfaust* 60. The bicycles may indicate that this unit is to be deployed in a tank-hunter role.
Bildarchiv Preußischer Kulturbesitz, Berlin

A *Volkssturmmann* on duty guarding a bridge in the Charlottenburg area of Berlin, February 1945. He is wearing a civilian greatcoat and a single-button black field cap (not the M43 *Panzer* field cap or standard HJ winter cap), and is armed with a Kar 98k rifle. **Bildarchiv Preußischer Kulturbesitz, Berlin**

CHAPTER SEVEN

Training

The first schedule of instructions for implementation of the *Führer* decree of 27th September, 1944 (Section II, paragraph 2) laid down that the *Volkssturm* was to be trained particularly in anti-tank and infantry combat; in the *Gaue* along the German borders positional warfare manoeuvres were carried out. *Volkssturmsoldaten* were called up for training in accordance with the second schedule of instructions for implementation of 12 October 1944 (Section II, paragraph 4) by the company and battalion commanders.

In accordance with the "Directive for Training the *Volkssturm*" of 16 October 1944 (Appendix XII) training was to take place at least once a week. This should only be interrupted if there were urgent reasons to do so. If training took place during working hours, those men taking part in it were not to suffer any financial disadvantage. They were entitled to continued payment of salaries, which employers could reclaim from the appropriate labour authorities.

As a result of the long working hours, which in the armaments industry could be as much as 72 hours per week, only Sundays were available for practical weapons and combat training. Training duty on Sundays was not to exceed six hours, including travel to and from home. Training duties themselves were not to last longer than four hours. In addition to Sunday training duties, units could, where local circumstances permitted, be assembled for parades, education sessions, instructional films and the like for about two hours on weekday evenings. Where the circumstances permitted, individual training with weapons could be undertaken by flying training units in the workplace during idle shifts.

For the training of officers and NCOs and for preparing for practical training sessions, two additional hours per week could be allocated for the individuals in question.

In addition to training within the home locality of individual units, there were also courses for officers and NCOs of varying duration. These were generally arranged within individual *Gaue* at Party schools or at other suitable locations. The training personnel and teaching equipment was commandeered for detached duty in agreement with the local defence command and senior SS and police authorities and was wholly or partly run by the locally available authorities of the Reserve Army, the *Waffen-SS*, and the police. The normal training of units was not to be interrupted by these special training sessions.

The *Führungsstab Deutscher Volkssturm* organised the 'Reich Training Courses for Battalion Commanders of the *Volkssturm*' at the Grafenwöhr troop exercise area in Bavaria, which in due course all battalion commanders had to undertake. Initially, these training courses lasted ten days. An end-of-course assessment was intended to inform *Gauleiters* of the suitability of those who participated in the courses. The organisers and training personnel on these courses consisted of Army frontline officers who had proved their worth on active service, were tested for their suitability, and in every respect carefully selected. The first "Reich Training Course" took place in the first half of December 1944. But as a result of the rapid deterioration of the military situation, particularly with regard to transport, they had to be discontinued as early as the end of January 1945.

The maximum length of any of these courses was not to exceed 14 days. The superiors and employers of the *Volkssturmsoldaten* called up to attend courses had to be informed in good time beforehand in order to be able to arrange appropriate cover for the temporary absence of their management and work personnel.

In carrying out the Sunday training sessions for the local *Volkssturm* units, it immediately became evident that the local officers and the training personnel detached from the military and police authorities were insufficient, in terms of numbers and quality, to provide any really useful training for so many units from the first and second levies. In addition, there was an almost total lack of teaching resources and above all of weapons for training purposes, and a complete lack of any training guidelines. There was also, for so many units, too little terrain on which to carry out exercises for frontline weapons and combat training, and there was an even greater shortage of firing ranges. For commanders of the active peacetime army, who before the war had had to make do with a shortage of exercise areas and firing ranges, these problems came as no surprise. But in the case of the *Volkssturm*, the resulting wastage of valuable training time which, instead of consisting entirely of weapons and combat training, was squandered in superfluous and forbidden drill, meant that the well-intentioned initial training orders issued by the Chief of Staff of the *Reichsführer-SS* for the most part remained little more than pieces of paper. But because any such wastage of valuable time in meaningless activities creates irritation and frustration and has a worse effect than any other form of service on the *esprit de corps* of troops, for the majority of the *Volkssturm* these training events also remained initially only a paper exercise. Thus, when, in situations of direst need, countless *Volkssturm* units were called up for service with the *Wehrmacht* and were quickly assigned unexpected military tasks, these units still had had no training of any kind.

In a much better situation with regard to training were those *Volkssturm* battalions of the first levy – it is true that the shortage of weapons meant that there were only a few of them – who from the end of October 1944 had been stationed as security garrisons in the border positions in the East. In Upper Silesia, for example, there were at first only six battalions. These units did receive their weapons, even if the weapons only came from captured stocks, and sufficient amount of equipment. During the period of their active deployment, which usually lasted from three to four weeks, they were able to undertake proper training. After this time they were relieved by fresh battalions from their individual *Gaue*, with weapons and other equipment or being handed over to the replacement units in their positions. Where dugouts or concrete bunkers had already been prepared, these units were accommodated within their positions, but more often than not they were accommodated in barracks or in the immediate locality in which their positions were situated. Food and drink were provided by the *Gaue* and were prepared in locally established cooking stations, often in the copper boilers usually used for washing clothes.

Because the Army's own training facilities were no longer sufficient to cater for this kind of training, and because they were also not very suitable for providing short term training for militia units such as the *Volkssturm*, at the end of October 1944 a special set of training instructions for the *Volkssturm* was under preparation by the Army Infantry Inspectorate in collaboration with the *Fuhrungsstab Deutscher Volkssturm*. But by the end of the war these instructions were still not ready for printing.

By contrast, it was possible to produce the first edition of a set of "Firing Instructions for the *Volkssturm*" which was based on the new Army firing instructions also under preparation at that time. These instructions combined guidelines for firing in situations of close combat, and general combat training for the individual infantryman within the framework of the section, in a skilful way which took account of the limited time available for training. Unfortunately almost the entire first print run of these instructions was destroyed by fire in an air raid on Berlin before they could be distributed.

Three periodicals were published as so-called "information material for commanders". These periodicals comprised *Der Dienstappell* (The Call to Duty), which appeared every week containing instructional material for company commanders, *Das Führungsblatt* (Commanders' Newsletter) which was to be provided every month for battalion commanders, and *Der politische Soldat* (The Political Soldier) information pamphlet which appeared every week and was intended to provide political and cultural education for unit commanders in the *Wehrmacht*.

In addition, on the instructions of the *Führungsstab Deutscher Volkssturm*, copies of suitable Army information films (300 copies of each film) were produced in sufficient numbers for training the *Volkssturm* and distributed to the *Gaue*. All the selected films – *Eingraben im Gefecht* (Entrenchment in combat), *Scharfschützen (Tarnung)* (Infantry Tactics [camouflage]), *Panzerfaust* and *Kampf um Dobrowska (Rundumverteidigung)* (Battle for Dobrowska [all-round defensive tactics]) – had been produced in 1944 but were very useful for the training purposes for which they were intended. All cinema proprietors had been instructed by the president of the Reich Chamber of Film to place their cinemas, when requested, at the disposal of units of the *Volkssturm*, with the expenses being borne by the Reich.

The nominations, in the *Führer* decree of 25 September 1944, of the Chief of Staff of the SA as Inspector of Firing Training and the Corps Commander of the NSKK as Inspector of Motor Vehicle Technical Training, had no practical significance for the training system itself.

Members of the *Volkssturm* are trained to use a
Panzerschreck, 23 October 1944. The men are
wearing Heer denim fatigues
Bundesarchiv 146/79/107/13

Target practise on the drill square, 23 October 1944.
Bundesarchiv 146/79/107/14

A member of the *Großdeutschland* division trains East Prussian *Volkssturmmänner*, November 1944. **Ullstein Bilderdienst**

Stabschef der SA Wilhelm Schepmann talks to a *Volkssturmmann*, 20 November 1944.
Museum of Modern History, Ljubljana, Slovenia

A *Volkssturm* member practising with a *Panzerfaust,* late November 1944. The target tank is a Soviet T-34/76.
Museum of Modern History, Ljubljana, Slovenia

This image of an elderly *Volkssturmmänner* discharging a *Panzerfaust* is particularly useful for demonstrating that weapon's fiercesome back-blast – a danger that inexperienced users were prone to forget in the heat of battle, sometimes fatally.
Alexandr Grinev

Members of the *Volkssturm* being trained in close-quarters anti-tank combat, photographed by SS-PK Feder, 11 January 1945. The focus of attention is on a man about to attach a hollow charge to a Panther tank. The use of hollow charges in anti-tank warfare required even more courage than the *Panzerfaust* - the later charges, as being used here, weighed 3.5kg, their magnets exerting an attachment force of 45kg. Detonating after 7.5 seconds, the charge could penetrate approximately 140mm of armour.
Bundesarchiv 146/71/33/9

Training with the *Panzerfaust*. During the last weeks of the war there is some evidence that a small number of women did receive elementary training on this weapon.
Bildarchiv ASL

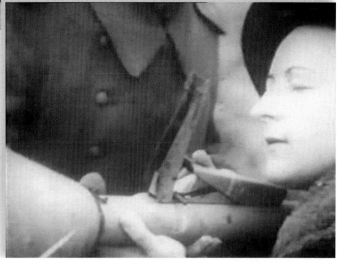

A **Volkssturm** *training exercise, Berlin 1945*

Two members of the *Volkssturm* take up firing positions during a training exercise in buildings of the Technical University (Berlin-Charlottenburg), February 1945.
Hilmar Pabel/Bildarchiv Preußischer Kulturbesitz, Berlin

A *Volkssturmmann* carrying a *Panzerfaust* during training exercises in the area of the Technical University, Berlin-Charlottenburg, February 1945.
Hilmar Pabel/Bildarchiv Preußischer Kulturbesitz, Berlin

Two *Volkssturm* men dash for cover during training exercises in the area of the Technical University, Berlin-Charlottenburg, February 1945. **Hilmar Pabel/Bildarchiv Preußischer Kulturbesitz, Berlin**

A **Volkssturm** *training exercise, Berlin 1945*

This well-known image is usually captioned as being a father and son awaiting the Red Army's advance into Berlin, end April 1945. However, it was actually taken by Hilmar Pabel during *Volkssturm* training exercises in the area of the Technical University, Berlin-Charlottenburg, February 1945. **Hilmar Pabel/Bildarchiv Preußischer Kulturbesitz, Berlin**

A Volkssturm *training exercise, Berlin 1945*

A *Volkssturm* MG42 team in position during training exercises in the area of the Technical University, Berlin-Charlottenburg, February 1945. They are wearing *Luftwaffe* issue uniforms (including probably the M44 *Luftwaffe* field blouse) with the *Volkssturm* rank insignia of *Gruppenführer* added. The caps are *Fliegermütze* or *Luftwaffe* enlisted ranks flyer's caps.
Hilmar Pabel/Bildarchiv Preußischer Kulturbesitz, Berlin

CHAPTER EIGHT

Legal status of members of the Volkssturm

The introduction to the Directive of 1 December 1944 concerning the Status of Members of the *Volkssturm* (Appendix XIII), which became law on its publication in the Reich Legal Gazette and in the Army statute book, reads:

> The *Wehrmacht* and the *Volkssturm* are the *Volk* in arms. Service in the *Volkssturm* is a service of honour to the German *Volk* in exactly the same way as service in the *Wehrmacht*. The *Volkssturmsoldat* has obligations and rights just as the soldier of the *Wehrmacht*.

The last sentence broadly outlines the legal status which had to be assigned to the members of the *Volkssturm* to correspond with the basic requirements of Paragraph 4 of the *Führer* decree of 25 September 1944 and Section III of the Schedule of Instructions for Implementation of 27 September 1944, and to give members of the *Volkssturm* the status of soldiers within the meaning of the Defence Act and of combatants within the meaning of the Hague Convention on Land Warfare.

With the issue of his paybook, the conscript – and also the volunteer – became subject to the obligations of a *Volkssturmsoldat*. By wearing the universal black, white, and red armband with the inscription '*Deutscher Volkssturm – Wehrmacht*', which was part of his uniform in whatever capacity he was serving, he was – even when not wearing uniform – externally marked out as a member of the *Wehrmacht* and as a combatant within the meaning of the Hague Convention on Land Warfare. Just as was the case for every soldier, he had to be instructed on the regulations with respect to combatants set out under the Hague Convention on Land Warfare.

The Allied headquarters recognised this fact in declaring, in an Associated Press Release of 24 October 1944, that "If the new German People's Army were to take up arms openly against the Allied invasion forces, members of that Army would be the granted the rights of combatants, even if they were not organised along military lines" (Archiv der Gegenwart 1944, Siegler-Verlag, Wien, page 6569).[34]

In accordance with this declaration, the enemy in the West treated the members of the *Volkssturm* as combatants within the meaning of the Hague Convention on Land Warfare. Of course, in the case of the enemy in the East, it was only if they were fortunate that German soldiers could expect to receive this kind of treatment. Certainly, at the outset, *Volkssturmsoldaten* were considered by the Soviet troops to be partisans and shot.

The legal directives, instructions and provisions which are attached as appendices placed the *Volkssturmsoldat* on a similar legal footing to the soldier of the *Wehrmacht* even in his basic relationship to the State.

The *Volkssturmsoldat* was obliged to obey the requirement to register and any orders requiring him to serve in any capacity in the *Volkssturm*. Any man who did not meet his obligations or did not meet them at the appropriate time could – without prejudice to any punishment on the basis of the applicable punishment code – be compelled by the police to present himself for service and carry out the duties which were required to.

In accordance with the "Directive concerning the Criminal Law pertaining to the *Volkssturm*" of 24 February 1945, the code of punishment applicable to members of the *Wehrmacht* was also to be applied to *Volkssturmsoldaten* both during training and in combat – in the case of young people also taking into account the Reich legislation with respect to young people. Thus the guidelines set out in the military penal code for punishable offences in the field only applied to members of the *Volkssturm* in cases where such offences were committed "in a situation of combat deployment".

With effect from 24 February 1945, the application of the penal guidelines became the responsibility of a jurisdiction which was created specifically for the *Volkssturm*, on the basis of the "Directive concerning a Special Jurisdiction in Criminal Cases for members of the *Volkssturm*". The courts of the *Volkssturm* replaced the field courts-martial and the Reich courts-martial, and *Wehrmacht* judges on special Army service were replaced by judges of the *Volkssturm*. These also had to be qualified judges and be suitable for service as officers in the *Volkssturm*. They were nominated by the *Gauleiter* and jointly appointed and dismissed by the Leader of the Party Chancellery and the *Reichsführer-SS*. As assessors, the presiding judge would appoint a company or battalion commander of the *Volkssturm* and another member of the *Volkssturm* of the same rank as the defendant. The presiding judges were the *Gauleiters*, and, in cases of offences committed in combat situations under the command of units of the Army or the Waffen-SS, were the presiding judges of the military units involved. The Superior Justice was the *Reichsführer-SS*, the Supreme Justice was the *Führer*.

To try criminal misdemeanours committed by members of the *Volkssturm* during training, in every *Gau* a court of the *Volkssturm* was set up. To exercise jurisdiction over the *Volkssturm* in combat situations, special *Volkssturm* judges were to be assigned to every Supreme Commander of an Army within which *Volkssturm* battalions were deployed.

Offences against military order and discipline committed by members of the *Volkssturm* were punishable in accordance with a service penal code specifically created for the *Volkssturm*

The "Directive concerning the Penal Code for the *Volkssturm*", the "Directive concerning a Special Jurisdiction in Criminal Offences for Members of the *Volkssturm*" and the first "Instructions for Implementation relating to the Directive concerning a Special Jurisdiction in Criminal Offences for Members of the *Volkssturm*" all came into force on 24 February 1945 with retrospective effect to 18 October 1944. All three directives (Appendix XIV) were announced in the Reich Legal Gazette 1945, Part I, pages 34/35. They had already been announced to the *Gauleiters* in "Directive 31/45" issued by the Party Chancellery on 1 March, 1945

The "Service Penal Code for the *Volkssturm*" (Appendix XV) was issued to the Supreme Command of the *Volkssturm* on 16 March 1945 as "Directive 40/45". It came into force with effect from that date.

It must have been found to be necessary to give the three Penal Code Directives retrospective effect because, in its "Circular" of 17 January 1945, the Party Chancellery had stated that it was undesirable to institute, through the normal judicial authorities, criminal proceedings for breach of *Volkssturm* obligations and other punishable offences associated with service in the *Volkssturm*. "Because of the only very small number of criminal misdemeanours associated with service in the *Volkssturm*, it seems appropriate to defer any punishments until the planned Directive concerning a Penal Code for the *Volkssturm* comes into force" (Circular 5/45 issued by the Party Chancellery on 17 January 1945).[35]

One of the reasons which argued for the creation of a special jurisdiction for the *Volkssturm* must have been the fundamental difference between militia units like the *Volkssturm* and the standing armed forces. For *Volkssturmsoldaten* any matters of fact relating to the military Penal Code doubtless required different and often gentler sentences.

The rights of the individual *Volkssturmsoldat*, set out in Paragraphs 5 to 11 of the "Directive of 1 December 1944 concerning the Status of Members of the *Volkssturm*" included, in particular, entitlement to health care, pay, food and accommodation when on active service, and to accommodation for family and care in the event of his being injured while on active service, and, finally, provision for any dependants.

Insofar as the provisions and instructions for implementation set out under the above paragraphs did not come under the remit of the leader of the Party Chancellery or the *Reichsführer-SS*, they were to be carried out by the appropriate Reich authorities and the Head of the *Oberkommando der Wehrmacht* in agreement with the leader of the Party Chancellery and the *Reichsführer-SS*.

The OKH directive of 27 December 1944 announced in the Army Legal Gazette, Part B, page 5 No. 7, the "Directive of 1 December 1944 concerning the Status of Members of the *Volkssturm*" and as an appendix also outlined provisions relating to the pay of *Volkssturmsoldaten* when deployed within the framework of the *Wehrmacht* and on courses of study which took place during the course of training with the *Wehrmacht*.[36]

Apart from a few special regulations, the *Volkssturmsoldaten*, while they were deployed within the framework of the *Wehrmacht* and when they were released, were treated in the same way as the soldier of the *Wehrmacht* with regard to pay, food, accommodation etc. Any period during which the soldier served under any *Wehrmacht* command authority (the shortened term for such service was *Wehrmachteinsatz*) was reckoned as service in the *Wehrmacht* irrespective as to whether this involved combat or other duties.

The special regulations included, in the first instance, service pay, the rate of which was set at 1 *Reichsmark* per day for all *Volkssturmsoldaten*, plus supplies of tobacco and other goods outside the Army Group districts. There were no special allowances for combat duties.

On courses of study and other training which took place within the framework of the *Wehrmacht* training, only free food and accommodation were provided, calculated in accordance with the set rates are for the schools and troop units and in exchange for appropriate food tokens.

Generally, for pay purposes, the *Volkssturm* units were assigned to a *Wehrmacht* unit. The allocation of pay and other allowances was the responsibility of the *Wehrmacht* command authority responsible for the *Wehrmacht* deployment of the individual *Volkssturm* unit. The Paymaster paid the current rates of pay with respect to service pay, front-line service allowances and if necessary special payments such as subsistence and overnight stay allowances to the commander of the *Volkssturm* units or his representative, who had to provide a receipt.

The first Schedule of instructions relating to the Directive concerning the Status of Members of the *Volkssturm* issued by the General Labour Plenipotentiary on 17 January, 1945 (Labour Law Provisions), and published in the Reich Legal Gazette 1945, Part 1, pages 15/17, contained regulations concerning compensation for loss of earnings resulting from proven service in the *Volkssturm*. The period counted as service also included any necessary time spent on transport and a certain period for rest and recuperation.

The compensation for loss of earnings and the other payments which were to be paid to the *Volkssturmsoldaten* by their employers were paid to them by the appropriate employment offices on receipt of appropriate claims. The compensation included employers' contributions to sickness, pensions, and unemployment insurance, which were up to be paid *pro rata* in respect of any loss of earnings compensation which was due.

Self-employed individuals including self-employed craftsmen, self-employed farmers and members of the professions were compensated in accordance with a scale of rates calculated per hour. These rates were calculated on the basis of the individual's last income tax statement, and, in the event that continuing operating costs for business were involved, could be increased by up to 50 per cent.

But employers only continued to pay wages as long as the overall period of *Volkssturm* service did not exceed six weeks. Every time an individual was called called up for service, this period began again. If the period of service lasted longer than six weeks, then from the beginning of the seventh week onwards the same employment provisions applied as for soldiers of the *Wehrmacht*.

Civil servants continued to be paid at civil service rates for the entire period of their service in the *Volkssturm*.

The Second Schedule of instructions relating to the Directive concerning the Status of Members of the *Volkssturm* issued by the Reich Labour Minister on 6 February, 1945 (Social Insurance and Welfare Provisions), and published in the Reich Legal Gazette 1945, Part One, page 24, clarified the position of members of the *Volkssturm* with respect to welfare provision.

The existing status of *Volkssturmsoldaten* with respect to social insurance remained unchanged by them being called up for service in the *Volkssturm* as long as wages for employment continued to be payable in accordance with the First Schedule of instructions outlined above. When this entitlement ceased, social insurance provision for the *Volkssturmsoldat* became subject to the same regulations which applied to individuals called up for service in the *Wehrmacht*.

Any damage or physical injury directly attributable to service in the *Volkssturm*, sustained either during travel or actually while on active service, was reckoned as a war injury within the meaning of the *Wehrmacht* legislation relating to welfare. Food and welfare were provided in accordance with the current *Wehrmacht* provisions for soldiers who had sustained war injuries, and their dependants.

Announcement 18/45, issued by the Party Chancellery on 8 February 1945 (Appendix XVI) provides a general overview and procedural guide for all regulations which were issued to guarantee family maintenance, health care, welfare and food for *Volkssturmsoldaten* and their dependants.

"*Anordnung* 34/35" issued by the Leader of the Party chancellery on 2 March 1945 provided that the main office for war victims of the NSDAP became responsible for the care of all members of the *Volkssturm* who sustained physical injury as a result of their *Volkssturm* service.

For gallantry and meritorious conduct, *Volkssturmsoldaten* could be decorated in the same way as members of the *Wehrmacht*.

To summarise, at the end of this section relating to the legal status of the individual member of the *Volkssturm*, it can be established that:

During his service with the *Volkssturm*, the individual *Volkssturmsoldat* had the status of a soldier as defined under the provisions of the Defence Act of 21 May 1935, irrespective as to whether this involved local training, courses of instruction/lectures, standing by or in action under *Wehrmacht* command. This status was unaffected by the fact that the development and the running of the *Volkssturm* organisation, to a certain extent on peacetime lines, had been taken over as such by the National Socialist German Workers' Party.

Outside *Volkssturm* service, there were only civilians liable for service in the *Volkssturm*, whose legal position with regard to their *Volkssturm* units was comparable to that of reservists in peacetime or of men in reserved occupations exempted from military service with their *Wehrmacht* reserve authority during the war.

A series of six Nazi propaganda photos portraying a variety of *Volkssturm* members at work. The original series was captioned "...and on Sunday with the *Volkssturm!*" whilst extolling the work ethic of the men shown, including *Kalkulator* Paul 'C', *Stadt-Oberinspektor* 'G' and *Ortsbauernführer* 'M'. **Museum of Modern History, Ljubljana, Slovenia**

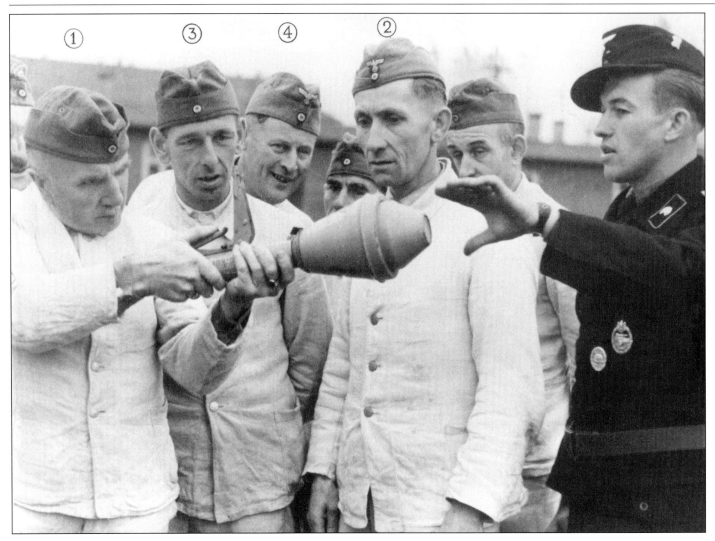

The same men are now shown wearing *Heer* denim fatigues and receiving instruction on the *Panzerfaust* from a member of the *Panzertruppen*. The latter is wearing the wound badge and *Panzerkampfabzeichen*.
Museum of Modern History, Ljubljana, Slovenia

A close-up of the later-pattern *Volkssturm* armband.
Friedrich Baier

CHAPTER NINE

Tasks carried out by the Volkssturm within the framework of the Wehrmacht

The "Führer Decree of 25 September, 1944 concerning the Formation of the *Volkssturm*" assigned to the *Volkssturm* the task of reinforcing the active forces of the *Wehrmacht* and maintaining a relentless battle against the enemy anywhere that the enemy attempted to enter upon German soil. Thus, if along the borders or in the interior of the Reich the military situation deteriorated to such an extent that the *Wehrmacht* in any given locality required temporary infantry support, then the local *Volkssturm* was to be called up for 'combat deployment'. We must always remind ourselves that such deployment could only possibly be temporary and restricted to a particular locality. Thus, for example, a telegram sent by Bormann on 16 November 1944 reads: "Basically, men capable of combat should be called up into the *Wehrmacht* by the normal procedure. The *Volkssturm* will be called upon where there is no time to follow this normal procedure and where the threat of enemy action makes it necessary to mobilise all local forces capable of combat".[37] It was not intended that the *Volkssturm* should simply be a fifth arm of the *Wehrmacht*.

As has already been stated, *Volkssturm* battalions from the first and second levy were available for service with the *Wehrmacht*. The battalions of the first levy could be deployed over a wider area than their immediate home locality, which generally meant that they could be deployed anywhere within their respective *Gaue*. The battalions of the second levy, because of the importance for the war effort of the civilian work carried out by their members, could only be provided in circumstances of the highest emergency and could generally only be deployed within their home district. The expression "usually" left the two concepts of "locally" and "more widely" open to interpretation depending on the situation and circumstances of deployment. But the intention was always for them to be deployed on a temporary basis. For them to be deployed for long periods in districts which were not under military threat, and which would involve these men being withdrawn from other important civilian activities, was not what the *Volkssturm* was meant for.

The military tasks which were considered as suitable for being undertaken by units of the *Volkssturm* within the framework of the *Wehrmacht* had been clearly outlined in meetings between the Army General Staff, the *Allgemeine Heeresamt* and the *Führungsstab Deutscher Volkssturm*. But it very soon became clear that the concept of *Kampfeinsatz*, or 'combat deployment', was too narrowly defined and would have to be replaced by the concept of *Wehrmachteinsatz*, or 'deployment in support of the *Wehrmacht*'. This concept included, as outlined in the previous section, any deployment of units of the *Volkssturm* under the command of a *Wehrmacht* command authority, irrespective as to whether this was for actual combat or for other purposes.

Detailed consideration was given to the modes of deployment outlined below, which were set out on 28 March 1945 in a decree issued jointly by the *Reichsführer-SS*, the Leader of the Party Chancellery and the Head of the OKW:

a) Security garrison duties in border positions or other positions away from the front line, and in fortresses and fortress areas.

It was intended that such security garrison duties, as the name suggests, should secure the positions in question against surprise attack, unexpectedly meet enemy forces which had broken through, and defend the positions until the *Wehrmacht* units arrived. It was intended to supply such security garrisons with heavy weapons, particularly anti-tank weapons, as support.

As long as these positions behind the lines were not seriously threatened or attacked by the enemy, the garrison units could continue their training and be used to extend and reinforce their positions. Examples of using the *Volkssturm* in this way are the situations in which *Volkssturm* units manned border positions in Silesia and Austria, which are described later.

b) Local defence against surprise breakthroughs by enemy point units.

The precondition for such cases was the availability of units which were ready for action and able to respond quickly to emergencies. If the localities under threat were occupied by combat troops of the *Wehrmacht* and particularly of the Army, the local units of the *Volkssturm* were placed under the command of the military combat commander. In places where there were no regular troops holding positions, combat by the local units of the *Volkssturm* was to be carried out independently under their own commander. The concept of combat troops thus included any unit of troops which was organised for combat, irrespective as to whether this belonged to the *Wehrmacht* forces in the field or the Reserve forces of the *Wehrmacht*.

c)   Securing anti-tank blockades.

On the basis of a *Führer* Decree issued at the end of September 1944, "the approaches to all localities west of the Rhine were to be provided with anti-tank blockades by military units or by appeals to the local population".[38] Later, such barricades were also set up in Eastern Germany and east of the Rhine. The local *Volkssturm* was called up to secure these blockades.

d)   Protection of specific targets.

e)   Construction and entrenching work.

Large numbers of *Volkssturm* units were drafted in to develop and maintain the border positions and other positions behind the lines in the East and in the West. *Volkssturm* battalions for whom there were no weapons available worked as construction battalions assisting in the defence of countless fortresses in the East. As examples of this, it is only necessary to mention Königsberg and Breslau.

f)   Provision of supply services in individual localities

g)   Evacuation and escort duties for refugees or for concealing and storing material important for the war effort.

h)   Anti-tank units, formed by volunteers, and made mobile by provision of vehicles or bicycles.

i)   Demolition/explosives units and other special units.

Because the essential preconditions for successful deployment of the *Volkssturm* were, in the first instance, provision of adequate training and trained officers, it was planned that this deployment should be focused on deep zone defence in areas behind the lines. Thus it was not intended that they should be temporarily deployed for defensive purposes on a quiet section of the front in order to release units of the Army for use elsewhere, or for them to assist in defending against enemy airborne troops. Such uses would have definitely been possibilities for a well-armed and trained militia.

But although it was quite clear what was needed for successful deployment in combat, the way that the military situation was developing forced the adoption of other solutions. This was principally because the *Volkssturm* in Eastern Germany had to be called up unexpectedly in support of the *Wehrmacht* before this had been intended, and countless *Volkssturm* units went into actual combat long before they were properly established, armed and trained.

It was the responsibility of the *Reichsführer-SS*, in his capacity as Commander of the Reserve Army, to deploy the *Volkssturm* in support of the *Wehrmacht* on the basis of requests made by the OKW, the OKH or other subordinate authorities of the *Wehrmacht*. In instances of immediate threat, the *Gauleiters* were also authorised to release *Volkssturm* units from their *Gaue* for service in support of the *Wehrmacht* in advance of any other formal order being issued. In this case the authority responsible for requesting such moves, outside the remit of the *Wehrmacht* in the field, was generally the deputy commanding general.

With the order for *Wehrmachteinsatz*, the *Volkssturm* units which were called up for service would be under the command of the appropriate *Wehrmacht* command authorities, both tactically, for supply purposes, and, until the special criminal jurisdiction for the *Volkssturm* was set up, also in terms of military discipline and penal law. With regard to the resulting question of supplies, the OKH Quartermaster-General, in his "Directive concerning the Provision of Supplies to the *Volkssturm*" of 12 December 1944, had given orders that the *Volkssturm* battalions should in all districts be supplied in the same way as *Wehrmacht* units.

The *Wehrmacht* was responsible for command of *Volkssturm* units called up to support it until such time as those command arrangements were changed in agreement between the *Reichsführer-SS* and the responsible *Wehrmacht* command authorities. But as time went on, the deteriorating situation meant that these provisions became insignificant in practical terms. The shortage of troops and above all of infantry was the principal reason which caused all *Wehrmacht* authorities to resist any attempts to release the *Volkssturm* under their command. Contrary to the intention for which it was formed, there was a growing tendency on all fronts to incorporate the *Volkssturm* seamlessly within the complement of military units simply as replacement manpower. Thus, for example, at the beginning of March 1945, in Army Group Centre (*Generaloberst* Schörner), the order was issued to call up all *Volkssturmsoldaten* into the *Wehrmacht*. Even though this order was successfully resisted, nothing could be done to prevent many *Volkssturm* battalions being arbitrarily dissolved and the younger *Volkssturmsoldaten* being transferred into fighting units and the older men being transferred to duties behind the line as members of the Army.

The shortage of troops caused the Army General Staff and the commander of the Reserve Army to constantly rethink how the *Volkssturm* could most effectively be used to support and reinforce the diminishing strength of the *Wehrmacht*. Thus, by the end of the war, men liable for service in the *Volkssturm* were used in three additional ways:

k) As early as mid-November 1944, the chief of the Army General Staff issued instructions to set up local autonomous fortress batteries to reinforce the garrisons of fortresses and fortress areas on German home soil. As a result of this, it was planned to form fortress pioneer units and fortress signals units.

These fortress units were – in agreement between the leader of the Party Chancellery and the *Reichsführer-SS* – set up as so-called *Rahmeneinheiten*, or skeleton units, in which only the core personnel, that is the most important command and administrative personnel posts, were continuously occupied by Army personnel, while locally based men of the second levy liable for service in the *Volkssturm* would be called up to complete the combat strength. By day, these men would follow their normal occupations, and they would only be called up for training in their local units in the evenings or on Sundays. They would only be called up for full-time duties if there was imminent threat of an enemy attack.

Exactly where such fortress batteries, which were generally equipped with captured guns, were actually set up, is no longer clear from the available source documents. In the East, they fought in all the larger fortresses. In the West, such *Volkssturm* batteries were involved in the battles for the Upper Rhine front. There were only exceptional rare instances of any fortress pioneer and signal units being formed.

l) In accordance with a decree issued to the deputy commanding generals in the defence districts on 20 January, 1945 by the *Reichsführer-SS* in his capacity as Supreme Commander of the Reserve Army (Ob. d. E./AHA/Stab II Nr. 4776/45 geh.),[39] personnel currently involved in guarding prisoners of war, and who were capable of being used in combat, were to be replaced by older members of the *Volkssturm* from the first levy and suitable men from the fourth levy, ands thus released for front line service. These men were called up for front-line service with *Volkssturm* equipment, but without weapons. But the shortage of men who were able to undertake guard duties for prisoners of war on a long-term basis gave rise to difficulties. Therefore, on the basis of instructions issued by the Supreme Command on 28 March 1945, the use of members of the *Volkssturm* to guard prisoners of war had "to be restricted to the situations specified to date".

m) Under the pressure of the serious military situation, in the middle of February 1945, the OKH ordered Grenadier Regiments to be formed from the schools and training courses for officer cadets and Reserve officer candidates.

In accordance with the "Special Regulations for Provision of Personnel for Grenadier Regiments 1233–44, 1246–50.1256," (GenStH/Org. Abt. Nr. IP/1707/45 geh. of 20 Feb 1945),[40] the schools and training courses had to provide the officers and NCOs for these regiments, while the units were to be built up to combat strength by the normal process of Army replacements which were assigned from the collection points for dispersed Army personnel and also by means of the *Volkssturm* which had been assigned by the *Gauleiters* of those *Gaue* in which the regiments were being formed.

The number of men liable for the *Volkssturm* who were assigned to these 18 Grenadier regiments, and probably also to other units which were formed, can no longer be determined. All these newly formed units, which were brought together into divisions with the names of 'Kurmark', 'Döberitz', etc., or into other divisions, saw front-line action before the end of the war, and some of them suffered very high and very bloody losses.

Both the long-term deployment of the *Volkssturm* on duties guarding prisoners of war, the drafting of men liable for service in the *Volkssturm* to form Army units and their long-term service within such units, in other words, regarding the *Volkssturm* simply as a source of replacements for *Wehrmacht* units, were totally out of keeping with the spirit of the *Volkssturm* and the aims of its training. This type of provision of replacements should have been the exclusive responsibility of the authorities responsible for the *Wehrmacht* reserves. Probably the authorities had recourse to the *Volkssturm* because it seemed simpler and quicker to do so. The military authorities were not authorised to recruit older men, and it took longer for an authority responsible for recruiting reserves to decide on questions relating to the possible exemption of men liable for military service than it did for the Party with the resources it had at its disposal. Using the *Volkssturm* route, it was possible to provide soldiers for the *Wehrmacht* more quickly than by going through the normal administrative procedures of the *Wehrmacht* Reserve authorities (in this connection, see also Appendix XXIV).

That such a procedure – at least until the beginning of March 1945 – did not correspond with Bormann's intentions is evident from a telegram which he sent on 28 February 1945 to one *Gauleiter* and which on 1 March 1945 he brought to the attention of all *Gauleiters* in the form of Party Chancellery Circular 30/45. This telegram reads as follows:

In your letter of 22 February 1945, you informed me that the Commanding General of II Army Corps had asked you to arrange for *Volkssturm* units to be deployed to man the anti-tank blockades being constructed in the eastern part of your *Gau*, and also for men of the *Volkssturm* to be called up to provide surveillance duties for prisoners of war or other security duties. On the other hand, as you write to me, 92 per cent of the armaments industry of your *Gau* is running on an emergency basis. I therefore repeat the following clarification.

A whole series of authorities, as is now repeatedly being demonstrated, has been under the mistaken assumption that the *Volkssturm* represent just another reserve to be drawn on.

This assumption is completely wrong.

Apart from the relatively few men who are no longer capable of active service, the *Volkssturm* could and can only recruit men whose work in the fields of the armaments industry, the Reich railways, the Reich postal system, manufacturing etc. is so important that throughout all the years of the war they could not be released for military service but had to remain exempted from it. If I call up these men for longer-term service in the *Volkssturm* then the benefit of their civilian work will be lost to the field of armaments, the Reich railways, agriculture etc. The implications of doing this have for the most part either not been considered at all, or have not been considered well enough.

In addition:

The industries which employ these men, that is, armaments, Reich railways etc have to release certain groups of men liable for military service to the *Wehrmacht* at specified intervals.

It is completely impossible for the authorities to release men both to the *Volkssturm* and to the *Wehrmacht*. If I draft into the *Volkssturm* men who have until now been exempted from military service, then they will no longer be available for regular military service.

All men who serve long-term in the *Volkssturm* will be fully taken into account against the numbers which the Army authorities request to be released for service with the *Wehrmacht*. In other words, if I provide a *Volkssturm* battalion, there will be one less battalion to be provided for the Army.

You must immediately make your Commanding General aware of this, because we must finally put a stop to *Volkssturm* battalions being mistakenly used in this way.

The only occasion on which it was intended to draft more men into the *Volkssturm* is if a direct and immediate threat of enemy attack brings local industry to a standstill. Only then – that is, in the case of the most serious threat to the local home district – should men who are working in the armaments industry, agriculture etc. etc. be provided and sent in *Volkssturm* battalions into action against the enemy.[41]

With this 'Circular 30/45' issued by the Party Chancellery on 1 March 1945 and quoted above, *Reichsleiter* Bormann once again quite clearly set out the task for which it was intended to use the second levy, that is, the majority of the battalions of the *Volkssturm*. Bormann was not fully correct in his assessment of the number and the significance of the so-called *Landsturm* age groups, the first levy. The men included in this levy, insofar as they were not employed in crucial functions of the armaments industry and administration, could not be drafted for service of the kind which had been suggested by the Commanding General of II Corps. Certainly, in this case the *Volkssturm* men would have to be properly armed, which was out of the question on account of the desperate situation with regard to the supply of weapons.

Members of the *Volkssturm* were not called up for all the tasks such as those outlined above. In particular, it had never been intended in any way that the *Volkssturm* should be assigned the task of a partisan army responsible for carrying out delaying guerrilla warfare of the sort which had caused German troops so much trouble in the occupied territories and not least in Russia.

The continuation of resistance in the enemy's rear by acts of sabotage of all kinds and by espionage was to be the responsibility of the *Werwolf* Organisation. This organisation was entirely composed of volunteers and had no connection whatever with the *Volkssturm*, a fact which is confirmed by the report on the *Werwolf* organisation made by the Institute for Contemporary History in 1956.

The fact that the *Volkssturm*, particularly when it was first formed, was assigned tasks for which it had neither been created nor was suitable, was due, in the first instance, to the unfortunate and unclear wording of the *Führer* Decree of 25 September 1944. Significant in this connection are the reports compiled by the Stuttgart *Sicherheitsdienst* (SD) in October 1944, which commented on the reception that the *Führer* Decree had met among the local population. In almost all the reports, there is a unanimous refusal to fight "in the manner of partisans", to "become bandits and guerrillas", or "to be officially classified as criminals". This misinterpretation of the task of the *Volkssturm* was no doubt one of the reasons for the universally poor reception which the appeal for formation of the *Volkssturm* had met among the population of Württemberg, and probably in other places too. In these reports, it is the exception rather than the rule to find comments such as "I am ready at any time to fight behind the lines, but would prefer not to have to fire on the enemy craftily concealed under cover as a harmless civilian",[42] itself a view which at least does not oppose the idea of fighting out in the open.

Very interesting series of images showing a *Volkssturm Panzerjäger* unit, January 1945. Note the foliage in the helmets, the camouflaged *Zeltbahns* and the Swastika armbands. **Emil Nagel**

CHAPTER TEN

Border areas of Silesia (December 1944–January 1945)

The Soviet advance on the Vistula bridgeheads in mid-December 1944 caused *Generaloberst* Guderian, the chief of the Army General Staff, to request the *Volkssturm* as a security garrison for the border positions in Lower and Upper Silesia.

The "deployment exercise" of the few *Volkssturm* battalions which had been manning the positions on the initiative of the appropriate *Gauleiters* since the end of October now became transformed into deployment in support of the *Wehrmacht* (*Wehrmachteinsatz*). The security garrison of these positions was reinforced to the strength of about 40 battalions, mainly from the first levy, which came from all political districts in both parts of Silesia. As before, the battalions were to be relieved by other battalions in a three to four-week rotation system in which weapons and equipment were to be handed over. Because there were no German weapons, the newly drafted battalions had to be supplied through the *Allgemeine Heeresamt*/Stab Ib with captured weapons, mainly of Italian origin. The problem was that there was only very little ammunition for all these weapons. There was an almost complete lack of heavy infantry weapons. It was similarly not possible to deploy *Wehrmacht* artillery and anti-tank weapons.

The battalions were introduced to the terrain and to their positions, given training with the weapons they were to use, and employed in constructing and extending the positions. They were, as previously, mostly accommodated in barracks or in local villages and only in some instances were they accommodated in the concrete bunkers which had been built. For the most part, there were no underground bunkers in these positions, which were mainly composed of a continuous system of trenches.

Although these *Volkssturm* battalions were deployed in support of the *Wehrmacht*, and were under the command of senior officers of the Army who had been installed as sector and sub-sector commanders, it had not been possible to organise supply arrangements for them, because none were available. The responsibility for supplying the battalions with food therefore largely fell to the Party. It also proved difficult to exercise tactical command, because the Army's sector commanders had neither fully operational staffs nor sufficient command resources. For this reason, introduction and training in battalion positions was largely left to the party authorities, and tactical combat command could only be exercised in an unsatisfactory manner.

After the Soviets had begun a large-scale offensive from their Vistula bridgeheads on 12 January 1945, and the German front had been broken through, only eight days later, advance enemy units were reaching the Silesian border positions. These continued to be manned by *Volkssturm* units or were not manned at all. There was still an almost complete lack of *Wehrmacht* artillery and anti-tank weapons. Although the Silesian *Volkssturm* had plenty of will for the fight, it was of course not capable of maintaining a sustained defence with its inferior weapons, without sufficient ammunition, and without any heavy weapons at all. As a result, the border positions were very quickly broken through in several places after only short periods of fighting.

There are accounts of the *Wehrmachteinsatz* of Silesian *Volkssturm* battalions by the former *Kreisstabsführer* Rudolf Pietsch from the Oppeln district (Appendix XVII) and the former commander of the *Volkssturm* Battalion Habelschwerdt (Appendix XVIII). The first account gives a representative overview of the formation, armament and eventual fate of the *Volkssturm* in a Silesian border district. The second account describes what happened to a battalion whose members came from a district in the west of Silesia. At first this battalion was employed in entrenchment work in the construction of the Silesian border positions, the so-called 'Operation Bartold', and in October 1944 was reorganised to form the *Volkssturm* Battalion Habelschwerdt. Under the pressure of the Soviet breakthrough in Silesia, it had to retreat with the *Wehrmacht* through Freystadt, to the west-north-west of Glogau, to the Neisse at Görlitz, and from there it was brought back to its home territory in Silesia, and then once more called up for action.

An account of another Silesian *Volkssturm* Battalion, the battalion 'Breslau-Land Nr. 3', which similarly was initially formed as a result of the general appeal for *Volkssturm* men in the East, is given by the former commander of this unit, *Oberstleutnant* (retired) D. Joachim Leder, now living in Schlüchtern, who was able to base his account on extensive notes he made in the summer of 1945.

The battalion 'Breslau-Land Nr. 3' had four companies with about 600 men and was equipped with about 100 Soviet, Italian and French rifles, for which, on average, there were 15 rounds per weapon. In addition, there were a few *Panzerfäuste*. The battalion was entirely commanded by elderly officers. The majority of its members wore civilian clothing.

On 18 January 1945, the battalion commander received orders from his district command to occupy a sector of the defensive positions to the east of Breslau. But this order was rescinded and on 24 January the battalion was brought by rail to Laugwitz near Brieg, where it was to be placed under the command of the 4th Panzer Army which was fighting there.

"Because there was also no authority in Laugwitz", continues the former battalion commander in his memoirs, "which could provide any information regarding how it was intended to use the battalion, and what the command arrangements were, on 25 January I went to Brieg to clarify the situation with the fortress commandant. But neither the fortress commandant nor the commander of the troops fighting between Linden and Brieg knew anything about what we were supposed to do. The garrison of the fortress (Brieg) consisted mostly of *Volkssturm*.

"After I got back to Laugwitz, the *Stabsleiter* (Chief of Staff) of the district command of Strehlen eventually arrived and informed me that the battalion had been placed under his command and had to take over responsibility for covering the evacuation of the district, which was currently in progress, against Soviet shock troops. Accordingly, for the next few days, we were to carry out reconnaissance duties as far as the areas of Mollwitz, Grüningen, Hünern, Heidau, Hennersdorf and Frauenhain, which were situated forward of Laugwitz and around which fighting was taking place. We mainly lived off the plentiful supplies left by the inhabitants.

"On 29 January, a reinforced reconnaissance unit in Hennersdorf unfortunately fell into Soviet hands and was completely wiped out. On that day the battalion set off westwards, was assigned to the Waffen-SS under *Oberstleutnant* Delfs and during the following days took part successfully in the defence of the Tempelfeld – Kl. Ols – Kallen – Weihmühle sector, against which the Soviets had mounted several unsuccessful attacks. But on 4 February, the enemy succeeded, with the aid of armoured support, in breaking through into Tempelfeld, and in rolling up the front sideways through Kl. Ols and Kallen as far as Mechwitz. The battalion suffered considerable casualties. I myself was seriously wounded (in the head, lower arm, and stomach). Transferred to the main dressing station at Heidersdorf, I was operated on the same evening.

"During the next few days, the battalion was withdrawn from the front line and assigned to construction duties on the defensive positions and to supply tasks, for which it was better suited. After my recovery, I visited the battalion on 2 May 1945. On this visit I was informed that, in recognition of the gallantry shown by the battalion itself and by me personally, on the orders of the Breslau Land district command it had been given the name 'Battalion Leder'. A few days later it was taken into the county of Glatz and there it was disbanded."

Members of the *Volkssturm* serving on the Eastern Front receive supplies of the early *Panzerfaust 30 klein*, 1945.
Bildarchiv ASL

Another view of the same *Volkssturm* unit.
Bildarchiv ASL

CHAPTER ELEVEN

Security garrisons along the Austrian border (December 1944-March 1945)

As a result of the increasing gravity of the military situation in Hungary, on 23 December 1944, in a telegram to the *Reichsführer*-SS, the Chief of the Army General Staff requested that the *Volkssturm* in Styria and the Lower Danube area be mobilised and that the positions on the Austro-Hungarian frontier should be manned.

Because at most only 30 *Volkssturm* battalions had been equipped with German and Austrian weapons and such captured weapons as could be obtained, which had been distributed to all the *Gaue* in Austria, it was not possible to mobilise a large number of battalions. Also, because it was expected that manning the frontier positions would be a long-term commitment, and it was unlikely that the *Volkssturm* of this area, some districts of which were thinly populated, could single-handedly defend the positions, the population and the local industry, it was decided to withdraw all the battalions from all the districts in the *Gaue* of Styria, Lower Danube and Vienna. Every week, a quarter of the personnel complement of these battalions was replaced by fresh men to ensure that the units remained in combat readiness. In addition, a few *Volkssturmsoldaten* who lived locally and thus knew the area were assigned to every unit. As in Silesia, weapons and equipment had to be handed over every time a man was relieved, and the time men spent in the trenches was used for training purposes.

On the morning of 24 March 1945, that is, only one week after the beginning of the Soviet offensive from the area to the north of Lake Velencze (south-west of Budapest), the Chief of Staff of the *Volkssturm* was summoned to Zossen to meet the Chief of the Army General Staff. Information had been received that the Austrian border position had been abandoned by the *Volkssturm* and was no longer manned at all. *Generaloberst* Guderian ordered it to be immediately reoccupied, and the Chief of Staff of the *Volkssturm* had to go immediately to Linz, Vienna and Graz to take the necessary action.

He called in to meet the *Gauleiters* of the Lower Danube and Vienna during the night and early morning of 24/25 March. What had happened – why had the decision been taken on local initiative to abandon the border positions?

When, in the middle of February, the farmers began their spring sowing and the workers were required in increased numbers in the factories, the three *Gauleiters* had initially substantially reduced the number of battalions deployed in the border positions, and at the beginning of March had withdrawn all the battalions. According to the *Gauleiters*, they had taken these measures in agreement with the Army Supreme Commander on the Hungarian front (Army Group South). The latter had promised to warn the *Gauleiters* of any imminent enemy attack so that it would still be possible to re-occupy the border positions. But neither the Chief of the Army General Staff nor the *Volkssturm* leadership had been notified that any *Volkssturm* battalions had been withdrawn from the border positions.

The two *Gauleiters* of Lower Danube and Vienna were ordered to immediately re-form the *Volkssturm* battalions which had been withdrawn, and to reoccupy the border positions. In the afternoon, the Chief of Staff of the *Volkssturm* informed Deputy General Command of XVII Army Corps at a meeting arranged in the local defence headquarters in Vienna. The minutes of this meeting on 25 March 1945 are attached as Appendix XIX. Apparently, the Deputy General Command, which was responsible for the border position, had not heard, or had heard too late, that the security garrison had been withdrawn from the position. In addition, no sector and sub-sector *Wehrmacht* staffs appeared to have been allocated to this border position. Similarly, no preparations must have been made for the transfer of local *Wehrmacht* to the border. Mention has already been made of the order to hand over usable weapons to the *Wehrmacht*, which appears in the last paragraph of the minutes of the meeting in Vienna.

In the early morning of 26 March, in Graz, the *Gauleiter* of Styria was also instructed to use his own *Volkssturm* battalions to reoccupy the southern sector of the Austrian border positions.

Only on 29 March 1945, that is, as always and everywhere, far too late, were *Wehrkreise* (local defence districts) XVII in Vienna and XVIII in Salzburg (for the region of Styria) placed under the operational and tactical command of Army Group South.

Because all the *Volkssturm* units in the three *Gaue* of Lower Danube, Vienna and Styria had first to be reassembled and re-formed, the weapons which had been distributed had to be collected, and finally most of the regiments had to march on foot to the border, they arrived just as late as the weak Army battalions from the two defence districts, the transfer of which into the area around the border positions had similarly been deferred for too long. It seems that the case was no different with flak units from the local *Luftwaffe*.

Before the majority of the local *Wehrmacht* and *Volkssturm* units designated as the security garrison were able to reach their destination, Soviet troops had already broken through the border positions which were still unmanned. The fact that Wiener Neustadt fell into enemy hands on 2 April and the city of Vienna itself only a few days later was not least the result of this sudden and unexpectedly lucky breakthrough made by the Soviets through the border positions to the south of the Neusiedler See.

A smartly-dressed and equipped unit of Tyrolean *Standschützen* marching through Innsbruck, November 1944. **Emil Nagel**

Left: A very un-military looking member of a *Volkssturm* unit in southern Germany, spring 1945. Note his M16 steel helmet. **Emil Nagel**

Below: Dramatic photograph of a Tyrolean *Volkssturm* unit in a snowstorm, winter 1945. **Emil Nagel**

CHAPTER TWELVE

East Prussia (October 1944–April 1945)

The excessively headstrong personality of the *Gauleiter* of East Prussia, Koch, and the fact that fighting was going on along the borders of East Prussia from mid-October 1944, are the reasons why East Prussia's *Volkssturm* represents something of a unique case among the *Volkssturm* as a whole. An overview of its organisation and equipment, together with details of the fighting in which it was involved, are provided in the account written by the former president of the Königsberg Chamber of Trade, which is attached as Appendix XX. This account also indicates Koch's efforts to remain independent of the *Wehrmacht*, which he deeply mistrusted. This mistrust is especially evident in his telegram to Hitler: "4th Army on the run into the Reich. Making a cowardly attempt to break out to the West. I continue to defend East Prussia with my *Volkssturm*."[43]

Among his so-called 'Supreme Command' in Königsberg, Koch created Sector and Sub-sector Staffs, which did not content themselves merely with organisational and training duties. They assigned to themselves military-style command authority and tried to fight as autonomous units both with and independently of the *Wehrmacht*. The former President of the Königsberg Chamber of Trade states in his account that "the Supreme Command of the East Prussian *Volkssturm* insisted on this autonomy and resisted any attempts to merge the *Volkssturm* with the *Wehrmacht*."

Another source states that the Party had forbidden their units to inform the regular Army commanders of military action they were taking. Thus, often the military commander – right up to the Commanding General, who after all was responsible for the defensive operation – did not know where the *Volkssturm* were. The location, strength, level of armament and duties of the various battalions had to be ascertained by asking around and by sending out officers. Only after many difficulties with *Gauleiter* Koch had been resolved were the *Volkssturm* units deployed at the front or in reserve placed under the command of the appropriate Divisional commander. Once the friction had been overcome, they worked well together.

In East Prussia, *Volkssturm* units were already in action before the *Führer* Decree concerning the formation of the *Volkssturm* had even been announced.

As early as 7 October 1944, the *Volkssturm* of Memel were already securing the periphery of the city and "despite shortages of equipment and no training set about the defence of Memel with marvellous spirit."[44] Then, when on 9 October the front was withdrawn into the city, together with the Army, the *Volkssturm* set about making preparations for the expected Soviet offensive against the *Festung*. "As dawn was breaking, the first large-scale Soviet attack began with massive preparatory fire of all calibres on the forward positions and on the periphery of the city. There stood the *Volkssturm*, who in good spirit let this fire break over them."[45]

> The Treuburg *Volkssturm*, which was formed between 16 and 21 October, was immediately involved in fighting in the north-eastern corner of the district to the west of Filipow … In the area to the east of Treuburg, still in Poland, in the forward trenches there appeared old men wearing the yellow armband of the *Volkssturm* and with Italian rifles, asking to be allowed to join reconnaissance and assault troops. 'The enemy mustn't get any further', these gallant men said in their broad East Prussian dialect, and joined in the fighting.[46]

On 20 October, seven East Prussian *Volkssturm* battalions were in action at the front. One month later, on 21 November, according to a report made by the East Prussian *Volkssturm* command, "almost 90 combat ready battalions with 80,000 men were standing under arms, or rather, under spades."[47]

The fate of the Goldap *Volkssturm* Battalion 25/235, which was formed on 17 October 1944, can be seen as representative of the fate of many East Prussian battalions. When it was formed, it comprised four companies with about 400 men, who were all 45 years old or older. The Soviet rifles with which the battalion was equipped had never been fired and did not work. The men wore civilian clothing and for the most part only ordinary shoes. They had no blankets, identity discs or packs of field dressings.

This Goldap *Volkssturm* Battalion first went into action as early as 18 October. Some of them had to hold the Goldap-Gumbinnen highway against enemy armour. On the early morning of 21 October, the battalion took up defensive positions in Daken – Schwadenfeld next to a *Wehrmacht* unit. In this position it came under mortar fire and was bombed by aircraft with high-explosive bombs. During the first three days of fighting, losses were 76 dead, wounded and missing. When on 23 October, the pressure from the enemy continued to mount, the battalion, which in the meantime had been placed under the command of the *Wehrmacht*, received orders to withdraw, together with the *Wehrmacht*.

There then followed a lengthy period of preparation and construction of defensive positions, which was used for training and for providing the battalion with better equipment and German weapons. The civilian clothing was replaced by grey, blue and even brown uniforms.

After renewed fighting, in January 1945 the battalion retreated to Königsberg, where at first it went into action in Ponarth and where it was provided with replacements from the Königsberg *Volkssturm*. At the end of March 1945, the battalion took part in an attempt to break out of Königsberg. After further hard and costly fighting in the Königsberg area, the remnants of the battalion were transferred to Denmark via Hela and there they were disbanded on 2 May. "When the times have quietened down, people will also remember the *Volkssturm*, and this diary is to help ensure that the East Prussian *Volkssturm* is not forgotten. The sacrifices which our battalion made are so enormous, and our comrades who were killed and wounded have a right not to be forgotten. Our battalion was twice brought back up to strength, and in the end only 70 men survived to tell the tale."[48]

At least eight combat battalions and many construction battalions of the *Volkssturm* with around 10,000 *Volkssturmsoldaten* took part in the defence of the fortress of Königsberg. The commander of the Königsberg *Volkssturm* was the *Kreisleiter* and *Leutnant der Reserve* Wag. The appeal of Memel's Kreisleiter Grau for men between the ages of fifteen and sixty to report to the Party offices within the city, dated 10 August 1944. (Alexandr Grinevner,[49] after *Gauleiter* Koch had fled the fortress. "The *Volkssturm* was also involved in the fighting for Neuhausen (6 kilometres to the north-east of Königsberg). At the aerodrome, one *Volkssturm* alarm unit came up against lorries full of Soviets, who turned and fled when the *Volkssturm* appeared. This action led to the award of the Iron Cross First Class to *Kreisleiter* Wagner, who took part in the action."[50]

On 28 February, the *Ritterkreuz* was awarded to *Volkssturm* commander Tiburzy for destroying five Soviet tanks with *Panzerfäuste*. Hans Graf von Lehndorff, in his *Bericht aus Ost- und Westpreußen 1945–1947*, pages 34/35, writes of this incident:

> Among the wounded that we are receiving, there are more and more of those who cannot be classified as proper, regular soldiers. Many of them are beyond the age for military service. As men of the *Volkssturm*, they are stuck into uniforms and immediately sent out against the enemy. Even so, many of them have achieved amazing things. One of them arrives with a six-man escort and a letter from the *Kreisleiter* which requests that he be shown special consideration. Despite being seriously wounded, he is almost wild with enthusiasm about his exploits, because he succeeded in destroying four Soviet tanks one after the other with the *Panzerfaust*.[51]

Even if, since the *Gau* of Danzig-West Prussia was formed, the city of Elbing had been attached to this *Gau* and removed from the *Gau* of East Prussia, the events in the eastern part of West Prussia and the siege of Elbing are indivisibly linked with the Soviet conquest of East Prussia. Therefore, the fighting for Elbing and in West Prussia will also be briefly mentioned at the end of this chapter.

To defend the city of Elbing, the commandant had at his disposal only the *Ersatz* units from the Division 'Feldherrnhalle', that is, one *Panzer-Grenadier-Ersatz* battalion, one *Panzer-Pioneer-Ersatz* battalion, one *Panzer-Ersatz-Abteilung* and one *Artillerie-Ersatz-Abteilung* together with a *Volkssturm* Battalion and two *Volkssturm* batteries. *Major* Kühneck, the artillery commander of the fortress, was soon able to form another three *Volkssturm* battalions with newly manufactured guns from the firm of Schichau.[52]

According to an account written by the former Lord Mayor of the city of Elbing, which is included among the documents held in the Bundesarchiv, on 23 January 1945, the Mayor was speaking over the telephone with the Chief of Staff (Ia) of the *Festungskommandanten*, during the course of which conversation the Ia assured the Lord Mayor that the military situation presented no threat at all. But even as the two gentlemen were speaking, seven Soviet tanks drove past the Town Hall, firing their guns and machine guns! The fact that despite this early surprise attack, the city managed to hold its own until 10 February deserves special mention.

In the *Gau* of Danzig West Prussia, sorting out organisation, armament and equipment for the *Volkssturm* was even more of a problem than it was elsewhere, with the result that, as was the case in Elbing, so also in the south eastern and southern part of the *Gau* only virtually unarmed *Volkssturm* battalions were available to reinforce the *Wehrmacht*. This shortage may well have been the result of the attitude of the *Gauleiter* who "had the most serious reservations about the idea of the *Volkssturm*, even in October, when the formation of the *Volkssturm* was proclaimed from Königsberg."[53]

But even the unarmed or very poorly armed *Volkssturm* of Danzig West Prussia does not seem to have been without its uses, as is indicated in an account written by the landowner Gunther von Flottwell from the district of Stuhm/West Prussia: "In the meantime, the *Volkssturm* had been mobilised. The men had to help with the evacuation and were at the disposal of the mayors for carrying out special duties. This order came just at the right time and averted a lot of potential disasters."[54]

The appeal of Memel's *Kreisleiter* Grau for men between the ages of fifteen and sixty to report to the Party offices within the city, dated 10 August 1944. **Alexandr Grinev**

Himmler addresses the East Prussian Volkssturm *October 1944*

Members of the *Volkssturm* listen to Himmler's speech at a rally announcing the organisation's formation, 18 October 1944, Bartenstein, East Prussia. As with the nationwide oath-taking ceremonies that occurred on 12 November, the date was carefully chosen by the Nazi hierarchy, recalling the victory over Napoleon at Leipzig, 18 October 1813.
Museum of Modern History, Ljubljana, Slovenia

Another view of Himmler's speech at the Marwitz Barracks, Bartenstein, East Prussia, 18 October 1944. The effect that the Party hierarchy are trying to convey to the audience is very evident from the full Nazi panoply on show.
Museum of Modern History, Ljubljana, Slovenia

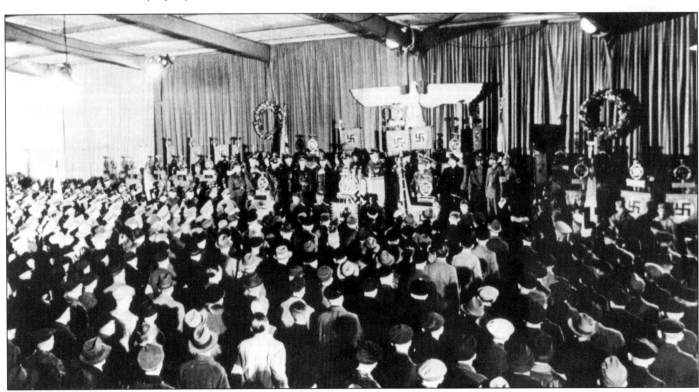

Himmler addresses the East Prussian Volkssturm *October 1944*

A close-up shot of Himmler during his speech on 18 October 1944. To his left is *Gauleiter* of East Prussia Erich Koch. Koch, who had served as *Reichskomissar für die Ukraine* between July 1941 and 1944, managed to flee East Prussia to Schleswig-Holstein at the end of the war. Finally captured by the British in Hamburg during 1949, he was extradited to Poland, where he was sentenced to death. This was later commuted to a life sentence - he finally died in 1986, still captive in a Polish prison, aged 90.
Museum of Modern History, Ljubljana, Slovenia

Himmler addresses the East Prussian Volkssturm *October 1944*

Left: A close-up view of some of the very first East Prussian *Volkssturm* pictured at Himmler's rally, Bartenstein, 18 October 1944. They carry rifles and wear the first-issue white armband – nothing else marks them out as members of an armed force. Party members are much in evidence.
Museum of Modern History, Ljubljana, Slovenia

Below: Another view of the same *Volkssturm* unit.
Museum of Modern History, Ljubljana, Slovenia

A fine study of a NSDAP *Obergemeinschaftsleiter* handing out first-issue armbands, East Prussia, October 1944.
Museum of Modern History, Ljubljana, Slovenia

Another image of the same East Prussian *Volkssturm* unit. The man on the right is a policeman, and wears the German sports badge and SA sports badge. This unit has been issued with Austro-Hungarian M1895 Steyr-Mannlicher rifles.
Museum of Modern History, Ljubljana, Slovenia

General der Infanterie Gollnik and NS *Kreisleiter* Grau visiting *Volkssturm* positions in the Memel bridgehead, East Prussia, autumn 1944. At the time, Gollnik was commander of XXVIII *Armeekorps*. *Kreisleiter* Kurt Grau was the Nazi Party's official in charge of Memel city itself. **Georg Hanisch/Bildarchiv Preußischer Kulturbesitz, Berlin**

Above: Men only recently called-up to the *Volkssturm* marching to their assembly point, East Prussia, 25 October 1944. They have thus far only been issued with early-pattern white armbands and rifles – many still carry their belongings in suitcases. **Bundesarchiv 146/74/120/20A**

Right: *Ritterkreuzträger Hauptmann* Franz Silzner (back to camera) confers with a SA *Sturmführer* and another man during *Volkssturm* operations in East Prussia, October 1944. Silzner, a reserve officer, was awarded the Ritterkreuz as a company officer with Inf. Rgt. 501, October 1942.
Museum of Modern History, Ljubljana, Slovenia

Interesting study of a *Volkssturm* headquarters during the fighting in East Prussia, October 1944. An officer dictates orders to a young girl drafted in to help with clerical duties. The officer appears to be wearing a four pocket *Heer* camouflaged field service jacket – a rare garment. It may well have been privately made for the officer in question – note the non-regulation National Emblem on his upper left sleeve instead of above the right breast pocket. A tank destruction badge is displayed on his upper right sleeve, and an early-pattern plain white armband is on his left arm. **Museum of Modern History, Ljubljana, Slovenia**

Members of the East Prussian *Volkssturm* train, November 1944. They still wear civilian clothing - their only military apparel is the first type of *Volkssturm* armband issued, black print on white. **Museum of Modern History, Ljubljana, Slovenia**

Men and boys of the East Prussian *Volkssturm* are sworn in, November 1944. The photographs were aimed at demonstrating the increased levels of uniformity, weapons and equipment prevailing amongst units than had been the case only a month before. They wear the M42 Army greatcoat and plain M43 field caps, but already have the second-issue *Volkssturm* armband. **Museum of Modern History, Ljubljana, Slovenia**

Another view of the swearing-in ceremony, East Prussia, November 1944. The weapons on display, including the *Panzerfaust* and *Panzerschreck*, are designed to lend maximum credence to the idea that *Volkssturm* units were equipped with the most up-to-date weapons available. **Museum of Modern History, Ljubljana, Slovenia**

A further good close-up view of these East Prussian *Volkssturmmäner*, November 1944. The simplicity of the uniforms is apparent. **Museum of Modern History, Ljubljana, Slovenia**

The East Prussian *Volkssturm* are inspected by *Generaloberst* Georg-Hans Reinhardt (CO *Heeresgruppe Mitte*) and *Gauleiter* Erich Koch, November 1944. **Museum of Modern History, Ljubljana, Slovenia**

Danzig was one of dozens of towns and cities throughout Germany in which oath-taking ceremonies took place on 12 November 1944. This photo shows the *Gauleiter* of Danzig-West Prussia, Albert Forster, and SA *Gruppenführer* Ohrt being sworn-in. Forster was later captured by the British in Hamburg on 28 May 1945, extradited to Poland and hanged in Warsaw on 28 February 1952. The four banners include two from Danzig, one from Marienweder and one from Deutsch-Eylau. Note the presence of *Heer*, *Polizei* and *Reichsarbeitsdienst* officials behind the banners. **Museum of Modern History, Ljubljana, Slovenia**

A member of the East Prussian *Volkssturm* reads letters next to his Christmas tree, December 1944. This image clearly shows the later-pattern armband worn on his left lower cuff, and the label attached to the explosive head of the *Panzerfaust*.
Ullstein Bilderdienst

Volkssturmmänner construct anti-tank barricades in the snow, East Prussia, winter 1944/45. **Bildarchiv ASL**

Volksturmmänner dug-in near Königsberg, East Prussia, 20 January 1945. The ubiquitous *Panzerfaust* is in evidence. The first phase of the assault on Königsberg began on 19 February; the city finally succumbed after a fierce three-day assault, on 9 April.
Bundesarchiv 183/R-98401

A *Gruppenführer* of the Angerburg *Volkssturm*, East Prussia, 1945.
Duncan Rogers

Volkssturm-Bataillonsführer and *Hauptsturmführer der* SA Ernst Tiburzy, the *Volkssturm*'s first recipient of the *Ritterkreuz*. Tiburzy was commander of *Volkssturmbataillon* 25/82 in *Festung* Königsberg. He received his award on 10 February 1945 for the destruction of five Soviet tanks with *Panzerfäuste*. **Friedrich Baier**

Another image of *Bataillonsführer* Ernst Tiburzy. **Friedrich Baier**

Both pictures above: Members of the Königsberg *Volkssturm*, spring 1945. **Friedrich Baier**

CHAPTER THIRTEEN

The Wartheland, east of the Oder and on the Oder
(January-April 1945)

On 12 and 13 January 1945, the large-scale Soviet offensive was unleashed from the bridgeheads on the Vistula south of Warsaw, Baranow, Pulawy, and Magnuszew. The fronts of the German 4th Panzer Army and the 9th Army were broken through so quickly that towards evening on 15 January, the leading Soviet armoured units were already approaching Krakow, Czestochowa and the Bora. The targets of the Soviet attack, the Upper Silesian industrial district and the Oder towards Kustrin, with Berlin as the eventual target, thus became clear. To give an account of the causes of this unexpectedly sudden catastrophe would be beyond the scope of the present work. It is enough to state that around midday on 14 January 1945, the *Volkssturm* Command Staff in the office of the *Reichsführer-SS* issued the order for the mobilisation of the entire *Volkssturm* in the East.[55] During the course of the afternoon, this order was passed on to the *Gau* Chiefs of Staff of the eastern *Gaue*. They were to begin by mobilising the first levy.

By the morning of 16 January, the Chief of the Army General Staff, *Generaloberst* Guderian, had summoned the Chief of Staff of the *Volkssturm* in the office of the *Reichsführer-SS*, SS-*Obergruppenfuhrer und General der Waffen-SS* Berger, and the military chief of the *Volkssturm* Command staff to his headquarters in Wunsdorf/Zossen .

Standing in front of his large wall chart, the *Generaloberst* sketched out the catastrophic developments which were taking place on the Eastern Front. Because "that man" (by which he meant Hitler) had strictly refused his request to abandon the senseless Kurland salient, now there were no reserves whatever to stabilise the existing front or to form a new front. To help overcome this dangerous shortage of troops, he said, the *Volkssturm* would have to play their part. "Any suggestions, gentlemen?"

At the request of the Chief of the Army General Staff, the entire *Volkssturm* in the East had already been mobilised on 14 January. But the *Generaloberst* had to add that for the time being the *Volkssturm*, of both the first and the second levies, had to be regarded as having no significant value as a fighting force. Thus, he said, for example, the second levy with its younger members had not yet been formed into battalions and as a result had had no training. But the principal problem was the shortage of weapons suitable for use in the field. Orders had been given for the few German weapons which the *Volkssturm* did have to be distributed to all the *Gaue* throughout the Reich, so that now, in the East, there was a shortage of weapons. As a result of this, in the eastern *Gaue*, only as many battalions of the *Volkssturm* could be mobilised in support of the *Wehrmacht* as could be provided with weapons, or could be used unarmed for construction work on the positions or for other duties. And, he said, there were only very few battalions which could be armed with weapons suitable for use in the field.

"What else can you do?" asked the *Generaloberst*.

In response to this question, the Chief of Staff informed him that the twenty *Gaue* in the interior of Germany could be instructed to form, initially, one and, later, a second *Volkssturm*-Battalion z. b. V. (for special service) for use outside the boundaries of their home *Gau*, and to equip these battalions with the weapons which were available in the *Gaue*. In particular, he said, the 30 light MG 34 or 42 machine guns, and six medium mortars *which had recently been allocated to each Gau* could be given to these battalions. After they were formed, he went on, the first twenty battalions could be brought by rail to the Oder and there – after about a week – could be placed at the disposal of the *Wehrmacht*.

The *Generaloberst* agreed with this proposal, but wanted to have these battalions transported to Posen, which had to be held "at all costs". In reply to this, the two gentlemen from the *Volkssturm* Command stressed that such units could be initially only be regarded as being suitable for deployment to the rear of defensive positions, where they could be given a certain amount of training before coming into contact with the enemy. They were, they said, completely unsuitable for offensive action and a war of movement, at least for the time being.

In addition, all experience to date, they said, led them to expect that these units would not arrive in Posen before the Soviets did. Despite these objections, the *Generaloberst* insisted on having his way. The first 20 Battalions z. b. V. had to be transported to Posen.

During the same afternoon of 16 January -in agreement with the Party Chancellery – the instructions to set up a *Volkssturm* Battalion for special use outside the boundaries of its home *Gau* were issued to the respective *Gaue* of Upper Danube, Bavaria, Franconia, Halle-Merseburg, Hamburg, Hessen-Nassau, Kurhessen, Magdeburg-Anhalt, Main-Franconia, Mecklenburg, Munich-Upper Bavaria, East Hanover, Pomerania, Saxony, Salzburg, Schleswig-Holstein, Swabia, Sudetenland, South Hanover-Brunswick and Thuringia. And on evening of the same day, the Chief of Staff of the *Volkssturm* Command Staff and the appropriate *Oberstleutnant* of the OKH General Staff agreed details of organisation, transport, and rail destinations.

While the target of the Soviet offensive forces coming from the Baranow bridgehead was Silesia, the enemy armies advancing from the bridgeheads at Pulawy and Magnuszew through Lodz and Posen were pushing towards the middle Oder. On 20 January, the enemy were already at the gates of the fortress of Posen, which they had completely surrounded three days later. Meanwhile, other enemy forces had circumvented the city to the north and to the south and, without pausing, were advancing on the Oder-Warthe bend. As early as 26 January the Soviets, with these forces, were already reaching the blocking line at Tirschtiegel, the most easterly line of the defensive positions to the east of Berlin constructed in the 1930s and later heavily extended. Thus, in just a fortnight, the Soviet armoured forces had covered about 350 kilometres as the crow flies, and had broken through 'Gau Wartheland' across its entire width of 270 kilometres.

The organisation of the *Volkssturm* in the Wartheland and the fate that overtook it in during the first two weeks of the Soviet offensive could hardly be better described than as they are in the 'Documents relating to the *Volkssturm* of the Wartheland', which are attached as Appendix XXI. All the accounts included among these documents were written in February and March 1945 and bear the stamp of experiences still fresh in the memory. Only the commentary written on the documents by the former commander of the Deputy General Command XXI Army Corps in Posen dates from 1953.

These documents illustrate the enormous difficulties which arose in connection with the formation of the *Volkssturm* in the Wartheland. Despite these difficulties, it was possible by 20 January to place under the local *Wehrmacht* authorities no less than 32 *Volkssturm* battalions from the Wartheland, each with an average strength of 450–500 men, even if those men were mostly only poorly armed. That these units were not able to carry out the tasks assigned to them was not in their power, and was not the fault of the *Volkssturmsoldaten*, who were for the most part keen and courageous.

Responsibility for defending *Festung* Posen was for the most part in the hands of makeshift regiments, the core of which was formed by School V for Officer Cadets. There was a complete lack of any artillery or anti-aircraft guns, and only small numbers of infantry guns and tanks were available. Which specific *Volkssturm* units were in action in Posen cannot be ascertained from the documents. "The spirit of the young officers, but also the spirit of the *Volkssturm* and police units, was excellent."[56] Posen held its own in hard fighting from 21 January to 23 February 1945, that is, for five whole weeks.

Not one of the special service *Volkssturm* battalions from the *Gaue* in the interior of Germany made it to Posen. The Soviets were faster. Some *Volkssturm* transport units crossed the Oder and came right up against the advancing enemy. Most of their members subsequently went missing. The special service *Volkssturm* battalion from Hessen-Nassau must have been pushed northwards, because in February it was fighting at Stargard in Pomerania and eventually was fighting at the Stettin bridgehead. Later chapters of this book will give accounts of the majority of the first 20 special service *Volkssturm* battalions whose transports were delayed and which, in agreement with OKH, were stopped and unloaded at the Oder.

As already mentioned, on 26 January the Soviets reached the blocking line at Tirschtiegel. Four days later, on 30 January, they brought up strong forces to the Oder-Warthe-*Stellung*, the main area of fighting in the Oder-Warthe bend. This permanent defensive position stretched from Landsberg/Warthe southwards along the Obra, reaching the Oder after about 75 kilometres between Grossen and Züllichau. Its concrete fortifications, well adapted to the natural obstacles of the landscape, offered permanent protection against shellfire up to calibres of 21cm and against temporary fire from heavier ordnance and bombing from aircraft. All the fortification works were arranged to provide all-round defence. In front of the positions were wire obstacles and a continuous anti-tank ditch. Transport and supplies within this area and to the rear could be maintained via tunnels. The Oder-Warthe-*Stellung* was one of the most strongly constructed fortified fronts in the Reich and, given sufficient men and material, was said to be impregnable.

Although during the war this position too had been extensively disarmed, not all weapons had been removed. In this sense, it was still, to a certain extent, defensible. Two *Ersatz* Divisional Staffs under the overall command of Defence District III, Berlin, were to command the garrison of the position which was largely composed of *Ersatz* units and *Volkssturm*. The *Gau* Chief of Staff of the *Gau* of Mark Brandenburg had taken the place of the peacetime border militia with around 25 *Volkssturm* battalions, and had led these battalions into the respective sectors which they were to occupy and defend if this became necessary.

On that same 30 January, on which the *Wehrmacht* Command Staff War Diary noted: "Soviets at Oder-Warthe-*Stellung*", it goes on to say: "Own forces to man these positions not yet here". Thus, as early as the night between 30/31 January, and on 31 January, the Soviets succeeded in breaking through the fortified area in its entire depth, almost without a fight. The result of this breakthrough was of that by 1 and 2 February the enemy were able to reach the eastern periphery of Küstrin, and the Oder on both sides of the city, and by 2 February were able to cross the river at Göritz, south-west of Küstrin, and establish a bridgehead there. The Soviet armour, which pushed in from the north around midday on 31 January in order to take possession of the fortress by a surprise attack, withdrew again after a Hitler Youth unit of the *Volkssturm* succeeded in destroying several tanks with *Panzerfäuste*.

How could such a collapse have come about?

It was only partly the case that on 30 January German forces to occupy the Oder-Warthe-*Stellung* had not yet arrived. Remnants of the Field Army which were withdrawing in the direction of the Oder had become involved in fighting between 26 and 30 January with the Soviets as they retreated. But they were seemingly unaware that there was an extended combat zone for not far away from them. Most of the *Ersatz* troop units under the command of Deputy General Command III Army Corps which were intended to occupy the position had not yet arrived, because the orders had supposedly been given too late. As a result, the crossing points over the anti-tank ditches had not been blown, and the blockade on the East-West routes had not been set up. Some of the *Volkssturm* battalions from the *Gau* of Mark Brandenburg had for a few days already been manning their allocated defensive sectors, a fact which is confirmed by the accounts in the Bundesarchiv. From among this material, the account of three *Volkssturm* battalions which had taken over their sectors in the Oder-Warthe-*Stellung* illustrate what problems and what difficulties these battalions found themselves facing.

On 20 January, the *Volkssturm* Battalion from Landsberg/Warthe which had been ordered to take up position in the bunker line on both sides of the Schwerin/Kustrin highway suddenly received the surprise order to march into its deployment area. On 21 January, it took up position. The men of the battalion were mostly wearing civilian clothing. In the position, training was carried out with Italian rifles, light machine guns, "on built-in [i.e. casemated] heavy mortars and Czech anti-tank guns". "The *Volkssturm* were to defend the concrete bunkers while units of the *Wehrmacht* were to occupy the areas between them".

By the line of burning villages to the right and to the left of the highway, the *Volkssturmsoldaten* were able to follow the progress of the Soviet advance. "The roads leading through the position were constantly flooded with retreating members of the *Wehrmacht* and columns of refugees".

In the night before the first Soviet attack, the aforesaid *Wehrmacht* unit, including its officers, disappeared from the *Wehrmacht* camp without informing the *Volkssturm*. The effect on the *Volkssturm* of being suddenly left on their own after weeks of working together in close agreement with the *Wehrmacht*, was considerable. But now it was at least possible to provide most of the men with *Wehrmacht* uniforms from the accommodation in the *Wehrmacht* camp.

During the morning of 1 February, the first tank shells began to explode around the bunkers, particularly on the highway (the battalion bunker), while by means of underground telephone communications, bunkers further to the south had already been overrun by the Soviets, and the only thing left for the men manning the positions to expect was to be taken prisoner. "A Divisional General with a company of infantry guns coming through the village in full order – even if without any ammunition – then ordered the now completely purposeless *Volkssturm* to withdraw in the direction of Küstrin."

On its march to Küstrin, the battalion had to survive an attack by Soviet armour and a temporary period of captivity. "In their lack of any will to fight, the *Wehrmacht* units fleeing to the rear, for the most part in small groups, had such a poor effect on morale that the *Volkssturm* units felt they had been betrayed and sold down the river".[57]

On 24 January a *Volkssturm* battalion from Küstrin was brought by railway to Trebitsch to man a section of the Oder-Warthe-*Stellung*. "While I was in Trebitsch, I honestly tried all I could to get weapons. It was no use. When, in the early morning of 30 January, I received a report that the Soviets were crossing the Obra, I went to the combat position, where, in the 'Ludendorff' bunker, I tried once again to get weapons or orders. The *Gefreiter* manning the telephone told me that the last officer had left and was not coming back. So then – still with only two rifles for the whole battalion – I gave orders to withdraw in the direction of Kustrin".[58]

The *Volkssturm* battalion from the Sternberg district was mobilised on 21 January. It had to occupy the Burschen – Starpel sector of the Oder-Warthe-*Stellung* and, if necessary, to defend it. The men of the battalion were still almost all in civilian clothing. Three machine guns, 17 rifles and 12 *Panzerfäuste* formed the total armament for the one company of the battalion, whose commander is the author of the account attached as Appendix XXII, which he wrote in the winter of 1946/47. "Nothing's going right. Our people are openly cursing the way things are, and want to go home. Too many soldiers are coming from the East, why doesn't someone hold them at our firm positions? This would be the best place to hold up the Soviet assault".[59]

When at the end of January the Soviets were approaching the Oder-Warthe-*Stellung*, the battalion from Sternberg occupied the defensive sector which had been assigned to them. Appendix XXII gives an account of their action in this position. The fact that the company in which the account's author was serving was able to hold its own for an entire month in its bunkered position, while the front had long since been running 60 kilometres further westwards along the Oder, is worthy of record. At the end of February, the author of the account, at the head of one of the last *Kampfgruppen*, managed to break out of the position and to return to his home village of Pinnow near Sternberg. But he was not spared the fate of captivity in Russia. After he was released on 31 July 1946, he decided not to return to his home district and settled in the West.

When the *Volkssturm* Command Staff in Berlin became aware that the special service battalions provided by the 20 *Gaue* in the interior of Germany were no longer able to get to the surrounded fortress of Posen, after the Chief of the Army General Staff had given his approval, the transport arriving in Küstrin and Frankfurt-an-der-Oder from 26 January onwards were stopped and unloaded. All these special service *Volkssturm* battalions of the first levy and later of the entire second levy were here placed under the command of the *Wehrmacht*. Then, together with emergency units formed on the spot from scattered troops of the Field Army, poorly trained *Ersatz* units, a few police units and some individual battalions from the *Reichsarbeitsdienst*, they were mobilised for the construction and defence of the Oder front, including the two cities of Küstrin and Frankfurt-an-der-Oder which had been declared to be *Festungen*.

Although, because of the nature of the terrain, to defend the Oder front required strong infantry forces to provide covering fire for the entire river, there were only enough available forces to man the positions at vital points. Added to this was the fact that at the end of January the Oder was frozen and had thus ceased to represent an obstacle. In the last days of January, the attacking Soviet units came up against this scanty and inadequate defensive force. With their first assault they established a foothold, even if this was at first only with weak forces, to the north of Fürstenberg (near Vogelsang), to the south of Küstrin at Göritz and north of the city at Schaumburg and Kienitz, and somewhat later also to the south of Frankfurt (near Schwetig). Because of the shortage of troops, these breakthroughs could not be immediately repulsed by those troops which were available, mostly *Volkssturm*, because they were in no position to counter-attack. With their usual tenacity, the Soviets dug their claws in and thus held on to what would form the basis for later bridgeheads.[60]

In addition to local *Volkssturm* units from both drafts, the following units, among others, were in action on the Oder front: The *Volkssturm* Battalions z. b. V. 'Hessen' and 'München' at Lebus, the *Volkssturm* Battalion 'Potsdam' at Klessin and a battalion of the *Reichsarbeitdienst* to the west of Göritz. On the Oder to the east of Lossow, *Volkssturm* Battalion z. b. V. 22/1 ('Oberdonau'), *Volkssturm* Battalions z. b. V. 15/1 ('Mainfranken'), 27/95 ('Dresden') and Battalion 16/156 ('Brieskow') together formed the Petersdorff Regiment which was part of *Kampfgruppe z. b. V.*(later Division) Raegener.

The brief history of *Volkssturm* Battalion *z. b. V.* 22/1 ('Oberdonau'), which is attached as Appendix XXIII, serves to give an illustration of the action and fighting in which one of these special service battalions was involved. In Appendix XXIV, the report of a member of *Volkssturm* Battalion z. b. V. 'Hessen II', the writer describes the formation, transport and initial combat deployment of this second levy special service battalion. The remarkable thing in this account written by a simple *Volkssturmsoldat* is the fact that immediately after their arrival in the combat area, the mostly untrained elderly men were immediately ordered to mount an attack.

The fortress of Küstrin was defended by two fortress regiments. These had been formed only at the end of January 1945 from emergency units of the Army and the *Luftwaffe*, police units, and two *Volkssturm* battalions, of which one came from Küstrin and the other from Lüneburg. The only heavy weapons available were a few artillery batteries and infantry gun units.

Mention has already been made of the Küstrin *Volkssturm* Battalion which was brought to take over a sector of the Oder-Warthe-*Stellung* near Trebitsch and was marched back again from there. Its commander gives this account: "On the evening of 31 January, after we had arrived in Kustrin, I was instructed to send the men home with the order to be available the following morning at 9 a. m. But not all of them came back; a large number of them belonged to the personnel of the Finance Ministry, all or some of whom were accommodated in the Stülpnagel Barracks. This authority vanished overnight, taking with it the people who belonged to the battalion. The rest of our people turned up loyally and bravely as ordered. Soon I received orders to relinquish 106 men to the artillery. It's true that there were guns and ammunition there, but there was no one to man them. Another part of the battalion I had to surrender to the 'Lüneburg' Battalion. The remainder of them were engaged in entrenchment work on the periphery of the town."[61]

A third Kustrin *Volkssturm* Battalion, for which there were also no weapons available, was used as a construction and work battalion. Some of the men from this battalion were later equipped with weapons from the dead and wounded and then sent themselves into action.

With these rag-tag groups of men, cobbled together, some of them poorly armed and untrained, because initially there was no organisation, Küstrin was held against countless and often very strong Soviet attacks from 30 January to 29 March 1945, that is, for two whole months. Only on 31 March did the *Wehrmacht* communiqué announce: "The gallant defenders of Küstrin have succumbed to superior enemy forces".[62]

Further to the south, the city of Frankfurt-an-der-Oder, situated east of the Oder, was held by a particularly brave commandant. He had cobbled together a garrison from hospital inmates, troops who had lost their units, *Volkssturm* and *Ersatz* troops, and this garrison, inspired by his own spirit, defended its bridgehead successfully against all attacks, and also held in check the Soviet bridgehead immediately to the south of Frankfurt.[63]

The Oder front was held until the middle of April 1945, that is, until the beginning of the last Soviet offensive. But the fact that it was possible to build it up out of nothing at the end of January 1945 would have been impossible without the *Volkssturm*, the local *Volkssturm* units and the special service battalions brought in from the interior of Germany. This result is all the more remarkable in the light of the intention of the Soviet high command, which had issued the following orders: "After breaking through the German defences and shattering the enemy forces in western Poland, we shall press on deep into Brandenburg, take Berlin with support from the neighbouring front and reach the line of the Elbe with armour and motorised units".[64]

In this situation, the special service battalions of the *Volkssturm*, quite apart from the local units, had not all yet been equipped with German weapons. Many *Gauleiters*, against the clear instructions of the *Reichsführer-SS* and his Chief of Staff, and also in complete and even criminal ignorance of the situation, retained the German weapons which they had in their *Gaue* to defend their own home territory. Thus, for example, the *Gau* of Schwabia sent a special service battalion which was only equipped with the poorest foreign rifles without sufficient ammunition, had no heavy infantry weapons, and as far as manpower was concerned was in a state which was completely unsustainable. The battalion had to be returned home and a better battalion requested, although it was precisely at the end of January and the beginning of February 1945 that every single man was desperately needed at the Oder front.[65]

At the end of February 1945, the *Gauleiters* of some *Gaue* in the interior of Germany made a request for their special service battalions which had been deployed on the Oder front to be returned. They justified this request on the grounds that many members of these battalions were now required for the emergency programme within German industry, and for the spring sowing. In addition, they supported their request by pointing out that it had been intended for the deployment of the *Volkssturm* in support of the *Wehrmacht* to be a temporary arrangement and generally not to involve deployment outside the borders of the respective unit's home *Gau*.

The request for the release of these *Volkssturm* battalions was then presented by the *Volkssturm* Command Staff in writing to *Armeeoberkammando* (AOK) 9. After the request had been refused, they tried to obtain the agreement of AOK 9 in verbal discussions. But it was no use. The Supreme Commander again refused point-blank to release the battalions, commenting that to carry out the tasks which he had been ordered, he already had too few soldiers and could not afford to lose a single man, even a man from the *Volkssturm*. This refusal was reported to the *Reichsführer-SS*, but the *Volkssturm* from the *Gaue* in the interior of Germany remained deployed at the Eastern Front. Many *Volkssturm* battalions were even dissolved, with their younger members being enlisted in the regular fighting troops, and their older members being conscripted for service in the rear areas.

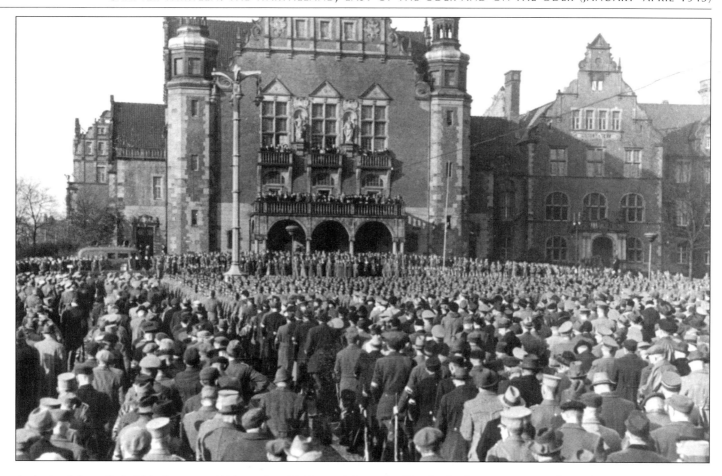

A photo of the rally held in Posen on 7 November 1944 to celebrate the *Tag der Freiheit* 1944 ('Day of Freedom 1944'), which commemorated the fifth anniversary of the founding of the *Reichsgau* Wartheland. Members of the recently-formed Wartheland *Volkssturm* listen to a speech by *Generaloberst* Guderian. Again, civilian dress predominates, along with first-pattern armbands; some Party and SA uniforms and headgear can also be seen being worn. **Museum of Modern History, Ljubljana, Slovenia**

This interesting photo shows members of the Wartheland *Volkssturm* parading in Posen, *Tag der Freiheit*, 7 November 1944. They are already wearing the official later-pattern Volkssturm armband. They are pulling what appear to be German 2cm flak cannon on improvised wheeled carriages, quite possibly MG151/20 cannon. This latter was a *Luftwaffe* 2cm aircraft cannon that was reused for ground service in the last year of the war. **Museum of Modern History, Ljubljana, Slovenia**

Another view of the Wartheland *Volkssturm* in Posen, 7 November 1944. *Gauleiter* Arthur Greiser, Himmler and Guderian (from left to right) review the men whilst standing on a SdKfz 7 half-track. Greiser was captured at the end of the war and hanged in Posen on 14 July 1946. **Museum of Modern History, Ljubljana, Slovenia**

Members of the newly sworn-in Berlin *Volkssturm* march past Goebbels towards the Brandenburg Gate, 12 November 1944. **Museum of Modern History, Ljubljana, Slovenia**

Another image showing the Berlin *Volkssturm*'s march-past on 12 November 1944. The original caption read 'Now the hour for strong hearts approaches!' **Museum of Modern History, Ljubljana, Slovenia**

A *Volkssturmmann* with a periscope rigged up to a *Panzerfaust*, east of Berlin, winter 1944/45.
Bildarchiv Preußischer Kulturbesitz, Berlin

A *Volkssturm* MG42 position at Frankfurt-an-der-Oder, 15 February 1945. **Bundesarchiv 183/J-28732**

Older members of the *Volkssturm* construct a tank barrier along the East-West Axis, Tiergarten area, Berlin, February/March 1945. **Arthur Grimm/Bildarchiv Preußischer Kulturbesitz, Berlin**

Volkssturmmänner wearing very basic uniforms dig an anti-tank trench on the Kaiserdamm, Berlin-Charlottenburg, February/March 1945. **Hilmar Pabel/Bildarchiv Preußischer Kulturbesitz, Berlin**

Berlin *Volkssturmmänner* at a rally at the Olympic Stadium, spring 1945. An absence of uniforms is still very apparent.
Friedrich Baier

The use of the ubiquitous *Panzerfaust* is demonstrated amidst the bomb-damaged ruins of Berlin, spring 1945.
Friedrich Baier

Fascinating and rare image of a train destined for the front being loaded with weapons for *Volkssturm* units at the Anhalter railway station, Berlin, 1945. **Arthur Grimm/Ullstein Bilderdienst**

Two members of the Berlin *Volkssturm* dig-in, spring 1945. Note the *Panzerschreck*. **History in the Making Archive**

Grainy but interesting photos showing a *Volkssturm* unit on the march, Frankfurt-an-der-Oder, spring 1945. This unit appears to be adequately armed and uniformed. The respite caused by the halting of the Soviet Vistula-Oder offensive gave the Germans a limited period of time in which to regroup and refit their units, an opportunity this unit appears to have benefited from. Note the prevalence of *Feldmütze* instead of the more common M43 *Einheitsfeldmütze*.
Friedrich Baier

Volkssturm marching through Küstrin, spring 1945. **Friedrich Baier**

Volkssturm positions near Küstrin, spring 1945. **Friedrich Baier**

Volkssturm *in action on the Oder*

This sequence of photographs shows a *Volkssturm* unit in action at Altdamm, the Oder, spring 1945. Note the use of the *Panzerfaust* as a form of grenade-launcher.
Bildarchiv ASL

The following series of three stark images shows Berlin
Volkssturm setting up concrete barricades and defences adjacent
to the Brandenburg Gate, Berlin, April 1945.
Ullstein Bilderdienst

CHAPTER FOURTEEN

Pomerania (February-March 1945)

At the same time as the Soviet forces broke through the blocking line at Tirschtiegel and the Oder-Warthe-*Stellung*, some elements of the Soviet forces began an offensive against the Pommern-*Stellung*. This front, which extended to the north of the Netze via Dt. Krone, had been constructed before 1939 with concrete emplacements and obstacles almost to the same strength as that of the Oder-Warthe-*Stellung*, and in the summer and autumn of 1944 had been reinforced. Large stretches of the country could be flooded. The first attacks by Soviet armoured units were repulsed on 30 January and 1 February 1945. But by 7 February, the Soviets had also broken through this strongly developed line of fortifications. One month later, on the morning of 4 March, the Soviets reached the periphery of the city of Kolberg, and in the night between 6/7 March finally reached the coast to the west and to the east of this city, thereby encircling the city on the land side.

With regard to the question as to how it was possible for the Soviets to break through such a well-developed position in such a short time, some extracts from contemporary accounts in the Bundesarchiv in Koblenz are illuminating.

According to the account of a former member of the Arnswalde district administration, at the decisive moment there were no *Wehrmacht* troops available to man the 'Pomeranian Wall'. "The few home garrisons, which were not in a state of combat readiness, had been senselessly deployed in front of the positions or in *Festung* Schneidemühl". In the two districts of Arnswalde and Friedeberg, seven *Volkssturm* battalions had been formed, whose commanders – former officers -had been trained with the *Wehrmacht* and in training battalions in the fortifications of the Pomeranian Wall. But because these battalions could not be armed, it is not likely that any order for deployment of the *Volkssturm* from these two districts was made. "Generally, though they were prepared to defend their homeland".[66]

In the district of Naugard, the formation of the *Volkssturm* had begun in November 1944. "The fact that the *Volkssturm* was unable to fulfil its task was largely due to the lack of ammunition. To my knowledge, rifles were available for only 10 per cent of the men of the *Volkssturm*. These rifles included weapons of five to six different systems and calibres, for which, often, only five rounds of ammunition per rifle were available. The *Volkssturm* in eastern Pomerania were mobilised on 21 and 22 January and sent into the field positions constructed in autumn 1944". Their task: to put the positions in order. "There was no question of them taking any part in the defence of these positions, because these units had no equipment whatever. On 1 March, these *Volkssturm* battalions were ordered to march back to their home districts. But this order came too late, because the Soviet offensive of 1 and 2 March largely cut off their retreat. As a result, the majority of the *Volkssturm* were taken prisoner. Some of them were pushed back to Kolberg".[67]

In the district of Pyritz, the formation of the *Volkssturm* had begun in October 1944. There was no equipment available apart from a few carbines and rifles of Dutch origin. "The *Volkssturm* was intended to be assigned to the military units in the eastern districts. In the district of Dt. Krone I saw nothing of any larger military units. After the Soviets had gone round them, these *Volkssturm* battalions withdrew and were disbanded ... In Pyritz, on the instructions of the Party, the *Volkssturm* were to hermetically seal the north-eastern exits from the town. Some tanks had pushed forward into the gardens of the suburbs. Mention should here be made of the fact that units of the Hitler Youth destroyed several tanks with their *Panzerfäuste*".[68] Then there came the word – "Every man for himself!"

The former district administrator of Dt. Krone district gives this account: "For many people, the fact that the Pommern-*Stellung* was so swiftly and completely overrun was incomprehensible. It had been disarmed after the war in Poland. But the positions could not be manned because there was a lack of personnel and weapons. As far as personnel were concerned, there was only the *Volkssturm*, who were almost entirely unarmed. There were no weapons". And the former district administrator writes elsewhere about the shortage of men to defend the positions: "Along this whole stretch I saw not one section of soldiers who were marching in the direction of the enemy. Quite the contrary: I saw everywhere soldiers with no weapons seeing to the columns of refugees and moving in the direction of Germany. In Küstrin and along the first few kilometres in the direction of

Landsberg, the roads were so packed with fleeing vehicles, mostly belonging to the *Luftwaffe*, that it took us at least 5 hours to get to Küstrin ... The German Army was in a process of complete disintegration".[69]

The city of Kolberg, which was raised to the status of a fortress by royal decree in 1872, was to be developed as a fortress again on the basis of an order issued in November 1944. But because there was a shortage of workforce and materials, when the second Fortress Commandant, *Oberst* Fullriede, arrived on 28 February 1945, all he found were parts of the planned anti-tank ditch and infantry positions.

When, on 4 March, the Soviets carried out their initial advance with the intention of taking the city by a surprise attack, the Fortress Commandant had the following troops at his disposal: one battalion of the *Feldausbildungs-Regiment Panzer* AOK 3 with regimental support units and regimental staff; one *Kriegsmarine Festungs-MG* Battalion, which arrived on 3 March; one poorly armed *Volkssturm* Battalion; one *Volkssturm* rocket launcher unit; parts of a Flak *Abteilung* with seven heavy and eight light anti-aircraft guns; 8 light field howitzers, with which it was only possible to form a battery on 3 March using observers and gunners from the infantry gun company and unarmed *Volkssturm* men; one *Panzergruppe* with a total of eight Panzer IV and *Hetzer* tanks, all of which needed repair, and had to be sent to Kolberg to be repaired. The *Volkssturm* rocket launcher unit had been formed in February 1945 from 60 *Volkssturm* men, to whom, by way of artillery, over 800 heavy rockets (28cm calibre) had been assigned. "The rocket launchers were manned entirely by men of the *Volkssturm*, who did their duty with unshakeable *sangfroid* and great success".[70]

Only after the fighting began was a second – poorly equipped – *Volkssturm* Battalion created. The two *Volkssturm* combat battalions carried out the defence of 'Combat Sector West' (Maikuhle) under the command of the local SA *Standartenführer*. Other mostly unarmed *Volkssturm* units were used for labour and guard purposes. After the fighting began, *Alarm* Battalion Hempel was formed from troops of the *Wehrmacht* who had lost their units.

As a result of the uninterrupted flood of refugees, the population of the town had grown from its original 35,000 to 85,000 inhabitants. Because the *Kreisleiter* had refused to evacuate the population before the town was encircled, on 7 March, a radio message from OKH was received forbidding any further attempts to keep open a supply route to the West, and giving orders to consolidate forces in order to provide protection for the evacuation of the population by sea.[71]

The *Volkssturm* played a large part in the defence of Kolberg: "In the West, on 9 March, a strong attack against the positions of *Volkssturm* Battalion Pfeiffer was repulsed" ... "Constant enemy attacks, supported by armour, against the *Volkssturm* sector in the west and against *Alarm* Battalion Hempel in the south-west were repeatedly repulsed in hand to hand fighting" ... "On 13 March (Tuesday) the enemy, with strong forces, attacked in the west at the Maikuhle" ... "At dawn on 14 March, a new, concentrated large-scale attack began with unusually strong artillery, tank, anti-tank, and mortar fire. It led to deep penetrations by the enemy into the Maikuhle, in the barracks in the suburbs of Geld, from the suburbs of Lauenburg into the interior of the city, and into the triangle of railway lines, which could only be blocked off with difficulty. The *Volkssturm* suffered very heavy casualties".[72]

After a struggle lasting 14 days, the defenders of the city had fulfilled the task which had been assigned to them. "Despite the lack of any support from the *Luftwaffe*, the combined deployment of armed forces from the Army, the *Kriegsmarine*, and the *Volkssturm* had succeeded in holding the city against all the concentrated attacks made by two Soviet tank units, reinforced by units of the 3rd, 4th and 6th Polish Infantry Divisions, by armoured, mortar and artillery units, including the 4th Artillery Regiment, sufficiently long enough to enable 70 to 80,000 refugees and the majority of the combat group (with the exception of 350 to 400 men who could not be evacuated) to be evacuated by sea to the West. German casualties dead, wounded and missing were estimated at 40 per cent, and in the case of the *Volkssturm* as high as 60 per cent".[73]

The *Volkssturm* were poorly equipped, sometimes armed only with ancient sporting or hunting pieces, poorly provided with ammunition, and for days at a time did not receive sufficient food. In addition to this, some of the *Volkssturm* were untrained men. Without any heavy weapons, these old men in the Maikuhle defended every inch of ground so that the port could be held open for the evacuation as long as possible ... The people of Kolberg will never forget how the men of the *Volkssturm* sacrificed themselves on their behalf. If, by 16 March, there were signs that *Volkssturm* units were beginning to disintegrate, who would dare to sit in judgment on them after the enormous physical and mental burden they had endured for 12 whole days? Even individual groups of the Army and the *Luftwaffe* temporarily left their positions. These kinds of incidents were only temporary and only affected some individual soldiers and *Kampfgruppen*, but not the majority of the defenders.[74]

In the early morning of 18 March 1945 a city completely devastated and burned to the ground fell into the hands of the enemy. In his letter of thanks to the defenders of the city, *Oberst* Fullriede wrote: "Under the hardest conditions, which required real men, you have proven yourselves to be the equals of those men who once fought under these same walls with Gneisenau and Nettelbeck".[75]

A rare Eastern Front photo from February 1945, showing *Oberst* Heinrich Remlinger, commander of *Festungstadt* Schneidemühl, and *Kreisleiter* Meil, commander of the town's *Volkssturm*. Note Remlinger's Knight's Cross, and the tank destruction badge on his right sleeve, and the fact that Meil is proudly displaying both his *Volkssturm* armband and wears collar patches indicating a rank of *Bereichsleiter* within the NSDAP. The defence of this town was conducted with some energy - a breakout was attempted on 14 February from which only 1,000 of the garrison escaped death or capture. **Ullstein Bilderdienst**

A *Volkssturm* coastal defensive position somewhere on the Baltic, Eastern Front, March 1945. **Ullstein Bilderdienst**

Youthful members of a Pomeranian *Volkssturm* unit, 1945. **Friedrich Baier**

Hitler Youth at an awards ceremony in Berlin, March 22 1945. **Emil Nagel**

Interesting photo showing *Volkssturmmänner* watching a remote-controlled 'Goliath' demolition vehicle, spring 1945. Note the fur caps and the decal showing the national colours on the right side of the steel helmet on the man second from left, a rare sight by spring 1945.
Bildarchiv ASL

The same *Volkssturm* unit on the march. **Bildarchiv ASL**

CHAPTER FIFTEEN

The Neisse Stellung *(February–April 1945)*

On 9 February 1945, the Chief of the Army General Staff informed the *Volkssturm* Command Staff that the main thrust of the Soviet pressure on Berlin was expected to come from the Glogau area through Sagan, that is, from the south-east. Because the troops fighting there would not be enough to withstand the pressure, the *Volkssturm*, he said, must immediately occupy a position to the rear of the front on the Neisse at Görlitz from Muskau through Forst and Guben to the Neisse estuary – with the focus at Forst and Guben. The holding garrison, he went on, would if necessary have to hold the position until sufficient Field Army units arrived.

The *Volkssturm* Command Staff responded by stating that the local *Volkssturm* along the Neisse had been registered, but in the absence of any weapons could not yet be equipped and trained, and that armed special service *Volkssturm* battalions from other *Gaue* were no longer available. In the light of the critical situation and the need to find some kind of solution, it was decided to mobilise all the *Volkssturm* in the Neisse area, from both the first and second levies, to support the *Wehrmacht*, to use them initially to develop the defensive positions which still needed to be established at some points, and then to arm as many battalions as could be armed by calling in weapons from everywhere. The Chief of the Army General Staff said that he would give the *Allgemeine Heeresamt* orders to place at the disposal of these battalions whatever weapons were available anywhere. In addition, Army sector and sub-sector staffs would be immediately formed and sent to the Neisse, and finally, he said, checks would be made whether, and if so, which, local *Wehrmacht* units could be released to serve as additional garrison troops for the Neisse positions.

By the early morning of the following day, 10 February 1945, the Chief of Staff of the *Volkssturm* Command Staff together with a few other officers, the *Gau* Chief of Staff of Mark Brandenburg, and a member of the Party Chancellery, drove to Forst, to which the five Chiefs of Staff of the *Kreise* in the Neisse area had been summoned by telephone. As a result of this meeting "32 battalions"[76] were immediately mobilised to support the *Wehrmacht*. On the arrival of the Army sector and sub-sector staffs, these battalions were placed under their command and set to work on extending the positions along the Neisse. In addition, the few *Volkssturm* battalions from other *Gaue* already occupied by the enemy which had fought their way through to the Neisse area and were armed, were immediately brought into the positions as a security garrison.

Examples of such battalions were the Kolmar *Volkssturm* Battalion 36/69 from the Wartheland, and one battalion from Posen. The former battalion, an account of whose initial fighting is given in Appendix XXI, went into action in Guben. The account attached as Appendix XXV describes the action taken by the Posen battalion near Gr. Breesen.

From its few remaining stocks of captured weapons, the *Allegemeine Heeresamt, Stab Ib*, assigned Dutch rifles of various manufacture, some Czech and Dutch machine-guns, plus a few German MG 34 machine-guns. There were a sufficient number of *Panzerfäuste* already available.

As luck would have it, it was also possible to secure 5,000 German 98K carbines for the Neisse battalions. One day during this period, a senior manager of the Mauser factory in Oberndorf-am-Neckar telephoned the *Volkssturm* Command Staff in Berlin. He said that there were 5,000 98K carbines at the factory for despatch to the *Gauleiter* of the Tyrol. These weapons, the manager said, had been manufactured from raw metal and using coal which the *Gauleiter* of the Tyrol had made available to them – probably using deliveries originally intended for Italy. Mauser had carried out the order, because if they had not they would have been forced to close the factory down because of shortage of coal. But they could, the manager said, imagine that in the current situation the carbines would be more urgently needed somewhere else other than in the Tyrol. The Command Staff immediately ordered that these weapons be requisitioned, and sent an officer to Oberndorf who organised their transport by rail to the Neisse.

The items of equipment assigned by the *Allgemeine Heeresamt* (weapons, ammunition and other items, which were mostly all stored in the west, north-west, and north of Germany) were transported into the preparation areas on the Neisse by lorry. Transport by rail had become unsafe because of the risk of air attack and on average took considerably longer than it had previously. The lorries were supplied by the *Volkssturm* transport squadrons which had been set up in all *Gaue* and which had been mobilised for a temporary period for this action in support of the *Wehrmacht*.

Within a week, almost all the weapons and all the other equipment were available on the Neisse for the *Volkssturm* battalions there. Whether there were enough weapons to equip all 32 battalions can no longer be ascertained from the available documents.

In order to make it easier and quicker to train the *Volkssturmsoldaten* on the foreign and German weapons, particularly on the machine guns, machine pistols and the *Panzerfaust*, the services of the 'Flying Training Groups' provided by the Senior Machine Gun Officer in OKH, which had already been active for some time at various places along the front, were enlisted. These training groups, which as a rule consisted of one officer and one service rank weapons master, carried out their training, which was always adapted to local circumstances, within the positions in the open air, in accommodation provided in local villages, schools and also in factory halls and other public rooms. They made a crucial contribution towards ensuring that the men of the *Volkssturm* were given at least a certain amount of knowledge of weapons which had hitherto been unknown to them.

In addition to instruction in the use of weapons, there were courses of instruction in positional warfare, combat training in the positions and construction of defensive works.

On 19 February 1945 the Soviets advanced to the line Forst-Guben. The units of the German Field Army which were withdrawing in front of the enemy and were extremely combat weary, were halted by the *Volkssturm* along the Neisse line. They reinforced the *Volkssturm* in those parts of the positions which were expected to be tactically important.

Only one day later, on 20 February, the *Volkssturm* deployed in Guben, on the eastern periphery of the city, succeeded in repulsing an advanced armoured enemy unit and in destroying two tanks by *Panzerfaust* in the process.

The following days were characterised by hard fighting around Forst and Guben. The *Wehrmacht* Command Staff Diary contains the following entries relating to these actions:

21.2 The enemy were repulsed at Guben.

22.2 Defensive actions on the Neisse; the enemy penetrated into Guben.

23.2 The enemy entered Forst, but were then thrown back out again; they were also thrown back at Guben. To the north of Forst the Soviets attempted to cross the Neisse.

24.2 The enemy pushed into Forst, but were repulsed again; between Forst and Guben there is another enemy bridgehead; the enemy were repulsed at Guben.

2.3 Fighting in the north-eastern part of Guben.

4.3 The enemy bridgehead north of Forst cleared out.

5.3 The situation has also improved north of Guben.[77]

After this there was a noticeable quietening of the Neisse front, which lasted until the large-scale Soviet offensive began on 16 April. This offensive is described as follows in the entries in the War Diary of the *Wehrmacht* Command Staff:

16.4 Large scale attack in the Muskau-Forst area, also on the Oder.

17.4 In the Forst area 1,000 air attacks by the Soviets.

18.4 Fighting going on in Forst. Enemy advance in Forst area.

19.4 Forst was lost.[78]

The *Volkssturm* battalions from the Neisse area remained deployed in support of the *Wehrmacht* to the end in their homeland. The deployment of the *Volkssturm* in the positions along the Neisse is a particularly instructive example for the use of a territorial militia within the framework of local defence. Despite sheer improvisation – within 10 days, men were called up into the unit, the unit was formed, the defensive position was prepared for defence, the unit was equipped with weapons, which first had to be brought in, training was carried out on these weapons and in the defensive positions – the *Volkssturm* on the Neisse were able not only to fulfil the task which had been assigned to them, to receive the retreating troops of the Field Army in their positions, but to go beyond this in successfully defending this position for two whole months with the units of the Field Army which were insufficient to do the job alone.

Silesian Volkssturm *January 1945*

This sequence of fascinating images was taken in Silesia, January 1945, and shows a *Volkssturm* unit being issued with weapons and on the march. Note the widespread wearing of *Heer*-issue fur caps to combat the severe winter of that year, and appearance of the ubiquitous *Panzerfaust* and *Panzerschreck*. Note also the horse-drawn transport. The collar patch insignia indicating the unit's commander is a *Bataillonsführer* is clearly visible. Contemporary and post-war recollections of members of the *Volkssturm* clearly indicate that such well-armed units were an exception, although many units were able to uniform themselves adequately.
Bildarchiv ASL

A *Volkssturm Batl.-Führer* talks to two of his men, Silesia, 22 February 1945. His two men wear a motley assortment of uniforms: on the left, a M43 *Heer* service tunic is worn with a black ski cap; his comrade wears a *Heer*-issue winter reversible jacket worn mouse-grey out with its accompanying hood. **Museum of Modern History, Ljubljana, Slovenia**

A lone *Volkssturmmann* on guard duty at a barricade in a Görlitz street, March 1945. Like many of his comrades, he appears to be wearing the later issue *Volkssturm* armband on his lower left sleeve, despite regulations stipulating it should be placed on the upper left arm. **Benno Wundshammer/Bildarchiv Preußischer Kulturbesitz, Berlin**

A *Volkssturm* unit makes its way through the shattered streets of Lauban, Lower Silesia, 30 March 1945. They wear basic uniforms and lack armbands. Lauban was the scene of fierce fighting during late February/early March – having fallen to elements of the Soviet 3rd Guards Tank Army on 28 February, it was recaptured by a German counter-attack on 1/2 March, spearheaded by 8th and 17th *Panzer* divisions. **Benno Wundshammer/Bildarchiv Preußischer Kulturbesitz, Berlin**

Two members of the *Volkssturm* manning a MG34, Rybnik, Silesia, early April 1945. They are wearing Czechoslovak pattern steel helmets, almost certainly requisitioned from storage due to the desperate shortages of arms, uniforms and equipment.
Bundesarchiv 183/J-28898

CHAPTER SIXTEEN

Breslau (January–6 May 1945)

Another impressive example of the way the *Volkssturm* were deployed in support of the German *Wehrmacht*, and of the effectiveness of local militia units, is provided by the siege of Breslau from January until the beginning of May 1945. The prime source for this is the remarkable book published by the two Generals von Ahlfen and Niehoff – *So kämpfte Breslau*.

Breslau was defended by a total of 40,000 to 50,000 soldiers, among whom at least 15,000 were members of the *Volkssturm*. As early as Autumn 1944, the OKH had ordered for Breslau the formation of six fortress batteries, one fortress pioneer company and one fortress signals company. These were entirely under the command of the Commandant of the city which had been declared to be a *Festung*. Personnel of these Army units consisted of Army officers who were not capable of being used actively in the field and of members of the *Volkssturm*. Before they were mobilised in support of the *Wehrmacht*, the latter had only received training on an individual basis within the framework of their weekly *Volkssturm* service training. The equipment consisted of French, Soviet and other captured guns, some of them without any optical equipment and without firing tables, which could only be brought in by air after the *Festung* was encircled. The fact that there was very little ammunition had severely affected the training of the fortress batteries.

The formation and the command and care of all *Volkssturm* units and *Volkssturm* members in Breslau was the responsibility of the *Gau* Chief of Staff for Lower Silesia, *SA Obergruppenführer* Herzog.

In addition to the fortress units, which mainly consisted of members of the *Volkssturm*, also involved in the defence of *Festung* Breslau were 26 combat battalions, 10 construction battalions and 2 training, or rather *Ersatz* battalions of the *Volkssturm*. The average strength of these units was 400 men. The majority of all the *Volkssturm* battalions deployed in Breslau had been recruited from the city itself; only five combat battalions came from the surrounding rural districts. Details of the individual battalions are given below, with the names of their commanders and home areas being shown in brackets. All battalions for which no specific home area is shown came from the City of Breslau itself.

a) Combat Battalions

Btl. 21 (Koschate, Pflan – zLiegnitz); Btl. 22 (Hanke – Schweidnitz); Btl. 23 (Kanter); Btl. 24 (Meinecke); Btl. 30 (Bannwitz); Btl. 31 (Göbel – Rothenburg); Btl. 32 (Böhm); Btl. 33 (Pöhlemann); Btl. 34 (Zöke); Btl. 35 (Sämann – Oels); Btl. 36 (Strauss); Btl. 37 (Torzewski); Btl. 41 (Klose, Kalusche, Dörsing [killed]); Btl. 42 (Stephan [killed], Merkle); Btl. 44 (Klüger); Btl. 46 (Peschke); Btl. 48 (Störel [killed]); Btl. 66 (Fischer); Btl. 67 (Graf Kayserling – Militsch, Trebnitz); Btl. 68 (Kayserling [killed], Stein [killed], Koch); Btl. 75 (Bischoff); Btl. 74 (Pölsch – formed at end of February from Breslau railwaymen); Btl. 76 (Herpischböhm – formed from the Breslau Postschutz); Btl. 52 (Mende – formed from the NSKK, served first as transport unit and was then employed on Pioneer duties); Hitler Youth (HJ) Btl. 55 (Seifert) and HJ Btl. 58 (Lindenschmidt).

Apart from the two HJ battalions 55 and 56, which through the initiative of their energetic and militarily experienced commander, HJ *Gebietsführer* Hirsch, were fully armed and equipped and whose training had been properly carried out by NCOs, a much earlier exceptional case with regard to organisation was *Volkssturm* Battalion 41 (Klose). This was because this battalion had been formed as early as October 1944, and had been equipped with the German 98 rifle and the 08/15 light machine-gun. What proved to be another advantage was that – also in October 1944 – this battalion, with its full complement of officers and NCOs, had already been introduced to what was expected to be the defensive sector which they would occupy, on the left bank of the Oder below Breslau (in the event, the battalion was actually deployed in this sector in January 1945).[79]

b) Construction Battalions

Btl. 38 (Augustin); Btl. 40 (Scharz, Schymeck); Btl. 43 (Stemmler); Btl. 45 (Schönwolf); Btl. 49 (Schriever); Btl. 50 (von Holleufer); Btl. 54 (Roll); Btl. 59 (Stricker); Btl 72 (Hain) and Btl. 73 (Nollau).

c) Training Btl. 71 (Mietsch) and Ersatz Btl. 51 (Buhr).

"Because, with the situation at the time making their organisation incomplete and deficient in many respects, to provide any – let's call them – 'Active Fortress Troop Units' at all would have been totally inconceivable without the *Volkssturm*."[80] Thus, the following episodes are mentioned in von Ahlfen's and Niehoff's book *So kämpfte Breslau*:

Within the framework of the Besslein Regiment, *Volkssturm* battalions 41 (Klose) and 42 (Stephan) had played a successful part in narrowing the Peiskerwitz bridgehead" ... "Therefore, to save pioneers, from the beginning of February gradually two-thirds of the regular pioneers were withdrawn from the Oder bridges and replaced by *Volkssturm* units which were gradually trained and introduced to the terrain" ... "Certainly, after crossing the boundaries of the city, the enemy very soon got a foretaste of the fact that we were not inclined to surrender Breslau, but more than any the youngest unit showed that the commanders could rely on their will being carried out with regard to the implementation of tasks. In the late afternoon of 20 February, Hitler Youth *Volkssturm* Battalion 55 (Seifert), moving up to counter-attack in the Südpark, and sustaining only slight casualties, threw the enemy back out of the city again." ... "Here (at the Gandau aerodrome) the work carried out by *Volkssturm* battalions in clearing away the wreckage of aircraft and in filling in bomb craters deserves the highest recognition." ... "At 3 pm, a fresh counter-attack by the Hitler Youth battalion, with us providing supporting fire, threw the Soviets back off the railway embankment." ... "In all this fighting which went on after Easter, *Volkssturm* battalions also played a large part in preventing the enemy from quickly gaining ground and penetrating into the city centre. Thus, the two Hitler Youth battalions 55 and 56 proved themselves worthy of their good reputation in the fighting around the Ruttgers factory and the Popelwitz station, and the same was true of the 'Railwaymen's Battalion' 74 (Potsch), formed at the end of February, which also fought at the Ruttgers factory, and proved its worth in the Mochbern shunting yards which were certainly well-known to the railwaymen. Battalion 21, under the command of *Gardejäger* Pflanz, which had already fought in January at Dyhernfurt, and after the regrouping which took place after the Easter battles was, after a very short period of rest, deployed with the Hanf/Velhagen Regiment. And in the fighting at the Nikolai Gate bridgehead on 18 and 19 April, Battalion 68, whose commander Kayserling was killed there, supported Battalion Commander *Major* Klose, the former commander of Battalion 41, known to us from the outset, who for some weeks had been commanding an Army battalion and was wounded here. Now, in recognition of the gallantry which he had shown from the time the fighting began in January, and his daring initiative and exemplary leadership, he was awarded the Knight's Cross.[81]

Another source states:

One Hitler Youth Regiment formed in the fortress became one of the bravest, but also suffered very high casualties.[82]

From the middle of February 1945 onwards, Breslau was encircled, and the fighting began at the end of February. Even after Hitler was dead, and Berlin had already fallen, Breslau still fought on. Only when it became clear to the *Festung* Commandant on 5 May 1945 that he could no longer count on being relieved by *Heeresgruppe Schörner*, did he decide to capitulate. Only the *Gau* Chief of Staff of the Lower Silesian *Volkssturm*, SA *Obergruppenführer* Herzog, distanced himself from this decision and urged that they should fight on. He believed that the Anglo-American forces would, within a few weeks, move with German *Freikorps* units against the Soviet Union.[83]

The *Festung* Commandant, *General* Niehoff, capitulated on the following day, 6 May 1945. The SA *Obergruppenführer* committed suicide. The last OKW report reads: "The defenders of Breslau, who defied Soviet attacks for two whole months, have, after a heroic resistance, at the last moment succumbed to the superior strength of enemy forces".

Volkssturmmänner strip and clean rifles, Breslau, 1944. **Museum of Modern History, Ljubljana, Slovenia**

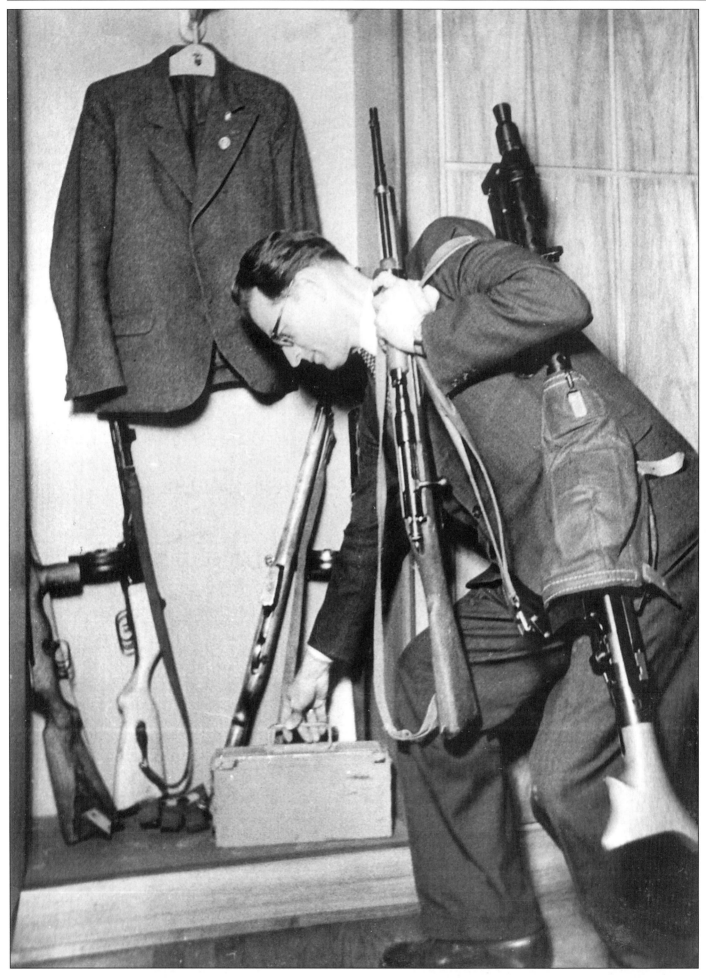

A member of the Breslau *Volkssturm* on his way to weapons training after work on a Friday evening, late 1944. The original caption was clearly intended to convey a 'business as usual' attitude. Note the Soviet PPsH sub-machine guns in the cupboard!
Museum of Modern History, Ljubljana, Slovenia

Volkssturmmänner are shown becoming acquainted with Italian Mannlicher Carcano M1891 rifles and the MG34, Breslau, 1944. **Museum of Modern History, Ljubljana, Slovenia**

The *Gauleiter* of Lower Silesia, Karl Hanke, greets men of the Breslau *Volkssturm*, spring 1945. Note the field caps being worn by some men - they are M43 field caps made from M31 *Zeltbahn* splinter camouflage material. Such caps were not standard issue, but were probably locally made in a Breslau factory. Despite being Under-Secretary of State in the Propaganda Ministry, Hanke enlisted in July 1939 and served as a *Panzerschütze*, the lowest *Panzer* rank, in the Polish and French campaigns. Becoming *Gauleiter* in 1941, he was appointed Himmler's successor as *Reichsführer-SS* on 29 April 1945. Hanke fled Breslau shortly before the Soviets captured it in May 1945, but is believed to have been killed by Czech partisans soon after. **Bildarchiv ASL**

A close-up of *Gauleiter* Hanke, clearly showing his NSDAP insignia. **Bildarchiv ASL**

Durchhalten (lit. 'endure', or 'hold out to the end') – a propaganda poster on a wall in Breslau, 1945. Already the image of a resolute *Volkssturmmann* with *Panzerfaust* is entering the mythology of the war. **Bildarchiv ASL**

Another propaganda poster extolling the *Panzerfaust* and *Panzerschreck*, Breslau, 1945. By November 1944 production of the former weapon topped 1.3 million per month, meaning that supplies were often plentiful. Indeed, it was not uncommon for some units to have a profusion of *Panzerfäuste* but virtually no small arms or the ammunition for them! All spent *Panzerfaust* tubes were supposed to be collected and returned to the factories for re-arming but during the chaotic days of 1945 it is doubtful this practise endured. **Bildarchiv ASL**

CHAPTER SEVENTEEN

Western Front (January–April 1945)

In accordance with the instructions issued by the most senior Party leadership, in October 1944 initial moves had also been made in the formation of the *Volkssturm* in the *Gaue* in the West. But the senior members of the *Volkssturm* authorities within the Party Chancellery and in the office of the *Reichsführer-SS* were agreed that the focus of activity had to be on the East. They wished to help prevent the Soviets penetrating more deeply into the territory of the Reich, and to spare the German population from Soviet atrocities. Certainly, after the atrocities committed by the Soviets in East Prussia at the end of October 1944, no-one was under any illusions as to what to expect if the Soviet advance could not be halted. What remained unspoken in these considerations was the tacit agreement that, in the event that all the Reich borders could not be held, it would be preferable to open the way to Berlin to the Western Allies than to the Soviets. Certainly, no-one reckoned with such a lack of political instinct as was demonstrated in the Morgenthau Plan and the later withdrawal of the Western Allies to the Elbe.

For this reason, even before the Soviet offensive in the East began in January 1945, the Eastern *Gaue* were accorded preferential status over those in the West in terms of organisation and equipment. And even later, it was only the most urgent requests from OKW and the *Oberbefehlshaber West* for *Volkssturm* support which were given any attention at all. Therefore, the *Volkssturm* in the West are not comparable to their counterparts in the East, either in terms of the scale of their deployment or the scale of their achievement.

According to entries in the *Wehrmacht* Command Staff War Diary, on 15 January 1945 there were deployed in support of the *Wehrmacht* 22 *Volkssturm* battalions from the *Gau* of Baden-Alsace, 9 battalions from the *Gau* of Westmark, and 6 battalions from the *Gau* of Moselland. According to another entry dated 6 February, on that date 14 *Volkssturm* battalions were under the command of *Armeeoberkommando* (AOK) 1.

The 22 *Volkssturm* battalions from Baden, a number of *Volkssturm* batteries with captured guns which had been formed as skeleton batteries using Army officer personnel, and six *Volkssturm* battalions from Württemberg were deployed in support of the *Wehrmacht* from January 1945 on the relatively quiet Upper Rhine front under the command of the 19th Army. These 28 *Volkssturm* battalions formed the majority of the infantry battalions available to the army,[84] earning the humorous nickname '19th (*Volkssturm*) Army'.

In the *Volkssturm* battalions from Baden, which were formed from the first and second levies, every one-and-a-half weeks a quarter of the *Volkssturm* personnel were replaced by fresh men. Thus, the individual liable for service in the *Volkssturm* remained six weeks in deployment at the front and then returned to his civilian occupation. The battalions from Württemberg were specially formed units. After spending an initial four weeks on the Swiss border and being trained there, these battalions spent another four weeks on the Upper Rhine front. Then they were relieved by fresh battalions coming from the Swiss border, and returned to Württemberg.

When these reliefs took place, weapons and equipment were handed over. In the case of the battalions from Baden, which were mostly equipped with captured weapons, the available weapons were sufficient for 22 battalions at most. In the case of the battalions from Württemberg, which were practically all equipped with German weapons, only six battalions could be fully provided with weapons. The *Gauleitung* in Stuttgart expected to be able to gradually train all the Württemberg *Volkssturm* by means of this process of relief and replacement.

After the Allied armies crossed the German border in the West, *Volkssturm* battalions were deployed in support of the *Wehrmacht* on the northern Western Front. Thus, for example, in March 1945 one battalion from the *Gau* Westphalia North was fighting on the Rhine, and by the end of March half-a-dozen battalions were deployed on the Dortmund-Ems Canal and on the Ems. On 6 April, a *Volkssturm* battalion surrendered to Canadian troops.

After the evacuation of the Upper Rhine front, in the eastern part of Baden and in Württemberg, the local *Volkssturm* also had to carry out combat duties. "As the front came nearer, the *Volkssturm* were given further important tasks, namely with the utmost haste to create defensive installations around the threatened towns, cities and villages, to construct machine-gun positions, to dig concealment trenches for anti-tank guns, and above all to set up anti-tank blockades. These anti-tank blockades were to remain open until the last German troops had passed through them, and then were to be closed as the enemy approached. Behind them, German defenders, mainly men of the *Volkssturm*, were to fight the approaching enemy armour".[85] But the accounts from various localities have very little to say about any real combat in which the *Volkssturm* was involved. In the West, the *Volkssturm* was too weak for that, and, above all, too poorly armed. Although, for example, in Stuttgart over 35,000 men liable for service in the *Volkssturm* were actually registered, in January 1945 only four *Volkssturm* battalions were ready for action, and shortly before the occupation of the city on 22 April, only four other battalions were in the process of being formed.

The former *Kreis* Chief of Staff of Sinsheim/Baden, to the south east of Heidelberg, gives this account:

"When towards the end of March 1945, the fighting front approached the *Kreis*, we set up anti-tank barriers at the entrance to the villages. During the last few days of the month, some rifles and some boxes of *Panzerfäuste* arrived. They were distributed to the battalions, and the men were trained how to use them. (Within the *Kreis*, 5 *Volkssturm* battalions had been formed, but not assembled).

When, in the night between 31 March/1 April 1945, American troops coming from the direction of the Neckar Estuary approached the *Kreis*, emergency units of the *Volkssturm* armed with rifles and *Panzerfäuste* were posted at the approaches to the villages. I myself was for a time with the Alarm unit in the town of Sinsheim. The *Volkssturm* had orders from the *Gau* leadership to withdraw if the *Wehrmacht* units in front of them withdrew. This happened during the evening of 1 April. The *Kreisleiter*, the *Kreis* Chief of Staff and the Alarm unit from the town of Sinsheim fell back in the night between 1/2 April to Weiler, where, in the afternoon of 2 April, the *Kreisleiter* was wounded by artillery fire. An hour later we began to withdraw through Eppingen and Muhlbach. At the border of the *Kreis*, the unit was disbanded by the deputy *Kreisleiter* and the men dismissed.[86]

From Backnang, one *Volkssturm* man gives this account:

On 19 April at 9pm major alarm, everyone somewhat excited and nervous. The artillery shells were already whistling over us. We withdrew into our positions, on which we had been working during the last few days, it was at the anti-tank barrier at Grossaspach. Our task was to knock out the first American tanks. We had no *Panzerfäuste*, only rifles with 10 rounds of ammunition.

In Crailsheim, anti-tank barriers had been erected, one (the outer barrier) on the Satteldorfer Strasse and the other (the inner barrier) at the cemetery. They were closed before the advancing Americans on 6 April between 3pm and 4pm. The seven-man guard which was manning the outer barrier withdrew to Karlsberg as the enemy armour approached. The Bosch company of the *Volkssturm* had been ordered to man this barrier, but only 46 men turned up. But there they met some other defenders, a group of officer candidates from Lenggries under the command of *Oberleutnant* Costa, and also some soldiers and *Gebirgsjäger* who had become detached from their units. These troops, in total about 80 men, were to hold the high ground from the Satteldorfer Strasse through the Beurlbacher Strasse as far as the Goldbacher Strasse. So then they began firing with their machine guns and rifles on the tanks rolling up from Satteldorf. But faced with the heavy enemy countering fire they withdrew. One *Volkssturm* man was killed in this action.[87]

In Schwäbisch Hall, some of the *Volkssturm* from Halle were deployed with the *Volkssturm* from Gmünd at the Theurershof towards Gottwollshausen, where on 16 April they first came into contact with the enemy. It had not been expected that the *Volkssturm* deployed here would be able to hold up the enemy for very long. "But these men fought bravely against the enemy for some time, some of them were wounded. After they had withdrawn into the city, a few days later the *Volkssturm* were disbanded shortly before the enemy marched in."[88]

In many other places the *Volkssturm* did not wait for the enemy to approach, but retreated beforehand with the political leaders or with the last German troops passing through the locality.

The soldiers passing through presented a shocking picture. Many were scarcely able to keep going, they are throwing away overcoats, steel helmets, cartridge cases and blankets, they are supporting themselves heavily on their makeshift walking sticks, and were pushing the pathetic remnants of their baggage in front of them on a cart or in an old child's pram … From 27 March onwards troop traffic was intense, but there were only a few units which were still intact, they had no heavy weapons and no armour, individual soldiers in various vehicles, wounded from disbanded field hospitals walked on foot, even amputees. Stark defeat stared out from the faces of all of them.[89]

Nevertheless, at one anti-tank barrier outside Cröffelbach, "a small band of Hitler Youth tried to put up a measure of resistance against the tanks, they fired a *Panzerfaust* which hit the caterpillar track of the first tank. Thereupon the other tanks turned round and withdrew back towards Wolpertshausen."[90]

And the *History of the American 100th Infantry Division* gives this account of the fighting for Heilbronn:

The enemy showed incredible fanaticism. Boys, old men, even cripples were firing on our soldiers. All told, it took eight days of the fiercest fighting. Working their way through one block of houses after the other, even house-to-house, our troops had to fight themselves a way through the town. Only on 13 April was the last SS man, the last *Volkssturm* man, the last Hitler Youth completely beaten and brought down.[91]

Sallow-looking *Volkssturm* men are trained in the use of the *Panzerfaust*, the Rhineland, late 1944. They are wearing M41 service tunics with a mix of ankle boots with Army trousers and riding boots with breeches, and old-pattern M34 *Feldmütze*.
Museum of Modern History, Ljubljana, Slovenia

Members of the Ludenscheid *Volkssturm* are sworn in. Ludenscheid was a manufacturing town in western Germany, in the North Rhine/Westphalia area. Note the variety of uniforms and equipment on display, including the puttees worn by the man on the left. **Bildarchiv Preußischer Kulturbesitz, Berlin**

A youthful-looking group of *Volkssturm* about to occupy a camouflaged bunker in the Moselle region, Western Front, December 1944. **Bundesarchiv 183/J-28489**

Above: Three Moselle *Volkssturmmänner* with a MG34 in a bunker on the West Wall, Saar, end December 1944. The young man on the left has been issued with the field-grey *Sturmartillerie* tunic, without insignia.
Museum of Modern History, Ljubljana, Slovenia

Right: Members of the Moselle *Volkssturm* carry *Panzerfäuste* into a bunker on the West Wall, December 1944.
Museum of Modern History, Ljubljana, Slovenia

Another view of Moselle *Volksturmmänner* unloading rifles from a lorry, West Wall, December 1944. The weapons are standard Kar 98k rifles.
Museum of Modern History, Ljubljana, Slovenia

Volkssturmmänner and *Wehrmacht* engineers at a tributary of the Rhine, March 1945.
Bundesarchiv 183/S-1223/502

CHAPTER EIGHTEEN

Fighting spirit, combat value, casualties

The American Professor Robert Koehl, Dept. of History, University of Nebraska, Lincoln, Nebraska, who served in 1944/45 as an interrogator of German prisoners of war, stated on 26 January 1961 that the *Volkssturm* in the West had fought worse than the Army. He said that especially the *Volkssturm* men from the Saarland, with whom he had had most contact, had given themselves up quickly and had often deserted to the Allies. They considered that the expected destruction of their homeland was a worse prospect than having to live with the French, whom, after all, they knew.[92]

General Brandenburger, a former *Oberbefehlshaber* of the 19th Army, wrote in his diary notes:

Their (i.e. the *Volkssturm*'s) armament and clothing were more than primitive, only a small number of them had uniforms, the majority only had printed armbands. Any hope that their combat value would be enhanced by the fact that they were defending their own hearth and home proved to be illusory. When it came down to it, the men of the *Volkssturm* had no intention of putting their own lives on the line. The thought that fighting in their home area meant that their own homes were under threat made them more inclined to run than to put up any resistance. Thus, when the collapse came, many of them very quickly made off home from their positions. But there were in the *Volkssturm* some sterling men prepared to make the final sacrifice.[93]

The former Chief of the General Staff of 19th Army, Staff *Oberst* Brandstaedter, made this comment when he was asked on 14 April 1947:

In the 19th Army area, *Volkssturm* battalions from the *Gaue* of Württemberg and Baden were deployed, namely 6 battalions from Württemberg and about 20 from Baden. In terms of strength, each battalion had about as many men as an infantry battalion, but the value of these men in any given battalion varied to an extraordinary degree. The general arrangements for registration of German men for military service or for work in war industries meant that the only people available for service in the *Volkssturm* were men who would otherwise never have been conscripted anyway, or highly-qualified people in the armaments industry ... The thought that they would be defending their home area and their own hearth and home which led to *Volkssturm* units being ordered to fight in their own home districts was the very thing which tended to make them particularly unreliable, and when the collapse eventually came, many men of the *Volkssturm* very quickly found their way home from their positions ... The shortage of suitable officers and NCOs had a very noticeable effect on the *Volkssturm*, and despite the best intentions of the occasional individual, for the Army the *Volkssturm* battalions were more a hindrance than a help.[94]

With German strength rapidly diminishing and the enemy's strength growing daily, among the German people as a whole, faith in Hitler and in his ability still to be able to avert unconditional surrender plummeted. And since the *Volkssturm* were part of the people in the strictest sense of the word, it would have been surprising if within its ranks confidence in a favourable outcome to the war did not diminish in the same way. As a result of this loss of faith and loss of confidence, there grew in many circles among the civilian population and also of the *Wehrmacht* the conviction – naturally unspoken – that any further destruction of the homeland by military action would be pointless, and that in the current political situation it was desirable for the armies of the Western powers to advance as quickly as possible. It was felt that the Western allies should in all events reach Berlin before the Soviets, and, if possible, that they should occupy the entire area of the Reich before the Soviets did. It is not surprising that in this frame of mind, the fighting spirit of the *Volkssturm* in the West – and not only of the *Volkssturm* – could not exactly be outstanding.

In the East, it was less the fighting spirit than the combat value, strongly affected as it was by material circumstances, which led to criticism.

Thus, in giving his opinion of the value of the *Volkssturm* on 10 February 1945, the Supreme Commander of Army Group Centre stated that "autonomous *Volkssturm* units did little to prove their worth in combat". He therefore suggested that "they should be incorporated within units of the Field Army, deployed on home terrain with which they were familiar, in positions to the rear of the front, for guard and security duties and construction of defensive positions", and suggested that "small groups of *Volkssturm* who knew the local area should be deployed on the flanks and to the rear of the enemy". If what he meant by "incorporating them within units of the Field Army" was not putting the *Volkssturm* battalions under the command of Field Army Command Staffs, but disbanding the *Volkssturm* units and conscripting individual *Volkssturm* men into the Army, then his first suggestion shows that the Supreme Commander of Army Group Centre was not aware of the basic idea behind the *Volkssturm* and the possibilities of using them. Why the *Volkssturm* were not suitable for "deployment on the flanks and to the rear of the enemy" has already been mentioned elsewhere.[95] On the other hand, the other suggestions made by the Supreme Commander fall completely within the overall remit of the tasks for which it was originally planned to use the *Volkssturm*. The fact that, under the pressure of the military situation and in the light of the fact that countless *Volkssturm* units were sent into combat immediately and prematurely, these tasks had to give way before other priorities, does not discredit the original planning of the *Volkssturm*, and, as will be evident from what has already been outlined, was not the fault of the *Volkssturm* leadership itself.

The same reasons led other Supreme Commanders in the East to bluntly and categorically state that men liable for service in the *Volkssturm* should be incorporated within the units of the Field Army, and many commanders began, on their own initiative, to incorporate them in just this way.

To examine and come to a critical evaluation of the combat value and fighting spirit of the *Volkssturm*, the following circumstances have to be taken into account:

The majority of all men liable for service in the *Volkssturm* belonged to the second levy from the *Gaue* in the interior of Germany, and these men were not deployed in support of the *Wehrmacht* because they were lacking in weapons and therefore the formation of regular battalions was not possible.

By contrast, in the *Gaue* along Germany's borders and above all in the *Gaue* in the East, the majority of the local men liable for service in *Volkssturm* had been assembled into *Volkssturm* battalions and deployed in action. The mobilisation of these *Volkssturm* units in support of the *Wehrmacht* almost necessarily followed under the pressure of the military situation, before these battalions were anywhere near complete in terms of men and material.

As a result of this premature mobilisation for action, by far the majority of these *Volkssturm* battalions could only be equipped with captured weapons, for which, as a rule, there was not enough ammunition, and could only be provided with other equipment which was completely insufficient. Since it was not possible to procure uniforms either, most of the *Volkssturmsoldaten* – at least in the initial period – had to fight in their civilian clothing, on which they simply wore the armband of the *Volkssturm*. Also, because of the shortness of time available, it was not possible to provide virtually any training at all; many a man of the *Volkssturm*, when he first went into action, was still completely untrained. The officers and NCOs were often inexperienced and often unsuitable for command. Instead of units which had been equipped and organised in a planned way – even if at short notice – it was usually hastily cobbled together 'bands' of men with improvised equipment which had to be thrown into battle.

Thus it was no coincidence that, for example, the specially selected *Volkssturm* battalions from Württemberg, which were equipped with German weapons and had a certain amount of training, performed better than the battalions from Baden, and that the skeleton batteries which were formed early on performed better than the pure militia battalions, the personnel of which was constantly changing. This experience was repeatedly confirmed in almost all similar circumstances.

It scarcely needs demonstrating that from this kind of improvised and inadequately equipped battalions only very limited combat value, or no significant combat value at all, could be expected, even if their members had excellent fighting spirit. So when many of these units, despite these disadvantages, played the man in actual combat, then this achievement deserves special recognition in itself.

Because poor weapons, primitive items of equipment, insufficient ammunition, civilian clothes instead of uniforms, inexperienced officers and lack of proper training, combined with a reduction in the combat value of the unit, almost always result in deterioration of its fighting spirit, the fighting spirit among the *Volkssturm* must necessarily be expected to be lower than it was in *Wehrmacht* units. And when, in addition to this, elderly *Volkssturm* men with captured weapons and with no heavy weapons are meant to hold a position while younger and better equipped members of the *Wehrmacht* and the police are rolling past them in vehicles of all kinds, with apparently only the single thought of seeking safety behind the front, then this would involve additional mental stress which could all too easily lead to failure to do their duty.

On the other hand, in eastern Germany psychological factors were at work which were not present in western Germany, and which influenced in a very positive way the fighting spirit of those *Volkssturm* men with home areas in the East. Added to these factors, which filled the *Volkssturmsoldaten* in Eastern Germany with a greater spirit of sacrifice than their counterparts in the West, and caused them to maintain the struggle for longer and defend their own homes, there was the knowledge that the individual had about the threat posed to his homeland and his nearest and dearest by the enemy in the East. This knowledge, and his conviction that he had to protect his homeland from invasion and from the bestial methods of the Soviets, meant that his general commitment – despite poorer armament and for the most part greater age – was more comparable to, and often exceeded, that of the soldier of the *Wehrmacht* in the East. Thus – even for the man of the *Volkssturm* – the desire not to surrender voluntarily a single inch of German soil to the Soviets, and to protect the German people from Asiatic atrocities, became the raison d'être of this last battle.[96]

It is perhaps sufficient, from the countless opinions which confirmed the correctness of this view and the difference between the *Volkssturm* in the East and the *Volkssturm* in the West, to select two opinions, one that of a member of a Sudeten *Volkssturm* Battalion, and the other the opinion of the former commander of *Volkssturm* Battalion Breslau Land No. 3:

> Certainly, our armament wasn't exactly top-notch, but the spirit of the men was good and intact. It was incredible how enthusiastically the *Volkssturm* men, mostly of riper years, took on the responsibilities assigned to them … It has to be said that the old men of the *Volkssturm*, with their inferior armament, and despite all the difficulties facing them, acquitted themselves surprisingly well in fighting against the young, well equipped Soviet combat troops.[97]

And:

> After I was driven out of my homeland, as far as I could gather here in the West from many descriptions of the fighting by officers and men of the *Volkssturm* who took part in it, here in the West it never came down to any serious fighting between the *Volkssturm* and the enemy. The *Volkssturm* units for the most part 'vanished into thin air' when the enemy approached. In the East, at any event in Silesia, things were very different. In spite of the much discussed difficulties, in many places the *Volkssturm* acquitted themselves gallantly against the attacking Soviets. This was particularly true for the *Volkssturm* garrisons in the towns and cities such as Oppeln, Brieg, Glogau, and outstandingly in Breslau, which were declared *Festungen*. Thanks to the unfailing commitment of their *Volkssturm* garrisons, they were able to hold out for months, right up to the general surrender, against all the raging assaults of the Soviets. To be sure, all these efforts and sacrifices proved to be in vain, but gallantry is never a matter of shame, on the contrary, it always honours the defeated![98]

Many officers and ordinary men of the *Volkssturm* received gallantry awards in the East. Among these were several awards of the Knight's Cross of the Iron Cross.

The different values to be attributed to the *Volkssturm* in the West and the *Volkssturm* in the East are also evident in the three search categories for the missing (VA, VB and VC) developed by the German Red Cross. The number of *Volkssturm* members who went missing in the West can of course not be taken as a benchmark. But the number of units listed in these search categories for the missing in the *Gaue* from Western and Central Germany pales into insignificance besides the battalions mobilised and sent into action in support of the *Wehrmacht* in the East.

To state the overall number of *Volkssturmsoldaten* who were killed is not possible, because it is also not known to the 'German Authority for the Notification of Relatives of Men Killed in the Former German *Wehrmacht*' in Berlin-Wittenau, and this authority is also not in a position to make any appropriate estimates. The number of members of the *Volkssturm* who were killed is also not known to the German Red Cross. Therefore the attempt must be made to gain a certain overview from the following information.

In the offices of the 'German Authority' in Berlin-Wittenau there is a *Volkssturm* card index which was created as a result of search requests from relatives and other authorities, and which contains approximately 175,000 index cards. Within this overall number it is estimated that there are 5,000 clear reports of deaths, which come in the first instance in the West from the International Red Cross in Geneva and from the War Graves lists of the war graves administrative authorities.

The search lists for the missing at the German Red Cross contain a total of 29,687 names of members of the *Volkssturm*, 11,182 of them with photographs, who are still registered as missing. But this number of the missing may be far too low, because it must be assumed that the relatives of many former members of the *Volkssturm* who are living in the Soviet occupied zone and in Austria have not submitted any requests for searches. Also, there are no requests for searches on the part of relatives of missing men whose place of residence was east of the Oder-Neisse line. In addition, those *Volkssturmsoldaten* who were members of *Wehrmacht* units are not recorded in the *Volkssturm* registers for the missing, but in the corresponding registers for the *Wehrmacht*.

According to the registers of the missing, the 29,687 missing members of the *Volkssturm* belonged to about 700 different *Volkssturm* battalions which are designated by their battalion numbers or by the names of their commanders. But because missing members of the *Volkssturm* are also recorded under the *Volkssturm* designation of their home *Kreis* -without any Battalion details – and also because details of the men recorded as missing in the 'fortresses' of Königsberg and Breslau are not shown within the context of their battalions, the overall number of *Volkssturm* battalions which were in contact with the enemy and suffered casualties is likely to be higher than 700. Certainly, many battalions which are indicated by their battalion numbers or by the names of their officers had only a few members or occasionally only one single member missing.

The following individual details may be of interest: as a result of the fighting around Königsberg there are still 2,400 *Volkssturmsoldaten* registered as missing, and from the fighting around Breslau 1,894 *Volkssturm* members are registered as missing. From Kurhessen *Volkssturm* Battalion 13/17, which saw action on the Oder, and from *Volkssturm* Battalion 36/161 (Warthbrücken), respectively 256 and 115 members of the battalions are registered as missing.

Another view of the later-issue *Volkssturm* armband.
Bildarchiv ASL

Reichsleiter der Deutschen Arbeitsfront Robert Ley visiting youthful members of the *Volkssturm*, November 1944.
Bildarchiv Preußischer Kulturbesitz, Berlin

Members of the *Volkssturm* are instructed in the use of the *Panzerfaust*. **History in the Making Archive**

Another view of *Panzerfaust* instruction, this time providing a clear view of how the explosive warhead fitted onto the hollow tube.
History in the Making Archive

The slogan painted outside this Berlin air-raid bunker reads 'Men between the ages of sixteen and seventy years belong in action – not in a bunker!'
Hilmar Pabel/Bildarchiv Preußischer Kulturbesitz, Berlin

CHAPTER NINETEEN

Conclusion

The underlying intention behind the formation of the *Volkssturm*, the general attempt to arm the population at the eleventh hour, was to provide all the available reserves of men and material to reinforce the operational forces of the *Wehrmacht*, to enable the *Wehrmacht* to prolong for a certain period the war which was already lost. There was a desire to prevent, for as long as possible, the enemy penetrating more deeply into the Reich in order to gain time until the promised new weapons were available, and to allow the expected political developments of a deterioration in the relations between the Western allies and Russia to become more intense.

Whether and to what extent these aims underlying the formation of the *Volkssturm* were actually achieved will be examined in these final observations.

In the West, the *Volkssturm* (although, for example, 19th Army in action on the Upper Rhine front had to rely largely on *Volkssturm* battalions and on a number of *Volkssturm* batteries) certainly had no delaying effect on enemy operations.

On the other hand, in the East, the enemy push to the Reich capital, which according to the intention of the Soviet high command was to be continued remorselessly across the Oder, would probably have succeeded as early as February 1945, if the masses of *Volkssturm* which had been mobilised directly in the path of the main enemy advance – one only needs to think of the fighting to the east of the Oder and the development of defences on the Oder and on the Neisse – had not made a significant contribution to halting this advance and forcing the enemy to regroup. In addition, it is thanks to the deployment of the *Volkssturm* that thousands more German people were able to escape the clutches of the Soviets than would otherwise have been the case.

The fact that in the course of the Soviet January offensive, the deep breakthroughs which were made into the eastern territory of the Reich could not be stopped despite the deployment of the *Volkssturm*, and the Soviets could then not be repulsed to give longer breathing space, was by the very nature of the situation in the first instance because the *Wehrmacht*, both the command and the units themselves, had been bled dry and exhausted, and were therefore physically and psychologically no longer capable of dealing with the difficult crisis situations.

Certainly, given the results that the Soviet militia divisions and the improvised *Volkssturm* were actually able to achieve, an intact, properly equipped, well trained and well established territorial militia would have provided such considerable reinforcement to the *Wehrmacht* that the planned operational goal could have been achieved with a degree of certainty which was almost definite. But the *Volkssturm* was not an intact territorial militia, because arrangements had been made far too late for its formation, and it had an almost complete lack of weapons of all kinds which could be suitable for use in the field, a lack of ammunition and, last but not least, a lack of time for anything approaching adequate training. As a result, the pressure of the situation forced *Volkssturm* battalions to be thrown into action prematurely as disorganised bands of men instead of as units which were more or less organised. The result of this approach was of course of that the plan largely failed, a failure which must be attributed not to the organisation in itself, but to the way in which it was implemented. A militia can no more be improvised than can a standing army, and certainly not if in the first place there is a shortage weapons, to procure which necessarily requires more time than it does to make men available.

It was therefore not without reason that the Soviet Union prepared its armed popular militia in peacetime, and continues to do so. And it is not without reason that in the Soviet-occupied zone of Germany, work went on for years in developing the SED *Kampfgruppen*. These groups were not, as is often assumed, simply for the purpose of maintaining internal order. Rather they were "to be reorganised into a well-functioning, disciplined and reliable territorial militia and to be deployed as a regular instrument in home defence at the side of the NVA (National People's Army)".[99] Thus, in the event of war, their purpose was to support the operational Army as a home defence territorial militia.

The age of total war increasingly forced the mobilisation for active home defence of the whole of the population capable of bearing arms, even those parts of the population which, because of their connection with civilian work vital to the war effort, were not available for service in the operational armed forces. The 'law of the big battalions' applies even more strongly in countries in a difficult geopolitical situation, and applies even more as the defensive zones become deeper.

More battalions, even if they had only been units of a territorial militia, would have made it easier to maintain momentum on the offensive wing on the Western Front when the war began in 1914, and in the East would have not established the defences quite so much on the basis of a Hannibal encountering a Varro. Perhaps the existence of the 'big battalions' would have meant that there would not have been a war at all. In his actions in 1938 and 1939, Hitler, even if he did not want to abandon his criminal policies, would, if a combat-ready territorial militia had been available, perhaps not have risked the fate of the Western Front on a single throw of the dice as he eventually did.

The Berlin *Volkssturm* are sworn-in by SA *Obergruppenführer* Grantz (far right), 12 November 1944.
Museum of Modern History, Ljubljana, Slovenia

Men of the *Volkssturm* on their way to training in an unknown German city, autumn 1944.
Museum of Modern History, Ljubljana, Slovenia

Last-minute training on the *Panzerfaust*, Eastern Front 1945. **Bildarchiv ASL**

Plate A – *First* Volkssturm *units 1944*

Volkssturmmann, East Prussia, October 1944

Volkssturmmann, East Prussia, November 1944

Plate B – Volkssturm *units* 1944–45

Volkssturmmann, Oder Front, February 1945

Gruppenführer, Silesia, January 1945

Plate C – *Army-uniformed* Volkssturm *units 1945*

Kompanieführer, Berlin, April 1945

Volkssturmmann, Saar area, Western Front, March 1945

Plate D – Miscellaneous Volkssturm units 1945

Volkssturmmann, Freikorps Sauerland, Ruhr Pocket, Western Front, March/April 1945

Zugführer, SA Volkssturm Panzerjäger unit, Eastern Germany, January 1945

Volkssturm *Uniforms and Equipment*

This section is not intended to provide a definitive reference regarding *Volkssturm* uniforms and equipment, but rather to supply the reader with some pointers indicating general trends that can be observed when studying combat gear worn. In any case, the supply situation vis-à-vis the *Volkssturm* was so haphazard that one can only make general comments and statements based on photographic evidence, as such a wide variety of clothing and weaponry was evidently issued.

The *Volkssturm* was issued with a very wide variety of uniforms, equipment and weaponry. In the limited space available, it would be impossible to pick out all items issued. In view of this, the artwork concentrates on the most commonly-observed uniforms and weapons, supplemented by a couple of figures demonstrating some of the more unusual *Volkssturm* formations.

Volkssturm *uniform variations 1944–45*

Broadly speaking, one can divide this section into four areas: a) civilian/NSDAP Party clothing, especially prevalent during the early stages of the organisation's history, b) period of greater uniformity, winter 1944/45, c) *Volkssturm* units provided with Army uniforms, d) special exceptions that fall outside the above three areas.

a) *Civilian/NSDAP Clothing*

Photographic evidence suggests that many *Volkssturm* units wore civilian or NSDAP (Nazi) Party clothing in one of three distinct situations. The very first units to be formed in the early autumn of 1944 were created so hastily that no uniforms could be provided. The supply situation at that time was particularly pressurised due to the enormous losses in men and material suffered during the Soviet summer offensives. Thus, the men could expect to receive little more than the first-pattern plain white armband. Civilian clothing could also expect to be used during training - uniforms were in such short supply that they were generally only issued immediately prior to deployment to a combat zone. Finally, those units which were formed when the Soviets were literally at the doorstep, could also expect to be given little more than armbands and sent into action.

Party uniforms seem to be very prominent in photographs taken during the autumn of 1944 but become far less frequently seen thereafter.

b) *Greater uniformity, winter 1944/45*

By the end of 1944 a lull on the Eastern Front combined with the limited role played by the *Volkssturm* in the West allowed the Germans to equip and uniform a number of units.

The most common item of uniform issued during this period was the greatcoat. Indeed, in many cases, it was also the only item apart from an armband to be issued. All manner of greatcoats were worn, although Army types predominated, including some dating from the First World War and *Reichswehr* periods. NSDAP, RAD and OT (*Organisation Todt*) greatcoats were also worn. There are numerous reports of *Volkssturmmänner* being shot out-of-hand by Red Army troops when captured wearing the latter, as their brown colour - similar in shade to those used by Soviet troops - led them to being accused of trying to disguise themselves as the enemy, or as partisans. Although orders stipulated that these brown greatcoats should be re-dyed field grey, this seems not to have happened in many cases.

The second-type *Volkssturm* armband was issued from late 1944, becoming regulation from 1 December. Although regulations stipulated that it was to be worn on the upper left arm, contemporary photographs suggest it was frequently worn lower down in the manner of a cuff-title.

c) Volkssturm *units provided with Army uniforms*

By late 1944 the Army was taking much more of an active role in training and equipping the *Volkssturm*. All manner of uniforms were issued, dependent upon available supplies in storerooms. In many examples this meant that obsolete, old or recycled uniform stock was supplied, even parade uniforms (with the inappropriate highly-tailored insignia removed).

When *Volkssturm* were issued with army clothing, the insignia was often removed, including the *Litzen* collar patches, national emblem and shoulder straps, partly due to it being under control of the Party and not the Army. Photographs show that in most cases the shoulder straps and *Litzen* collar patches were removed or tunics were issued directly from stores without them. The national emblem was frequently retained.

d) Variant units

A wide range of paramilitary and other Party formations came under the *Volkssturm* banner, including *Freikorps Sauerland*, *Standschützen* units, Hitler Youth, *SA-Wehrmannschaft*, *Allgemeine SS* etc. Sometimes they were their own uniforms (as in the case of the Hitler Youth), sometimes clothing from other organisations, such as the RAD, NSKK or OT.

Freikorps Sauerland was in the NSDAP *Gau* of Westfalen-Süd, an area covering part of the industrial Ruhr basin and in the main consisting of rugged, hilly and forested country containing many deep and fast-flowing rivers, highly defensible. It was a NSDAP paramilitary formation consisting of several battalions, that existed prior to the *Volkssturm* and was incorporated into it. Consisting of well-trained and equipped personnel it could be regarded as an élite formation. The unit was distinguished by a special shield decal on their helmets and a badge on their tunics. Mention has been made of a cuff-title as well, although there is no evidence for this being worn. Instead, the official *Volkssturm* armband was worn on the lower left sleeve. Information on this unit's uniforms is sketchy. Photographic evidence suggests olive-brown RAD uniforms were worn, notably the second type of RAD tunic. This was a hybrid that appeared between the first M35 type tunic and third (and final) M39 tunic, and there were probably many in stores and available for use. However, as with all *Volkssturm* units it is worth remembering that uniforms issued may have differed between the various battalions!

The uniforms of most branches and organisations were worn by *Volkssturm* units at one time or another, including Army, *Kriegsmarine*, *Luftwaffe*, NSKK, NSFK, OT, Police, SA and NSDAP items. The *Volksopfer* programme also contributed thousands of items of clothing donated by civilians.

Medical orderlies and doctors were required to wear a red cross armband on the upper left sleeve.

The origin of *Standschützen* units is described in Chapter 1. To continue the tradition and provide *esprit de corps*, the *Volkssturm* raised in the Tyrol and Vorarlberg were also named *Standschützen*. They were also entitled to wear a special badge on their upper left sleeve, consisting of a dark green diamond-shaped cloth piped in white or yellow bearing a red Tyrolean eagle and the unit's name embroidered in pale green. *Edelweiß* badges were also sometimes worn on the left-hand side of the cap.

Figure 2 in plate D also provides a reconstruction of a SA *Panzerjäger* wearing an interesting combination of items, including Swastika armband and *Zeltbahn*.

Volkssturm *headgear*

As with the items of uniform issued (or not, as the case may have been), headgear worn by *Volkssturm* units also varied very widely. Civilian caps were very common if other civilian clothing was being worn. All manner of steel helmets can be seen in photographs, ranging from standard M42s to more unusual items such as the M44 *Luftschutz* helmet, or recycled *Luftwaffe* M18 helmets. *In extremis* captured helmets previously assigned to the *Luftschutz* were also pressed into service, including French 'Adrian' and Soviet M36 and M40 helmets. M16 and M35 helmets could also be worn. In many cases, the helmets continued to bear the insignia of their previous users, including the Army, *Luftwaffe*, *Kriegsmarine*, *Luftschutz*, Fire Service and Police. Field caps, including the M38 and M42 *Feldmütze* and the M43 *Einheitsfeldmutz* or general service issue field cap were all worn. Army-issue fur caps are also worn in a number of photographs taken during the severe winter of 1944/45.

Volkssturm *ranks and insignia*

Volkssturm ranks and their associated insignia are set out in the table below.

Rank	Insignia
Bataillonsführer	Black collar patches each bearing four aluminium pips
*Kompaniefführer**	Black collar patches each bearing three aluminium pips
*Zugführer***	Black collar patches each bearing two aluminium pips
*Gruppenführer****	Black collar patches each bearing a single aluminium pip
Volkssturmmann	Black collar patches

* Additional ranks at the same grade and with the same insignia: Adjutant, *Ordonnanzoffizier, Bataillonsarzt. The latter* rank also added a snake and staff (caduceus) to his insignia.

** Additional ranks at the same grade and with the same insignia: *Zahlmeister, Waffenmeister.*

*** Additional rank at the same grade and with the same insignia: *Sanitätsdienstgrad.*

Due to shortages, the pips were sometimes affixed directly onto the collar without a collar patch. Some officers unofficially added piping of twisted aluminium cord.

Volkssturm *armbands*

There were two basic types. The first issue was most commonly a very basic plain white or pale yellow armband bearing the words *Deutscher Volkssturm* and the national emblem. Some examples also carried the legend *Wehrmacht* below, but this was not always the case. This was superseded by a later pattern, stated as regulation by 1 December 1944. This used a combination of the colours black, white and red (Germany's national colours), the national emblem and the legend *Deutscher Volkssturm* and *Wehrmacht*.

Summary

Overall, the *Volkssturm* formations created during 1944 and 1945 wore an extremely wide variety of uniforms and equipment. Due to the dreadful supply situation that prevailed at that time, it could literally be said 'anything goes' and units wore whatever they could lay their hands upon, or whatever they were issued with. It is hoped that the notes in this section, combined with the colour plates and the many photographs throughout the book will assist the reader in building up a reasonably comprehensive picture of what the *Volkssturmmänner* wore.

Captions to the colour plates

Plate A – *First* Volkssturm *units 1944*

Figure 1 Volkssturmmann, *East Prussia, October 1944*

Some of the first *Volkssturm* units were drafted in East Prussia to aid in the defence of its borders against the Red Army. Photographs suggest that in many cases the only form of military clothing issued was a plain armband. This man is representative of these short-term measures, although he has also pinned a small NSDAP Party badge to his coat lapel. He is armed with a Mannlicher 95 rifle of First World War Austro-Hungarian provenance. Ammunition and other essentials would have been carried in his coat pockets.

Figure 2 Volkssturmmann, *East Prussia, November 1944*

This man is also representative of members of some of the early *Volkssturm* formations. Presenting a slightly better-equipped appearance than his comrade, he is wearing a NSDAP greatcoat, beneath which a standard NSDAP uniform would be worn - his belt and boots are also Party-issue. Note the variant first-pattern armband. His helmet is the M44 *Luftschutz* originally used by Air Raid Protection units. He is armed with a Kar 98a rifle and a *Panzerfaust* 60. He has one set of rifle ammunition pouches, as regulations stated for second-line troops.

Plate B – Volkssturm *units 1944-45*

Figure 1   Gruppenführer, *Silesia, January 1945*

By the winter of 1944/45 some (but by no means all) *Volkssturm* units were beginning to receive improved supplies of uniforms, equipment and weapons. This *Gruppenführer*, or section leader, has been issued with an old *Reichswehr* greatcoat under which he wears a standard Army field grey uniform, although in many cases greatcoats were worn directly over civilian clothing. He has also been fortunate enough to acquire a pair of Army marching boots. Many *Volkssturm* units reported great problems caused by inadequate footwear being worn in the harsh winter conditions of 1944/45. He is sporting the second and regulation issue armband, being worn in the correct position on his upper left arm. His headgear is an Army fur cap.

Equipment is still minimal - a M31 Army bread bag, Army belt and Kar 98 ammunition pouches. These pouches were frequently worn regardless of the weapon carried, which in this case is a VG 1-5 assault rifle.

Figure 2   Volkssturmmann, *Oder front, February 1945*

Many of the better equipped *Volkssturm* units appear, from photographic evidence, to have served along the Oder front, benefiting from the halting of the Soviet Vistula Oder offensive in early spring 1945 that allowed the Germans to refit and re-equip their forces along this last natural barrier before Berlin was reached.

This man is again wearing a variety of uniform items originating from a number of organisations. He has a M42 Army greatcoat, worn over a NSKK uniform. His gaiters and ankle boots are typical. The regulation armband is being worn in a non-regulation (but nevertheless very popular) lower left sleeve position. His headgear is a recycled M18 *Luftwaffe* steel helmet. Note the reissued M34 Army *Feldmutz* or field cap tucked into his waistbelt.

His personal equipment has again been sourced from a variety of organisations - the waistbelt is *Luftwaffe* whilst the cross-strap is NSDAP. The belt also carries a tool box for the MG42 he is armed with. He also has a M34 backpack with rolled blanket.

Plate C – Army-uniformed Volkssturm *units 1945*

Figure 1   Volkssturmmann, *Saar area, Western Front, March 1945*

Although the *Volkssturm* undoubtedly saw less action in the West than the East, a large number of men were drafted and as with those in other parts of the country, an attempt was made to find as many items of uniform for them as was possible within the circumstances.

This soldier has been clothed primarily from Army stores, and wears a M43 tunic and M44 trousers with ankle boots, as well as possessing a M42 steel helmet. Note that the *Litzen* on the collars and the shoulder straps have been removed from the tunic, but thte national emblem remains above his right breast pocket. He also wears the regulation armband, and has pinned a SA sports badge to his left breast pocket.

Equipment is mixed, including a NSDAP belt on which standard Kar 98 ammunition pouches, an entrenching tool and a M39 'egg' grenade hang. His weapons are a Kar 98k carbine and a *Panzerfaust* 30 *klein*. The latter was the first type of its kind issued, and production had been halted by 1945, although it is evident supplies continued to be sent out for use from stores right up until the end of the war. Its armour penetration performance was inferior to later types, up to 140mm compared to the 200mm achieved by the later *Panzerfaust* 30, 60 or 100.

Figure 2   Kompanieführer, *Berlin, April 1945*

Presenting quite a tidy appearance, this *Volkssturm* company commander is wearing a M36 Army tunic (note officer tunic modifications to hip pockets) with standard officer's breeches and boots. The tunic has been altered to *Volkssturm* specifications by having the shoulder straps removed and his rank is clearly shown on his collar patches. The ribbon for the First World War Iron Cross 2nd Class is also worn above his left breast pocket. He also has a M43 Army officer's field cap bearing silver piping on the crown.

A standard Army officer's belt is worn, along with a set of machine-pistol magazine pouches, and a pair of 6x30 binoculars are slung around his neck. He is armed with a Spanish Astra pistol reissued from captured stocks and a MP41 machine-pistol. This latter was a wooden-stocked weapon based on the successful MP40, although it was never officially accepted into service.

Plate D – *Miscellaneous* Volkssturm *units 1945*

Figure 1 Volkssturmmann, Freikorps Sauerland, *Ruhr Pocket, Western Front, March/April 1945*

As discussed above, the *Freikorps Sauerland* was a NSDAP paramilitary formation that was incorporated into the *Volkssturm* in late 1944. This man wears RAD clothing, including the 2nd type RAD tunic originally issued sometime between 1935 and 1939 and RAD trousers, along with ankle boots and gaiters. Note the *Freikorps Sauerland* arm badge on his upper right sleeve, whilst the second-pattern *Volkssturm* armband is worn on the lower right sleeve. His M42 steel helmet also bears the unit's distinctive insignia on its decal.

Equipment is fairly plain - an Army belt from which are suspended standard rifle ammunition pouches, bayonet, bread bag, field canteen and a M24 stick grenade.

Figure 2 Zugführer, *SA* Volkssturm Panzerjäger *unit, Eastern Germany, January 1945*

This very interesting figure belonged to an evidently well-equipped and uniformed unit serving somewhere in the East, 1945. He wears an olive brown SA uniform, with white cuff rings indicating that the man in question was a SA member before 1933, and his *Volkssturm* rank pips on black collar patches. Note also that a SA Swastika armband is worn, not the *Volkssturm* issue armband. There is evidence of the latter being worn over the former. SA breeches and boots are also worn. This particular unit were also issued with a variety of *Zeltbahns*; this figure has been portrayed wearing a *Waffen-SS* one, although other types were also worn. A M35 steel helmet is worn with a bread bag shoulder strap pressed into service to hold foliage.

On his SA-issue belt are suspended MP44 magazine pouches. Heavily armed, he carries a *Tellermine 43*, *Panzerfaust* 100 and has a slung MP44 assault rifle.

The publishers wish to acknowledge the kind assistance given
by Stephen Andrew in preparing this information

Appendices

Instruction to the Party Chancellery 12/44 dated 1 September 1944

Action to be taken by the Party Chancellery in the consolidation measures

1. I authorise the Leader of the Party Chancellery to issue the necessary instructions in my name to the *Gauleiters* responsible for the consolidation measures or called upon to support such measures.

   Other authorities within the NSDAP Reich leadership are not authorised to take effective measures without being instructed to do so by the Leader of the Party Chancellery.

2. The *Gauleiters* are responsible for taking all measures to ensure that construction works on defensive positions are implemented as soon as possible.

3. The Leader of the Party Chancellery shall nominate for the integrated management of the overall action representatives who shall be directly responsible to him and report directly to him. He is authorised to bring in suitable Party comrades from other authorities within the Party.

4. The *Reichsorganisationsleiter* shall make available NSDAP management and supervisory personnel as instructed by the Leader of the Party Chancellery.

signed: Adolf Hitler

Directive 278/44, issued by the Party Chancellery on 27 September 1944

Re: Maintenance and security of defensive positions

As ordered by the *Führer*, I hereby charge the *Gauleiters* responsible for the construction of defensive positions with the following responsibilities:

1. The maintenance and security of the positions constructed by them and not yet occupied by our troops, including all material stored within them and built into them.

2. The formation of security garrisons which on the approach of the enemy shall defend the positions until a planned defence can be organised by the armed forces.

The necessary measures are to be taken in agreement with the responsible Deputy General Commands; the security garrisons are to be set up within the framework of the *Volkssturm*.

signed: M. Bormann

Decree of the Führer 25 September 1944 concerning the Formation of the *Volkssturm*

(Reich Legal Gazette 1944, T. I. S. 253)

After five years of the hardest fighting, and as a result of the failure of all our European allies, on some fronts the enemy are close to or at the German borders. They are summoning their strength to smash our Reich, and to annihilate the German people and its social order. Their ultimate aim is to exterminate the German.

As in autumn 1939, we are now once again facing the united front of our enemies completely alone. In a few years we once succeeded, by the first major effort of the power of our German *Volk*, in solving the most important military problems, and guaranteeing that the Reich, and thus Europe, would continue for years to come. While now the enemy believe that they are about to strike the final blow, we are resolved to carry out the second great effort of our *Volk*. We must and we shall succeed, as we did in the years 1939–1941, building only upon our own strength, not only in breaking the will of the enemy to exterminate us, but in throwing them back and keeping them out of the Reich until a peace can be secured which will guarantee the future of Germany, the future of its allies, and the future of Europe itself. In the face of the well-known desire of our Jewish-international enemies to exterminate us, we set the total commitment of all German people.

To reinforce the active forces of our *Wehrmacht* and in particular to carry out a merciless struggle wherever the enemy wishes to enter upon German soil, I call to arms all German men capable of wielding them.

I order that:

1. In the *Gaue* of the Greater German Reich, there shall be formed, from all men between the ages of 16 and 60 years of age who are capable of bearing arms, the *Volkssturm*. It shall defend German home soil with all weapons and means as shall seem to be suitable.

2. The formation and command of the *Volkssturm* within their *Gaue* shall be the responsibility of the respective *Gauleiters*. In carrying out this responsibility, they shall principally make use of the most capable organisers and leaders of the tried and tested Party establishments, the SA, SS, the NSKK, and the HJ.

3. I nominate SA Chief of Staff Schepmann as Inspector of Firing Training, and NSKK *Korpsführer* Kraus as Inspector of Motor Vehicle Mechanical Training of the *Volkssturm*.

4. During the period of their service, the members of the *Volkssturm* shall be considered to be soldiers within the meaning of the Defence Act.

5. The membership of *Volkssturm* members in other organisations shall remain unaffected. However, service in the *Volkssturm* shall take priority over any other service.

6. The *Reichsführer-SS*, in his capacity as Supreme Commander of the Reserve Army, is responsible for the military organisation, training, armament and equipment of the *Volkssturm*

7. Combat deployment of the *Volkssturm* shall be ordered on my instructions by the *Reichsführer-SS* in his capacity as Supreme Commander of the Reserve Army.

8. Military instructions for implementation shall be issued by *Reichsführer-SS* Himmler in his capacity as Supreme Commander of the Reserve Army, and political and organisational instructions shall be issued on my behalf by *Reichsleiter* M. Bormann.

9. The National Socialist Party is meeting its highest obligations of honour to the German *Volk* by placing its own organisation as the first line champion of this struggle.

Führer Headquarters, 25 September 1944.

The *Führer* Adolf Hitler
The Leader of the Party Chancellery
M. Bormann
The Head of the *Oberkommando der Wehrmacht*
Keitel
Reichsminister and Head of the Party Chancellery
Dr. Lammers

APPENDIX III

Instructions for implementation relating to the *Führer* Decree concerning the formation of the *Volkssturm* 27 September 1944

National Socialist German Workers Party

Party Chancellery
The Leader of the Party Chancellery

Führer Headquarters, 25.9.44

Directive 277/44

Re: Instructions for implementation relating to the *Führer* Decree concerning the formation of the *Volkssturm*

I. Organisation:

1. The *Gauleiters* shall immediately register, for the formation of the *Volkssturm*, all *Volksgenossen* capable of bearing arms and aged between 16 and 60 years.

2. In mobilising men for the *Volkssturm*, regard shall be had to the vital war tasks of armaments, food, transport and communications.

3. The *Volkssturm* shall be formed by the appropriate authorities on the basis of *Kreise* and *Ortsgruppen*. It is to be organised in companies and battalions.

   In dealing with all questions relating to the formation of the *Volkssturm* in the *Gaue*, and the selection of battalion and company commanders, the *Gauleiters*, if they do not principally take action themselves, shall nominate an assistant. This assistant must be a convinced, fanatical and thus totally committed National Socialist, a troop commander who has a proved his worth in frontline service, and a good organiser, and thus be able on the instructions of his *Gauleiter* to carry out the formation of the required units and the selection of suitable commanders as quickly as possible.

   The names of such assistants are to be notified to me by telegram no later than 30 September 1944, giving details of the individual's career, both military and within the Party.

4. The appropriate authorities shall assume responsibility for the management and training of political advisers with experience at the front, members of subsidiary organisations, police officers or other *Volksgenossen*. They are to be selected on the basis of the following criteria : loyalty to the *Führer*, steadfastness, and military ability.

II. Equipment and Training

1. The armament of the *Volkssturm* shall be carried out in collaboration with the *Gauleiters* by the authorities directly subordinate to the *Reichsführer-SS* in his capacity as Supreme Commander of the Reserve Army.

2. The *Volkssturm* shall receive particular training in anti-tank and infantry combat. In the *Gaue* on the borders of Germany, training manoeuvres are to be carried out on the actual terrain of existing defensive positions.

3. The training of members of the *Volkssturm* shall be carried out at least once per week; if possible, such training shall not disturb the normal civilian occupations of *Volkssturm* members.

III. Recognition of Volkssturm members (Volkssturmsoldaten) as combatants as defined under the Hague Convention on Land Warfare

1. The members of the *Volkssturm* shall be recognised as having the status of combatants as defined under the Hague Convention on Land Warfare.

2. The *Reichsführer-SS*, in his capacity as Supreme Commander of the Reserve Army, shall organise the preparation of the required insignia. He shall organise the issue of combatants' identity papers.

3. The members of the *Volkssturm* are to be instructed on the definitions relating to combatants set out in the Hague Convention on Land Warfare (see attached).

signed: M. Bormann

APPENDIX IIIA

To: *Gauleiters*
For information: *Reichsleiter, Verbandsführer*
Extract from the Hague Convention on Land Warfare:

Article 1

The laws, rights and obligations of war apply not only to the army, but also to the militias and volunteer corps, if they fulfill all the following conditions:

1. That someone is in a position of command who is responsible for his subordinates,

2. That they wear a specific insignia which can be recognised from a distance,

3. That they carry weapons openly, and

4.   That in their operations they observe the laws and customs of war.

In those countries in which militias or volunteer corps form the army or part of the army, such corps are included under the definition of 'army'.

Article 2

The population of an unoccupied territory which on the approach of the enemy take up arms on their own initiative in order to fight the invading troops, without having had time to organise their forces in accordance with Article 1, shall be considered to be legitimately waging war, provided that they carry weapons openly and observe the laws and customs of war.

APPENDIX IV

Instructions for implementation relating to the *Führer* Decree concerning the formation of the *Volkssturm* 10 October 1944

National Socialist German Workers' Party
Party Chancellery

The Leader of the Party Chancellery

Führer Headquarters, 12 October 1944

Directive 318/44

Re: 2nd schedule of instructions for implementation relating to the *Führer* Decree concerning the formation of the *Volkssturm*.

The *Gauleiters* and *Kreisleiters* are responsible for the command, registration, development and organisation of the *Volkssturm*

I. Command

1.   This Directive expands the scope of my Directive No. 277/44, to further direct that *Kreisleiter*s shall also designate an assistant. The assistants to the *Gauleiters* and *Kreisleiter*s are in the first instance only to be responsible for day-to-day management and administration, I retain the right to confirm their appointment.

The assistants shall be designated *Gau* (or *Kreis*) *Stabsführer* (Chief of Staff).

2.   The *Gauleiters* and *Kreisleiter*s are responsible for the proper selection of suitable *Battalionsführer, Kompanieführer, Zugführer* and *Gruppenführer*.

3.   Men to be selected as officers in the *Volkssturm* must be reliable and steadfast National Socialists, who, if at all possible, have had front-line infantry action experience in the present war. They must have proved their worth in a position of command in such a way that they can be expected to fully discharge their command duties in the *Volkssturm*.

II. Registration

1.   The registration process shall ensure that all men capable of bearing arms are mobilised for service in the *Volkssturm*.

2.   The men in the age groups mobilised by the *Führer* shall be registered in their place of residence by the NSDAP *Ortsgruppe*. All documents suitable for assisting in this registration shall be used to (NSDAP Party Index, population indexes, food rationing indexes, etc)

In registering 16 to 18 year-olds, the *Ortsgruppe* of the Hitler Youth shall be used.

The registration lists must contain details of: name, forename, date of birth, address, telephone number, place of work, current profession and any other professional qualifications, membership of the NSDAP, its subsidiary affiliated organisations, membership in other organisations, military service, knowledge of weapons, war experience, decorations, and military rank last held.

3.	In registration appeals, the men called up for service will be assigned to the respective drafts in accordance with their availability for service. Men who are not fit for *Volkssturm* service will be exempted.

Those men whose fitness for service is doubtful on health grounds, shall be examined by a medical officer appointed by the *Kreisleiter* without taking account of any other medical recommendations.

4.	The men so registered shall be mobilised by the company and battalion commanders for service in the units of the *Volkssturm*.

A paybook shall be issued to them through the companies. On receipt of the paybook, the man who is called up for service shall be considered as having the obligations of a *Volkssturmsoldat*.

5.	Membership of the *Volkssturm* shall lapse on a man being called up for service in the *Wehrmacht*. Membership in the *Volkssturm* of men liable for service in the *Volkssturm* shall not interfere with or delay enlistment for regular military service.

III. Development

1.	The *Volkssturm* shall be organised into four levies. This division into levies is for internal administrative purposes only; it shall not be publicised.

2.	The first levy of the *Volkssturm* shall comprise – insofar as the definition is not superseded by any of the following qualifications – all men in the age group with dates of birth between 1884 and 1928 who are fit for military service and who can be used in the *Volkssturm* without jeapordising vital services on the home front.

Units deployed to man defensive positions shall come from this first levy.

3.	The second levy of the *Volkssturm* shall comprise – insofar as the definition is not superseded by any of the following qualifications – all men in the age group with dates of birth between 1884 and 1928 who work on the home front in organisations vital to the war effort, vital industries, communications or transport services or any other vital functions, and are therefore not included in the first levy. In organising and assigning duties to the second levy, account must be taken of the vital services and/or operations in which men are engaged. The organisation of the second levy is to be on an elastic basis agreed with the appropriate authorities within industry and the special administrative bodies. Further instructions relating to these arrangements will be issued under separate cover.

4.	The third levy of the *Volkssturm* shall comprise all men in the age group with dates of birth between 1925 and 1928, insofar as such men have not yet been called up for active military service.

5.	The fourth levy of the *Volkssturm* shall comprise all those men no longer fit for military service who can be used for guard and security duties.

IV. Organisation

1.	The *Volkssturm* shall be organised into the following units:

	a) *Gruppe* (average strength 1/9 men)

	b) *Zug* (3 to 4 *Gruppen*)

	c) *Kompanie* (3 to 4 *Züge*)

	d) *Bataillon* (4 *Kompanien*)

In the *Volkssturm* there are neither large staffs nor lines of communication.

2.	On the basis of the units of the *Volkssturm* detailed above, the following service ranks shall be introduced:

	a) *Volkssturmmann*

	b) *Gruppenführer*

	c) *Zugführer*

	d) *Kompanieführer*

	e) *Bataillonsführer*

All members of the *Volkssturm* are *Volkssturmsoldaten*.

3.	The *Gruppenführer* shall be appointed by the *Kompanieführer*, the *Zugführer* by the *Bataillonsführer*, the *Kompanieführer* by the *Kreisleiter*, and the *Bataillonsführer* by the *Gauleiter*. These appointments shall in the first instance be temporary, to be confirmed after a period of probation.

4. The organisation of the *Volkssturm* corresponds with the district organisation of the NSDAP. The integrity of the *Ortsgruppe*, and, as far as is possible, that of the *Zelle* and the Block, should be maintained.

    Unless there are exceptional circumstances, these guidelines shall not be departed from even in the organisation of the second levy.

5. Units shall be assembled without any regard to any memberships held by *Volkssturmsoldaten* in the subsidiary organisations of the NSDAP or any other organisations. In assigning men to units, account shall be taken of any special or professional skills and/or knowledge.

6. As a fundamental principle, units of NSDAP subsidiary or affiliated organisations shall not be incorporated en bloc into the *Volkssturm*.

    Special units within the NSDAP subsidiary organisations or other organisations shall, in accordance with the military implementation instructions issued by the *Reichsführer-SS* in his capacity as Supreme Commander of the Reserve Army, be incorporated into the *Volkssturm* to carry out special tasks.

    The *Stadtwacht* and *Landwacht* shall continue in existence until such time as the *Volkssturm* shall be able to take over their duties.

V. Clothing and Equipment

1. All *Volkssturmsoldaten*, irrespective of service rank, shall provide their own clothing and equipment.

2. Suitable items of clothing are all uniforms and weatherproof sports and work clothing. Special importance is to be placed on stout footwear and overcoats. Equipment must be limited to the most essential items. These should include (even if the items are makeshift):

    Rucksack, blanket, crockery, haversack, water bottle, drinking cup and cutlery.

    If necessary, items should be obtained from the *Nachbarschaftshilfe* organisation.

3. The *Gauleiters* shall place at the disposal of the units of the *Volkssturm* all available stocks of uniforms and items of equipment.

4. The uniforms of the Party and its subsidiary organisations shall be dyed to a colour suitable for service in the field. More detailed guidelines with dye samples will be sent to the *Gauleiters*.

5. The *Volkssturmsoldaten* shall wear the following service rank insignia:
    The *Gruppenführer* – one silver-coloured star,
    The *Zugführer* – two silver-coloured stars,
    The *Kompanieführer* – three silver-coloured stars
    The *Battalionsführer* – four silver-coloured stars.

6. While on duty, all *Volkssturmsoldaten* shall wear the armband issued by the *Reichsführer-SS* in his capacity as Supreme Commander of the Reserve Army, with the legend 'Deutscher *Volkssturm-Wehrmacht*'.

                                                            signed: M. Bormann

To: *Gauleiters*

For information to: *Reichsleiter, Verbändeführer*

APPENDIX V

Instructions for implementation relating to the *Führer* Decree concerning the formation of the *Volkssturm* 3 November 1944

National Socialist German Workers' Party

Party Chancellery
The Leader of the Party Chancellery

Führer Headquarters, 3 November 1944

Directive 379/44

Re: 4th schedule of instructions for implementation relating to the *Führer* Decree concerning the formation of the *Volkssturm*. (Guidelines for mobilisation into the first and second levies of the *Volkssturm*)

In accordance with my directives 277/44 (I, 1 Section. 2) and 318/44 (III, 1, 2), the first and second levies of the *Volkssturm* are composed as follows:

The first levy of the *Volkssturm* includes all those men with dates of birth between 1884 and 1924, who are fit for military service, and whom it is possible to use for a limited period without jeopardising vital services on the home front.

The second levy of the *Volkssturm* includes all those men with dates of birth between 1884 and 1924 who are fit for military service but who, because of their civilian activities in vital war work, cannot be mobilised into the first levy.

In agreement with the *Reichsfuhrer-SS* in his capacity as Supreme Commander of the Reserve Army, I issue the following guidelines for mobilisation to these levies of the *Volkssturm*.

I.

Overall responsibility for conscription into the first and second levies of the *Volkssturm* belongs to the *Gauleiter*, who may delegate responsibility for implementation to the *Kreisleiter* and *Ortsgruppenleiter*.

II.

The *Gauleiter* shall ask the employers of all men who cannot be conscripted into the first levy because of their civilian employment in vital services to send a *Z-Karte* (*Zuteilungskarte* – allocation card) to the appropriate *Kreiskommission* at the men's place of residence. The *Z-Karte*, for which there is a standard form, shall contain the following details:

1. Name
2. Forename
3. Date of Birth
4. Address
5. Place of Work
6. Current occupation and any other professional skills
7. Local *Ortsgruppe*

In addition the *Z-Karte* must contain an officially signed and stamped statement from the employer or supervising authority that the man in question is carrying out vital work and cannot be replaced.

III.

Classified as vital work within the meaning of paragraph 2 are the manufacturing processes of armaments and war production which cannot be dispensed with under any circumstances, and also the indispensable functions of ensuring the supply of food, transport and communications services, administration and the Party. The employers and the supervising authorities shall define as narrowly as possible the field of tasks which shall be protected. Special instructions are being issued relating to the conscription of men from individual employer groups (armaments, transport).

The practice of retaining some men in vital work should prevent men being conscripted into the first levy who will not immediately be available for service.

IV.

Monitoring of *Z-Karten* is the responsibility of the *Kreis* Commissions formed as a result of the Joint Directive for the implementation of total war issued by the Reich Plenipotentiary for Total War Mobilisation and the Leader of the Party Chancellery

The *Gauleiters* shall decide whether the *Kreis* Commissions need to reach a decision on every individual said card or whether they will simply test allocations to the second levy of the *Volkssturm* by means of random testing and by checking cards in important individual cases, and, if necessary, by revising decisions.

In special circumstances the *Gauleiters* may provide different regulations concerning decisions relating to allocations to the first and second levy.

The *Z-Karten* which have been received will be sent by the *Kreis* Commissions to the *Ortsgruppenleiter*. Men for whom there is an accepted *Z-Karte* shall not be drafted by the *Ortsgruppenleiter* into the first levy.

V.

The number of men for whom a *Z-Karte* is prepared shall normally not exceed 50% of the total number of men within the *Gau* liable for registration for the *Volkssturm*.

signed: M. Bormann

To:
Reichsleiter
Gauleiter
Verbändeführer

APPENDIX VI

Telegram from *Reichsleiter* Bormann 1 October 1944

Reichsleiter Bormann
To *Oberbefehlsleiter* Friedrichs
Berlin
Party Chancellery

Führer Headquarters, 1 October 1944, 12.45pm

Re.
Organisation of the *Volkssturm*
Propaganda Plan for the *Volkssturm*

You send me *Parteigenosse* Schuett's Propaganda Plan of 30 September and add that the *Volkssturm* would be given real momentum if the *Führer* were to speak after it was formed.

However, the precondition for the *Volkssturm* being formed is the issue of the organisational service guidelines.

So long as these most basic initial guidelines are not available, it is not possible for organisation and development to be carried out in an integrated way, or, rather, they can only be carried out in a disorganised and incoherent way.

But it would be an enormous and irretrievable error if we were to mobilise the *Volkssturm* and if then, because of a lack of clear guidelines issued by the responsible *Reichsleiter* M. Bormann, nothing else whatever happened.

It is thus urgently and crucially important that clear service guidelines be prepared, because it is on them that the correct action of the *Gauleiters* depends.

If *Pg.* Berger does not provide the military documents with the requisite haste, we shall have to produce these kinds of documents ourselves, quickly but faultlessly.

Reichsführer-SS Himmler will be grateful for any support.

The *Gauleiters* are waiting, with justifiable impatience, for clear service guidelines and organisational guidelines to be issued quickly.

Heil Hitler!
Signed: M. Bormann

APPENDIX VII

Circular regarding the *Volkssturm* 23 February 1945

National Socialist German Workers' Party
Party Chancellery

The Leader of the Party Chancellery

Führer Headquarters, 23 February 1945

Circular 28/45

Re: Military suitability of *Kreisstabsführer* and unit commanders of the *Volkssturm*

Often not enough care is being taken in selection.

Therefore, in order to avoid any misunderstandings, it must be again stated that loyalty to the *Führer* and National Socialist steadfastness are the prime conditions for any leadership position within the movement. The unit commanders and *Kreisstabsführer* of the *Volkssturm* must, in addition to these qualities, also demonstrate the necessary military knowledge and, if possible frontline experience in the present war, but in any event must have proved themselves and distinguished themselves as a military commander in one of the two World Wars. They are then to be selected solely on the basis of their suitability without taking any account of their position within the Party, within the State, or within industry.

Signed: M. Bormann

The numbers of the *Gaue*

1 Baden	2 Bayreuth	3 Berlin
4 Danzig-Westpreussen	5 Düsseldorf	6 Essen
7 Franken	8 Halle-Merseburg	9 Hamburg
10. Hessen-Nassau	11. Kärnten	12 Köln-Aachen
13 Kurhessen	14 Magdeburg-Anhalt	15 Mainfranken
16 Mark Brandenburg	17 Mecklenburg	18 Moselland
19 München-Oberbayern	20 Niederdonau	21 Niederschlesien
22 Oberdonau	23 Oberschlesien	24 Ost-Hannover
25 Ostpreussen	26 Pommern	27 Sachsen
28 Salzburg	29 Schleswig-Holstein	30 Schwaben
31 Steiermark	32 Sudetenland	33 Süd-Hannover-Braunschweig
34 Thüringen	35 Tirol-Vorarlberg	36 Wartheland
37 Weser-Ems	38 Westfalen Nord	40 Westmark
41 Wien	42 Württemberg-Hohenzollern	43 Auslandsorganisation

Incorporation of various groups and workers into the *Volkssturm*

Incorporation of members of the German *Reichspost* into the *Volkssturm*

I. Levies

1. All men of the German *Reichspost* shall be included in the first levy, in so far as this is not superseded by any of the following.

2. In the second levy will be included:

    a) the telegraph services,
    b) the other doubly exempted men of the *Reichspost*,
    c) the members of the postal security service and
    d) up to 30 per cent of the remaining male personnel of the *Reichspost*.

II. Incorporation

1. The employees of the *Reichspost* who are included in the first and second levies shall be incorporated into the local units of the *Volkssturm* insofar as this is not superseded by any of the following provisions.

2. Within the framework of the local units – with the approval of the *Gauleiter* – the telegraph services shall be brought together to form employment related units. The employment related units shall also be under the command of the officer responsible for their area, who shall organise the selection of officers and development of units in accordance with the general regulations. The training and organisation of these units are as the same as that for the other *Volkssturm* units, but shall be adjusted to meet the requirements of the *Reichspost* service in terms of time.

    Otherwise the employment related units will be deployed in the same way as the local units of the *Volkssturm*.

III. Postschutz

1. The existing formations of the *Postschutz* shall be incorporated within the *Volkssturm* as discrete units. The service provided by the *Postschutz* units shall be implemented with reference to the military and political guidelines and instructions issued by the *Reichsfuhrer-SS* in his capacity as Supreme Commander of the Reserve Army and by the Leader of the Party Chancellery. The senior officers of the Party shall determine in which local *Volkssturm* units the *Postschutz* formations shall be incorporated. They shall be mobilised for combat deployment with these *Volkssturm* units. The *Postschutz* senior officers, who shall provide the senior officers of the Party with reports on the strength of the units together with the required personal details concerning the members of the individual *Postschutz* formations, and shall keep these lists up-to-date, shall take part in the current service meetings of the respective *Volkssturm* units.

2. The special duties of the *Postschutz* (security of postal and telegraph installations) shall continue. The *Postschutz* shall also continue to be the responsibility of the *Reichspostminister*.

   Weapons and equipment provided to the *Postschutz* shall also remain at the disposal of the *Reichspostminister*. He shall also determine the leaders of the *Postschutz* units.

3. Every effort must be made to ensure the closest collaboration between the authorities of the party and the senior officers of the *Postschutz* in all questions relating to the *Volkssturm*.

IV. Responsibility

In cases of doubt, decisions shall be taken by the *Kreisleiter* (*Kreis* Commission) in agreement with the head of the equivalent authority (Departmental Head) of the *Reichspost*. In cases of appeal to higher authority, decisions shall be taken by the *Gauleiter* in discussion with the President of the *Reichspost* Directorate.

Incorporation within the *Volkssturm* of employees of industries which are under the control of the *Reichsminister* for Armaments and War Production

I. 1st Levy

In every *Gau* there shall be allocated to the first levy 30 per cent of the employees of the industries under the control of the *Reichsminister* for Armaments and War Production (armaments, war production, mining, industries controlled by the General Plenipotentiary for the Chemical Production Plan, building, *Organisation Todt*, *Transportkorps Speer*)

   Within this framework, the percentage for individual industries need not be equal. The managing authorities can, for instance, attribute a lower percentage to some industries because of their particular products or because they employ a large proportion of foreign workers, and attribute a balancing higher percentage to other industries.

II. 2nd Levy

The remaining workforce shall be allocated to the second levy, particularly if they are involved in the following industries or services:

a) *Flak* weapons and *flak* ammunition

b) High-performance aircraft

c) Shipyards

d) Public utility supply industries (electricity, gas, water).

   In addition, employees who are doubly exempt shall be allocated to the second levy.

III. Local Units

The employees of the industries under the control of the *Reichsminister* for Armaments and War Production who are included in the first and second levies, shall be incorporated into the local units of the *Volkssturm* insofar as this is not superseded by any of the following provisions.

IV. Betriebsgebundene Einheiten (Employment-related units)

Within the framework of the local units, employees of industries included within the second levy can, with the approval of the *Gauleiters*, be assembled into employment-related units (platoons, companies, battalions), if the running of the industry makes regular participation in the service of the local units impossible. In particular, employment-related units are to be formed if workforces live together in camps or residential communities, or work on a mobile basis, for example, with the *Organisation Todt*, construction units, survey sections, supply units, signals units, security command units, mobile winter service.

Men from outside the specific industries should also be assigned to the employment-related units insofar as local circumstances permit.

The employment-related units are under the command of the responsible authorities within their specific area, who shall organise the selection of officers and general organisation in accordance with the general regulations. Training and service organisation is the same as that of the other *Volkssturm* units, but is to be adjusted to suit the requirements and possibilities of the industries in question in terms of time.

V. Responsibility

In cases of doubt, decisions shall be taken by the *Kreisleiter* in discussion with the controlling or equivalent authority (*Rüstungskommandatur* or *Oberbauleiter*).

VI. Exceptions

The members of the *Front-OT* (*Organisation Todt*) and the *Wehrmacht* section of the *Transportkorps Speer* are exempted from service in the *Volkssturm*.

Conscription of members of the *Ordnungspolizei* (civilian police) into the *Volkssturm*

I. Levies

1st Levy

a) There shall be included in the first levy the members of the *Ordnungspolizei* and its auxiliary organisations whose service allows them to be deployed in the first levy without seriously affecting the implementation of the war-related tasks of the *Ordnungspolizei*, particularly the members (uniformed and non uniformed) of the civilian police,

   the members of the voluntary and statutory fire services (without motorised fire appliances),

   the members of the general *Technische Nothilfe* without technical deployment units,

   members of the civilian police who work outside the police (for example, armaments and industry), are to be conscripted into the *Volkssturm* in the same way as all other *Volksgenossen*.

b) The conscription of members of the voluntary and statutory fire services for training within the *Volkssturm* shall be carried out in discussion with the local responsible officers of these organisations in such a way as to guarantee the continuance of technical Fire Service training and constant availability of the fire services. In general, during training in the *Volkssturm*, about one-third of the fire service must remain as a discrete unit in the locality and carry out the necessary technical fire service training.

c) The local authorities of the *Technische Nothilfe* shall, insofar as this is possible and desirable, make available to the first levy a course of supervisory staff from the technical deployment units who shall form and train pioneer units.

2nd Levy

As exceptions, the following members of the *Ordnungspolizei* shall be incorporated in the 2nd levy:

a) The motorised fire service units, the headquarters staff, the fire service technical inspection staff, the fire chiefs and the voluntary fire service mechanics and also the works fire brigades.

b) From the general *Technische Nothilfe*, the technical deployment units.

c) The police surgeons.

II. Incorporation

1. Local units of the Volkssturm.

The members of the *Ordnungspolizei* who are included in the 1st and 2nd levies shall be incorporated individually in the local units of the *Volkssturm*, insofar as nothing else is stipulated in the following provisions.

2. Employment-related units

Exceptionally, the following are to be incorporated within the local units as employment-related units:

a) the motorised fire service units,

b) the technical deployment units of the general *Technische Nothilfe*,

Men from outside the specific services should also be assigned to the employment-related units insofar as local circumstances permit. The employment-related units are under the command of the responsible authorities within their specific area, who shall organise the selection of officers and general organisation in accordance with the general regulations. Training and service organisation is the same as that of the other *Volkssturm* units, but is to be adjusted to suit the service requirements of the *Ordnungspolizei* and its other auxiliary organisations in terms of time. In the event of the voluntary and technical emergency services needing to be deployed, such deployment shall be in parallel with training in the *Volkssturm*.

III. Exceptions

The members (active and reserve) of the following are excepted from the *Volkssturm*:

1. the *Schutzpolizei*, including the other uniformed Police units (*Schutzmannschaften*, German Police Volunteers),

2. the *Gendarmerie*

3. the *Feuerschutzpolizei*

4. the *Luftschutzpolizei*

IV. Responsibility

In cases of doubt, decisions shall be taken by the *Kreisleiter* in agreement with the appropriate responsible police administrator (police commander). In cases of appeal to higher authority, decisions shall be taken by the *Gauleiter* in discussion with the senior SS and police leaders.

V. Landwacht and Stadtwacht

The *Landwacht* and *Stadtwacht* organisation has been dissolved. Former members of the *Landwacht* and *Stadtwacht* are therefore unrestrictedly at the disposal of the *Volkssturm*. To carry out the tasks previously carried out by the *Landwacht*, at the request of the *Gendarmerie*, suitable members of the *Volkssturm*, principally the former members of the *Landwacht*, shall be made available to the *Gendarmerie*. The request shall be made by the local responsible *Gendarmerie* authorities to the local commander of the *Volkssturm*.

The former *Landwachtposten* and shall be taken over by the *Volkssturm* as *Volkssturmposten*. The service instructions applicable to the *Landwacht* shall apply to the *Volkssturmposten*.

To carry out the tasks previously carried out by the *Stadtwacht*, when necessary, at the request of the locally responsible commander of the *Schutzpolizei*, the required units of the *Volkssturm* shall be placed at his disposal. The request shall be made to the *Kreisstabsführer*, and in urban *Gaue* to the *Gaustabsführer*.

The weapons formerly used by the *Landwacht* and *Stadtwacht* shall, in discussion between the senior SS and police chiefs – the senior commanders of the *Ordnungspolizei* – *and the Gaustabsführer*, be transferred to the units of the *Volkssturm*.

VI. Concluding instructions

Instances of conscription or incorporation which do not comply with the above specifications are to be cancelled or to be adjusted to comply with the above specifications.

Special regulations are to be issued concerning the relationship between the *Verwaltungspolizei* and the *Volkssturm*.

Enlistment in the *Volkssturm* of agricultural and food industry and agricultural administration employees

I.

1st Levy

In every *Gau*, the following shall be assigned to the 1st levy of the *Volkssturm*:

30% of those employees (liable for service in the *Volkssturm*) in the agricultural and food industries and the agricultural administration within the areas of responsibility of the *Landesernährungsämter* and *Landesbauernschaften* (regional foodstuffs departments and regional farmers' associations),

70% of those junior and middle-level employees in the other agricultural administrative departments.

II.

2nd Levy

The other employees (liable for service in the *Volkssturm*) within the foodstuffs sector shall be enlisted in the 2nd levy of the *Volkssturm*, in particular

1. In agricultural establishments (including horticulture):

    Establishment managers
    Milkers
    Tractor Drivers
    Shepherds
    Piggery employees

2. In foodstuffs establishments (e.g. in bakeries, butchers' establishments, mills, cold stores, tinned food and foodstuffs factories, distribution establishments and goods associations, and also in campaign operations such as sugar factories, distilleries, potato and vegetable drying establishments):

    Establishment managers
    Senior officials
    Essential specialist staff
    (including the specialist staff within the establishment responsible for the transport of foodstuffs)

3. In the State-operated stud establishments:

    Stud managers
    Stud employees

4. In the agricultural administration:

    (a)   within the area of the *Landesernährungsämter* and *Landesbauernschaften*:

Landesbauernführer (heads of regional farmers' associations) together with essential staff (including those in business associations)

(b) *within the area of foodstuffs departments and Kreisbauernschaften*:
Kreisbauernführer and essential staff (including those in survey offices), *Bezirksbauernführer*, *Ortsbauernführer*,

(c) within the other areas of agricultural administration in particular rural estates administration (estate management, fisheries management) the staff required to carry on the most essential tasks.

III.

Procedures and allocation of responsibilities

Applications (*Z-Karte*) in respect of men to be enlisted in the 2nd levy shall be submitted to the *Kreiskommission* of the local NSDAP *Ortsgruppe*

1. in the case of agricultural and food industry establishments, via the *Kreisbauernführer*,

2. in all other cases via the departmental manager (e.g. *Landstallmeister*, head of the *Landesernährungsamt* (regional foodstuffs department), *Generallandschaftsdirektor*)

In cases of doubt, the *Kreisleiter* shall have the final decision, in agreement

(in the case of (1) above) with the *Kreisbauernführer*
(in the case of (2) above) with the departmental manager

In cases of appeal, the *Gauleiter* shall have the final decision, in agreement

(in the case of (1) above) with the *Landesbauernführer*
(in the case of (2) above) with the manager of the responsible middle-level department or head of the *Landesernährungsamt*

APPENDIX X

Volkssturm weapon requirements 30 November 1944

The *Reichsführer-SS*
Supreme Commander of the Reserve Army
Chief of Staff, *Volkssturm*

Berlin-Grünewald, 30 November 1944
Douglasstraße

Schedule of Weapons Requirements

a) According to reports received to date, the *Volkssturm* will comprise

1st to 4th levies	6,000,000 men		
3rd levy	about 600,000 men		
4th levy	about 1,400,000 men	=	2,000,000 men
1st and 2nd levies together	about 4,000,000 men		

of these 1st levy 30%:1,200,000 men in about 1,850 battalions and
2nd levy 70%:2,800,000 men in about 4,860 battalions.

b) Subject to confirmation of strength, the following weapons requirements are envisaged for one *Volkssturm* battalion:

	1st Draft	2nd Draft
Small-arms	649	576
Rifle grenade launchers	27	27
Light machine-guns	31	30
Heavy machine-guns	6	3
Medium mortars	6	3
Anti-tank guns	3	–
Panzerschreck	6	6

c) For the time being, no weapons are required for the 3rd levy. The 4th levy must manage with the capture weapons and hunting weapons available in the *Gaue*.

d) This produces the following overall requirements for the *Volkssturm*: for ...

	1st levy, 1850 battalions	2nd levy, 4860 battalions	Total
Small-arms	1,200,000	2,800,000	4,000,000
Rifle grenade launchers	49,930	131,220	181,150
Light MG	57,350	145,800	203,150
Heavy MG	11,100	14,580	25,680
Medium mortars	11,100	14,580	25,680
Anti-tank guns	5,500		5,500
Panzerschreck	11,100	29,160	40,260

After weapons have been directed to the *Volkssturm*, consideration must be given to the needs of the *Gaue* which are immediately under threat, and some *Gaue* in which fighting is already taking place, viz: for ...

	1st levy, 400 battalions	2nd levy, 1050 battalions	Total
Small-arms	261,390	609,91	871,300
Rifle grenade launchers	10,800	28,350	39,150
Light MG	12,400	31,500	43,900
Heavy MG	2,400	3,150	5,550
Medium mortars	2,400	3,150	5,550
Anti-tank guns	1,200		1,200
Panzerschreck	2,400	6,300	8,700

After the above programme has been completed, the following supplies of weapons will be delivered to the *Gaue* under less immediate threat, beginning with those for the first draft: for ...

	1st levy, 200 battalions	2nd levy, 550 battalions	Total
Small-arms	134,250	313,250	447,500
Rifle grenade launchers	5,400	14,850	20,250
Light MG	6,200	16,500	22,700
Heavy MG	1,200	1,650	2,850
Medium mortars	1,200	1,650	2,850
Anti-tank guns	600		600
Panzerschreck	1,200	3,300	4,500

e)   The following German weapons have been reported as available by the *Gaue* under immediate threat:

> 9,690 rifles
> 32 light machine-guns
> 1,517 pistols
> 38 machine-pistols

f)   The *Gaue* under less immediate threat report the following stocks of German weapons:

> 3,971 rifles
> 121 light machine-guns
> 27 heavy machine-guns
> 842 pistols
> 457 machine-pistols

pp.*Reichsführer-SS*
Signed: Kissel
Oberst

APPENDIX XI

Armament of the *Volkssturm* 8 December 1944

Main Weapons Committee
In the office of
Reichsminister for Armaments
And War Production
Berlin

Chairman: Dir. Dipl. -Ing. K. Weissenborn

Berlin NW7, 8 December 1944
Unter den Linden

Secret!

To the
District Representatives of the Main Weapons Committee
Re: Armament of the *Volkssturm*
To date, with respect to small-arms, it has been planned to provide 2 weapons:

1.   the *Volksmaschinenpistole*

2.   the *Volksgewehr*

The following sets out an outline of the planned production programme:

1. *Volksmaschinenpistole.*

The weapon is being produced in two main groups

a)   in small German workshops

b)   in industrial groups or groups controlled by industry.

The first orders for both groups have been placed by OKH, WaH, Wu G2. Further orders are being placed by the *Reichsführer-SS*. Production management will be carried out by the Main Weapons Committee. The special committee responsible for this is W 12, Director, Dr. Schnitger, Berlin-Borsigwalde, Eichenborndamm 167/209, Tel. 49 24 81, Teletype 01 1247. The main client for the weapons being produced in small workshops is the *Reichszentrale für Handwerkslieferungen*, Berlin SW 68, Friedrichstrasse 10, Tel. 1757 11. Contact: Herr Lenk.

The *Reichszentrale* has issued sub-contracts to 30 small workshop production associations and 14 assembly locations.

Further orders are being produced at various different establishments which have themselves received direct orders from OKH.

The first production run will be in December.

It is absolutely necessary that the widest possible support is given by all authorities to the production of the *Volksmaschinenpistole*, so that the largest possible number of weapons will be produced by this programme in the shortest possible time.

2. Volksgewehr.

The District Representatives were first informed by the following telegram, which is repeated here:

The following information supplements the letter of 27 November 1944 from Herr *Reichsminister* Speer to the *Gauleiters* and Reich Defence Commissioners :

1. The orders for the weapons for the *Volkssturm* will be placed by the *Reichsführer-SS*, the Chief of Staff of the *Volkssturm*, *SS Obergruppenführer und General der Waffen-SS* Berger.

2. The production of the *Volksgewehr* will be organised on a decentralised basis throughout the Reich by the Main Weapons Committee. To assist in this process, the district representatives in their individual areas and in agreement with the appropriate authorities shall specify a suitable managing company which shall be recommended by the Main Weapons Committee to the *Gauleiter* who shall confirm the recommendation. The managing company shall be the main contractor. With the support of all appropriate authorities, this company shall record every potential manufacturer, even the smallest, shall plan the production process, place sub-contracts and manage the whole work process.

3. Final detailed drawings of the weapons will be available on 8 December 1944 from the Main Weapons Committee, Arbeitsstab Ge-Pi, Berlin NW7, Unter den Linden 38, IV, Room 404, and can be collected from there by courier on 8 December 1944.

4. At 9 am on 17 December 1944 a production meeting will take place at the firm of Carl Walther in Zella-Mehlis. At this meeting, every firm involved in producing the weapon shall be handed a completed weapon as a pattern. The responsible manager of the management firm responsible for production of the *Volksgewehr* shall be sent to the meeting for this purpose.

Further information follows by letter.

The following supplementary information should be noted:

a) Organisation

The production process itself will be carried out by the designated managing firms, who will work in the closest collaboration with all authorities, the Defence District Representatives, the Armaments Commissions, Armaments Inspectorates, Armaments Commands, *Gau* industrial offices, chambers of trade, *Gau* Labour Offices etc. But this alone is not sufficient.

I ask the *Gauleiter* to form and manage a '*Volkssturm* Armaments Staff '. The task of this Staff is, by short circuiting all authorities and cutting out all red tape, to resolve all difficulties which arise and support the responsible managing firm.

In this connection, the following areas are of particular importance: procurement of materials, labour force, energy and other industrial materials, transports.

By the direct action of representatives of the Armaments Commands, Labour Office etc as members of this Staff, it will be possible to resolve directly all difficulties which arise.

At the designing firm of Karl Walther, Zella-Mehlis, a '*Volksgewehr* Works Committee' has been formed under the chairmanship of Herr Fritz Walther, Tel. Zella-Mehlis 651, Teletype 06 81 84. This Committee is responsible for all questions relating to design and production. The Walther Company is forming its own production line, which will serve as an exemplar and training operation and will provide advice, improvements etc to all industries involved in the production process. Contracts and production management will be provided by the *Reichsführer-SS*.

b) Production

1. Planning

The size of the monthly output to be planned will depend upon the technical circumstances of the individual *Gaue*. Every *Gau* must deliver complete weapons, with support being given in the production of gun barrels during the first two to three months. As a general planning guideline, work should be carried out on the basis that throughout the area of the Reich 100,000 to 150,000 weapons must be produced by this scheme every month. Thus every *Gau* is required to produce 3,000 to 4,000 weapons per month, and the more industrial *Gaue* will of course considerably exceed this figure. In planning the individual weapons parts and groups, to achieve industrial scale production rates, it will be necessary to assemble small producers into a production line. In this, the management will be assisted by the individual master craftsmen, who can build effective and efficient groups by appropriate use of unskilled labour and use of the machinery within their individual operations. In this process, the assistance of the *Gauhandwerkmeister* will be of crucial importance. Plans should be also made to use groups of craftsmen trained in this way as 'godfathers', by assigning to them an industrial-scale plant which can support this group using its greater organisational and industrial potential.

With regard to technical drawing documentation, 10 sets of final drawings are being issued on 8 December 1944. One set each of these drawings shall be handed by the District Representatives to the *Gauleiter*, the Defence District Representative and the Chairman of the Armamaents Commission. Working drawings and operational drawings are under preparation at the Carl Walther Company, Zella-Mehlis. It is expected that the design work will be completed on 20 December 1944. Every *Gau* must provide its own industrial resources.

Planning should take account of the basic premise that it is not possible to provide new machinery. Any requirements for machinery must be covered by sharing arrangements within the individual *Gau*. After planning is completed, requests and production/delivery estimates are to be notified to the Main Weapons Committee, Arbeitsstab Ge-Pi.

Deadline for these reports: 21 December 1944

2. Procurement of Materials

Material, at least for the gun barrel, must be procured within the *Gau* itself by scouring the last corner of all stores, by using, for example, material already worked from contracts which have been stopped, by use of material from other manufacturing processes which has not been needed in recent months. It is essential that the *Gaue* provide each other with mutual help in this process. Surplus materials and shortages of materials are to be reported to Arbeitsstab Ge-Pi.

In addition, material will be provided by the Central Procurement Group of the Main Weapons Committee. Requests should be sent to Herr Direktor Habicht, Berlin-Grünewald, Wernerstrasse 15a, Tel. 89 05 67, Teletype 01 15 30. Any difficulties in obtaining materials should be reported to Arbeitsstab Ge-Pi.

3. Transports

Transport must similarly be carried out using the resources of the individual *Gau*; the Hitler Youth can provide invaluable assistance in this by carrying out and escorting courier deliveries.

4. Communications

Good communications are the precondition for smooth collaboration. I would request that up-to-date details of addresses, telephone and telegraph numbers of all managing firms and the other managing authorities be regularly notified to Main Weapons Committee, Berlin Office, Arbeitsstab Ge-Pi, Dipl. -Ing. Riese, Teletype 0120 49 and 01 15 02, Tel. 11 27 45.

General

These manufacturing programmes have the same urgency as the Infantry Armaments Programme. There are no special conditions of secrecy applying to the production process.

The current weapons programme is not to be impeded in any way by the action for arming the *Volkssturm*. Thus, only additional capacity should be used without affecting other weapons production.

The weapons themselves were designed in such a way that the required tolerances can be maintained with the normal machine plant of any small or medium-sized workshop without special equipment.

In terms of construction, the *Volksgewehr* is a similar weapon to the infantry rifle. No German soldier or *Volkssturmmann* should therefore receive a weapon which is unsafe because some of the production process was carried out by firms or individuals with no experience in producing weapons.

Main Weapons Committee
Office Berlin
Weissenborn

Distribution:

Main Weapons Committee District Representatives	22

For information to:

Chief of Staff *Volkssturm*	20
Gauleiters and Reich Defence Commissioners	42
OKH, Chief HRüst and BdE	10
Defence District Representatives	27
Chairmen of Armaments Commissions	27
Armaments Inspectorates/Armaments Commands	97
Technical Authorities	20
Armaments Staff	20
Reichshandwerkmeister	60
Main Weapons Committee	10
Managing firms	50
Reserve	85
	490

APPENDIX XII

Order for the Formation of the *Volkssturm* 16 October 1944

The *Reichsführer-SS*
Commander of the Reserve Army
The *Volkssturm*
Chief of Staff
Pa/Ji. VS. Tgb. Nr. 6396/44 geh.

Berlin-Grünewald, 16 October 1944
Douglasstraße 7–11

Order for the Formation of the Volkssturm

A. Basic principles

1. The *Führer* has ordered the formation of the *Volkssturm* to reinforce the active forces of our *Wehrmacht* and in particular to carry on a remorseless struggle everywhere that the enemy tries to enter upon German soil.

2. This wish by the *Führer* represents the exclusive and sole purpose for the formation of the *Volkssturm*.

3. The formation process will be divided into

    a) a process of ideological motivation in accordance with the guidelines produced by the Leader of the Party Chancellery;
    b) training in weapons and use of terrain (including special training in field pioneer service, signals service and motorised vehicle service).
        This process must be so far advanced by 31 March 1945 that all drafts of the *Volkssturm* are capable of being deployed in combat.

4. The urgency of the task makes it necessary to begin the process of training immediately within the scope of the manpower immediately available.

5. Necessary organisational work (for example, registration of the *Volkssturm* men, procurement of additional training equipment etc) are to be completed in parallel with training, and should not be regarded as having greater priority than training itself.

5. The training shall take place at least once a week (exceptions are Hitler Youth, *Reichsarbeitsdienst* and NSKK in accordance with special orders). The available time will depend upon the claims made on the *Volkssturm*

men by other important war work, and will vary, for example between districts with more agricultural population and those with more industrial population.

6.   Training personnel and training equipment
         As necessary, these are to be borrowed from the regular Army in agreement with the Defence District Commands and senior SS and Police authorities, without causing the training of regular troops to suffer. The Defence District Commands and senior SS and Police authorities will be provided with appropriate information from this office.

B. Weapons Training

1.   Weapons training shall comprise

   a)   training in the use of the rifle, the light machine-gun, the mortar, the hand grenade, close-quarters anti-tank fighting (including use of the *Panzerfaust*) and in use of terrain.
   b)   instruction in the use of the machine-pistol, the pistol, and in temporary laying and clearing of mines.

2.   As a fundamental principle, any kind of drill shall be excluded. The necessary training in forming up and in military order will generally be sufficient for the *Volkssturm* man.

3.   Drill shall only find a place where it is required for weapons training (for example, in loading and securing the rifle). Otherwise it will damage inward preparedness.

4.   The basic principles of training are:

   •   Practical training for practical application!
   •   No long explanations, but let's get our hands on the training equipment!
   •   No rambling explanations, but practice with the weapons themselves!
   •   No boredom, but discipline of spirit and body!

   Training shall take place on an individual basis, with no unit training. Only the training in the use of terrain is intended to educate men in reconnaissance for reconnaissance units.

5.   Training in the use of the rifle shall achieve complete mastery of the rifle and safe firing of the weapon up to 150 metres. The emphasis here is on firing training. From an early stage, this should take place outdoors in field conditions.
         The important thing is accuracy with individual shots. The man should gain absolute confidence in his rifle. Increasing training targets in firing practice should generally only be done when the individual rifleman has performed well with the easier practice.

6.   Training in the use of the machine gun shall have as its aim complete mastery of this weapon. Here too training is to be moved out doors into field conditions as soon as possible. The individual is to be trained to fire in short bursts. At first, firing practice should be with blanks, because the current stocks of ammunition do not permit using live ammunition.

7.   Training on the light mortar has as its aim the complete mastery of this weapon. So far as is permitted by the ammunition situation, firing should be done in combat conditions.

8.   Training with hand grenades. This should train the *Volkssturm* man in throwing grenades high, far, and at specific targets, and also in close-quarters combat conditions.

9.   Training in close quarters anti-tank warfare shall comprise both the complete mastery of the *Panzerfaust* and also training with the other close quarters anti-tank warfare devices.

10. In training in the use of terrain, the *Volkssturm* man should learn how to make the best use of the terrain for himself and to carry out the tasks which he has been assigned, to set up temporary barriers and to be able to dig in quickly for himself and for his weapon.
         Further training will be carried out in a entrenching, camouflage, and in solving small reconnaissance tasks. In connection with the latter, trainees shall learn the basics of simple reporting.
         In any training carried out in the open, thus, for example, in shooting, great value is to be placed on the use of spades, camouflage, and the use of terrain.

11. Instruction in the use of the machine pistol, the pistol, and in laying and clearing of mines should give the *Volkssturm* man some knowledge of the equipment involved, so that he is able to use it if necessary.

Signed: G. Berger
SS-Obergruppenführer

APPENDIX XIII

Directive of 1 December 1944
Concerning the status of Members of the *Volkssturm*

(RGBl. 1944, T. IS. 343/344)
(H. V. Bl. 1945, T. B. S. 5 Nr. 7)

The *Wehrmacht* and the *Volkssturm* are the *Volk* in arms. Service in the *Volkssturm* is a service of honour to the German *Volk* in exactly the same way as service in the *Wehrmacht*. The *Volkssturmsoldat* has obligations and rights just as the soldier of the *Wehrmacht* has.

On behalf of the *Führer* and in agreement with the *Reichsminister* and head of the Reich Chancellery and the head of the *Oberkommando der Wehrmacht*, the following orders are therefore made:

1.

Men called up for service in the *Volkssturm* are obliged to meet the requirement for them to register for the *Volkssturm* and to obey any orders are requiring them to serve in any capacity in the *Volkssturm*.

Anyone who does not meet his obligation to present himself for registration and serve in the *Volkssturm*, or does not do so at the proper time, can, without prejudice to any punishment under the provisions of the current penal code, be constrained by the police to present himself for registration and/or service in the *Volkssturm*.

2.

Offences against discipline and order shall be punished according to the provisions of a Penal Code for the *Volkssturm*.

3.

In accordance with a judicial order, a penal jurisdiction for the *Volkssturm* is to be created.

4.

1) The *Volkssturmsoldat* shall supply his own clothing and equipment.

2) In addition, it is the duty of honour of every German to help *Volkssturmsoldaten* who do not possess suitable items of equipment and clothing.

5.

The *Volkssturmsoldat* shall be decorated for gallantry and for meritorious conduct in the same way as the member of the *Wehrmacht*.

6.

1) The *Volkssturmsoldat* shall receive welfare in accordance with the provisions of more detailed regulations, and when on active service, shall receive provisions and accommodation as a member of the *Wehrmacht*.

2) All *Volkssturmsoldaten* shall receive soldier's pay at the same rate.

7.

The maintenance of the family (family maintenance) of the *Volkssturmsoldat* deployed on active service shall be a maintained to the same extent as the maintenance of the family of the member of the *Wehrmacht*.

8.

Should a *Volkssturmsoldat* sustain an injury in the course of his service, on receipt of an appropriate claim, care and provision shall be provided for him and his dependants in accordance with the regulations applying to members of the *Wehrmacht*.

9.

1) The *Volkssturmsoldat* should, if possible, be trained outside the working hours of his normal occupation.

2) Should training be carried out during his normal working hours, then no economic disadvantage had should accrue to him and his family as a result. Working salary shall continue to be paid.

10.

To the extent that working salary continues to be paid, the amounts will be compensated on receipt of a claim.

11.

Regulations which have been issued for the members of the *Wehrmacht* to avoid legal disadvantages and to facilitate legal actions shall apply in a corresponding manner for combat deployment.

12.

Regulations which are necessary to implement the basic principles set out under Figures 4 to 11, insofar as these do not fall within the responsibility of the Leader of the Party Chancellery or the *Reichsführer-SS*, are hereby issued by the responsible senior Reich authorities and the Head of the *Oberkommando der Wehrmacht* in agreement with the Leader of the Party Chancellery and the *Reichsführer-SS*.

Führer Headquarters, 1 December 1944

The Leader of the Party Chancellery
M. Bormann

The *Reichsführer*-SS
H. Himmler

APPENDIX XIV

Legal Directives of 24 February 1945 concerning the *Volkssturm*

Legal Directive of 24 February 1945 concerning criminal law relating to the *Volkssturm*

(*Volkssturm-Strafrechtsverordnung* – VoStVO.)
of 24 February 1945
(*Reichgesetzbl.* 1945, T. I S. 34)

On behalf of the *Führer* and in agreement with the *Reichsminister* and head of the Reich Chancellery and the head of the *Oberkommando der Wehrmacht*, the following orders are made:

§ 1

During deployment on active service and in training, the criminal law regulations applying to members of the *Wehrmacht* shall, insofar as no other provisions are made, be applicable to the members of the *Volkssturm*. In the case of minors, such application shall be in conjunction with the Reich Youth Jurisdiction Act.

§ 2

The provisions of the military penal code relating to non-commissioned officers shall apply in the case of the *Volkssturm* to *Gruppenführer*, the provisions relating to officers to *Zugführer*, *Kompanieführer*, *Bataillonsführer* and their superiors.

§ 3

1) The provisions of the military penal code relating to punishable offences in the field shall apply to the members of the *Volkssturm* only in respect of punishable offences committed in a situation of combat deployment.

2) Punishment in accordance with the provisions of the military penal code or the imposition of other minimum sentencing sanctions for military misdemeanours can be waived if the punishment or the applicable minimum sentence could be seen as being unreasonably harsh and are also not required on the grounds of maintenance of order or the defence of the Reich.

§ 4

This Directive shall come into force with effect from 18 October 1944.

Führer Headquarters, 24 February 1945

The Leader of the Party Chancellery
M. Bormann

The *Reichsführer*-SS
H. Himmler

Directive Concerning a Special Jurisdiction in Criminal Cases for Members of the *Volkssturm*

(*Volkssturm-Strafgerichtsordnung* – VoStO.)
of 24 February 1945
(*Reichgestzbl.* 1945, T I. S. 34)

On behalf of the *Führer* and in agreement with the *Reichsminister* and Head of the Reich Chancellery and the Head of the *Oberkommando der Wehrmacht*, the following orders are made:

§ 1

1) The members of the *Volkssturm* shall, for all criminal acts which they commit in a situation of combat deployment or in training, be subject to the jurisdiction of the *Volkssturm*.

2) In the case of offences which contravene the general penal laws, the justice shall hand over the proceedings to the general jurisdiction, provided that this is not precluded on grounds of general order and the defence of the Reich. The decision to hand over cases is irrevocable.

§ 2

Criminal proceedings shall be applied analagously.

§ 3

The field courts-martial and the Reich courts-martial shall be replaced by the courts of the *Volkssturm*.

§ 4

1) *Wehrmacht* judges on special military service shall be replaced by judges of the *Volkssturm*. They must be qualified judges and suitable to serve as officers in the *Volkssturm*. They shall carry out their office on an honorary basis.

2) As assessors, the presiding justice shall appoint a company commander or a battalion commander and another member of the *Volkssturm* of the same rank as the defendant.

§ 5

1) The presiding justices are the *Gauleiters*, and, in situations of combat deployment under the command of units of the Army or of the Waffen-SS, the presiding justices of those units.

2) The Superior Justice is the *Reichsführer-SS*.

3) The Supreme Justice is the *Führer*.

§ 6

The *Reichsführer-SS* can revoke a legally valid judgment and order a fresh trial if he considers that serious doubts about the correctness of the judgment render a new decision necessary.

§ 7

Clemency shall be exercised by the *Führer*, and by the *Reichsführer-SS* on the *Führer's* instructions.

§ 8

Terms of imprisonment can, at the request of the presiding justice, be carried out by the authorities of the general criminal jurisdiction.

§ 9

1) The organisation of the jurisdiction of the *Volkssturm* and the selection and appointment of judges shall be managed by the Leader of the Party Chancellery in agreement with the *Reichsführer-SS*.

2) The *Reichsführer-SS* and the leader of the Party Chancellery shall jointly issue explanations, supplements, amendments and instructions for implementation of this Directive.

§ 10

This Directive shall come into force with effect from 18 October 1944.

Führer Headquarters 24 February 1945.

The Leader of the Party Chancellery
M. Bormann

The *Reichsführer*-SS
H. Himmler

First Schedule of Instructions for Implementation relating to the Directive concerning a Special Jurisdiction in Criminal Offences for Members of the Volkssturm

(Formation of the Jurisdiction of the *Volkssturm*)
of 24 February 1945
(*Reichgesetzbl.* 1945, T. I. S. 35)

To implement the *Volkssturm* Criminal Jurisdiction Directive, I determine, in agreement with the *Reichsführer-SS*:

§ 1

Exercise of Jurisdiction over the *Volkssturm* in situations of combat deployment

1) To exercise jurisdiction over the *Volkssturm* during situations of combat deployment, judges of the *Volkssturm* shall be assigned to every Supreme Commander of an Army in whose command area *Volkssturm* battalions are deployed.

2) The *Reichsführer-SS* shall be responsible for the appointment of the judges.

3) Insofar as a *Volkssturm* judge cannot be immediately reached, and sentencing cannot be delayed, then the nearest available *Wehrmacht* or SS Judge can act in his place.

§ 3

Designation of the Courts

The Courts of the *Volkssturm* shall be designated as follows:

• During training:
    Gau ... (e.g. 27)
    Court of the *Volkssturm*

- During combat deployment:
  Court of the *Volkssturm*
  in the command area of ... Army.

§ 4
Place of Jurisdiction

1) The members of the *Volkssturm* shall be subject to the presiding justice under whose special jurisdiction they fall.

2) In cases of doubt, the *Reichsführer-SS* shall decide.

§ 5
Legal Status of the Judges of the *Volkssturm*

1) The judges of the *Volkssturm* shall be appointed and dismissed on the recommendation of the *Gauleiter* jointly by the Leader of the Party Chancellery and the *Reichsfuhrer-SS*.

2) In disciplinary terms they shall be subject directly to the *Reichsfuhrer-SS*

3) The superiors of the Justices of the *Volkssturm* shall be determined by the Leader of the Party Chancellery in agreement with the *Reichsfuhrer-SS*.

4) Otherwise the Directive of 17 June 1944 (*Reichgesetzbl.* 1 s. 35) concerning *Wehrmacht* judges in special military service shall analogously apply.

§ 6
Officers of the Court

To carry out the tasks of the officer of the court, the Presiding Justice for the units in training in every *Kreis* shall appoint one or more suitable members of the *Volkssturm*, and for every battalion a *Zugführer* or *Kompanieführer* as officers of the Court of the *Volkssturm*.

§ 7
Swearing in

The judges and the officers of the Court of the *Volkssturm* shall be sworn in by the Presiding Justice.

§ 8
Recording services

The judges and officers of the court of the *Volkssturm* can appoint any suitable member of the *Volkssturm* to provide recording services.

Führer Headquarters, 24 February 1945

The Leader of the Party Chancellery
M. Bormann

APPENDIX XV

Directive of 16 March 1945
concerning service penal code for the *Volkssturm*

Deutscher Volkssturm

The Supreme Command

Führer Headquarters, 16 March 1945

Directive 40/45
Service Penal Code for the Volkssturm

Responding to the call of the Fuhrer, at this moment of great threat to the Greater German Reich, the men of the German homeland have formed themselves together into the *Volkssturm* in order, together with the men of the *Wehrmacht* and the *Waffen-SS*, to defend the soil of the Reich with every means at their disposal, loyal, obedient and steadfast. To this end, during the time they have free from work, they wish to practise in the use of weapons and thus while they are training give the proper obedience to their superiors.

The superiors are building on this will shown by the men to subject themselves voluntarily to the law of duty, and they will preserve the necessary discipline and order in the *Volkssturm*.

If, exceptionally, a member of the *Volkssturm* are is not willing to fulfil his duty towards the community, **he must** be compelled to do so by force.

Therefore, on the orders of the *Führer*, this service penal code shall give those superiors responsible for discipline and order within the *Volkssturm* special penal powers:

Item 1
Scope of applicability

1) In combat deployment and in training, the members of the *Volkssturm* are subject to this penal code.

2) Service punishments can be imposed for all offences against discipline and order.

Item 2
Service Punishments

1. Service punishments are:

    a. Reprimand
    b. Simple and close arrest for other ranks and *Gruppenführer*.
    c. Simple and close house arrest against officers, from *Zugführer* upwards
    d. Removal from post.
    e. Warning with threat of being handed over to a special section of the *Wehrmacht* or *Waffen-SS* or to the Police for other ranks and *Gruppenführer*
    f. Removal from the *Volkssturm* and handing over to a special section of the *Wehrmacht* or *Waffen-SS* or to the Police.

2. In the case of imposition of arrest punishments in training, the need for this kind of punishment and the consequences of any resultant loss of work shall be balanced against each other.

3. The minimum duration of the arrest is one day, the maximum duration three weeks.

4. In addition to arrest, orders can be given for removal from post, warning and removal from the *Volkssturm*.

Item 3
Penal powers

1. Superiors with service penal powers are:

     a.   The *Führer* and the superior officers designated by him.
     b.   The *Gauleiter*, and in combat deployment the respective commander.
     c.   The battalion commander.
     d.   The company commander.

2.   The company commander can impose:

on other ranks:	reprimand simple and close arrest up to two weeks
on *Gruppenführer*:	reprimand removal from post simple and close arrest up to one week

3.   The battalion commander can impose:

on other ranks:	reprimand simple and close arrest warning
on *Gruppenführer*:	reprimand removal from post simple and close arrest
on *Zugführer*:	reprimand simple and close house arrest up to one week
on *Kompanieführer*:	reprimand

4.   The authorities superior to these can impose all punishments on officers and men of the *Volkssturm*.

Item 4
Temporary arrest

Any superior officer can temporarily arrest a member of the *Volkssturm* if this is required to maintain discipline and order. The temporary arrest is to be immediately reported to to the arrested man's nearest superior.

Item 5
Exercise of penal powers

1.   The superior officer exercising penal powers shall carefully examine every defence against discipline and order and shall give the accused the opportunity to put his own case.

2.   The superior officer exercising penal powers can waive a service punishment if a warning, rebuke or reprimand is sufficient.

3.   In situations of combat deployment, but not in training, the superior officer exercising penal powers is authorised to impose punishment in respect of a legally punishable offence if the case is sufficiently clear and this is sufficient to establish the guilt of the perpetrator and the consequences of the offence. The superior officer shall report punishment imposed under these provisions to the presiding judge giving details of the circumstances of the punishable offence. If the penal solution adopted does not comply with the facts or with the law, the presiding judge shall impose a suitable sentence. He can also revoke the punishment if it is too lenient and replace it with a harsher punishment. The new punishment shall take account of the milder punishment already sustained.

4.   The service punishment shall be imposed on the perpetrator in giving sentence. The sentence is to be previously set out in writing, giving details of the time and nature of the offence committed.

5.   A service punishment can only be revoked or altered by a more senior officer with penal powers.

Item 6
Appeal by the recipient of punishment

1)   The recipient of punishment can appeal regarding the punishment being imposed to the next most senior officer with penal powers. The appeal must be submitted within seven days after the imposition of the punishment. One night must have passed a since the punishment was imposed.

2)   The decision of the next most senior officer with penal powers is final.

Item 7
Execution of Service Punishments

The officer who imposes a service punishment shall also execute it. He can also ask the authorities of the *Wehrmacht*, the *Waffen-SS*, the police or the judiciary to execute the punishment.

1. The reprimand is executed by making it before all the assembled men of the unit, from the rank of the recipient of the punishment upwards.

2. Removal from post shall become effective when sentence is passed on the recipient of the punishment.

3. a) Before arrest is executed, one night must have passed and the recipient of the punishment must have had the opportunity to appeal. Should the recipient of the punishment appeal before the execution of the punishment has begun, the execution can be deferred until a decision is reached on the appeal.

   b) Otherwise, for the execution of arrest, the execution regulations of the requested authority shall apply analogously.

   c) Arrest can also be executed by subjecting the arrestee to restrictions on his personal freedom or by requiring him to undertake special duties for the duration of the arrest. During training, regard is to be had any work being undertaken by the man being punished, by, for example, executing the arrest during the man's free time.

4. The warning shall be executed by the expression, before the assembled men of the unit, of a threat to hand the recipient over to a special unit of the *Wehrmacht*, the Waffen-SS, or the police.

5. Removal from the *Volkssturm* is executed by handing over to a special unit of the *Wehrmacht*, the *Waffen-SS*, or the police.

Item 8
Clemency

Clemency shall be exercised by the *Führer* and by the superior officers designated by the *Führer*.

Item 9
Supplements to the Service Penal Code

The provisions of the *Wehrmacht* Disciplinary Penal Code (DSTO) of 6 June 1942 are to apply analagously as supplements.

Führer Headquarters, 24 February 1945

The *Reichsführer-SS*
Signed: H. Himmler

The Leader of the Party Chancellery
Signed: M. Bormann

APPENDIX XVI

Announcement regarding
enlistment in the *Volkssturm Deutscher Volkssturm*

The Leader of the Party Chancellery
Chief of Staff

(1) Berlin, 8 February 1945
Wilhelmstrasse 63
Telephone 11 74 11

Announcement 18/45

Re: Enlistment for service in the German *Volkssturm*.

Subject: Maintenance of families, health care, welfare and maintenance

In order to save the *Volkssturmsoldat* enlisted for service in the German *Volkssturm* any concern about the maintenance of his family, to provide free health care for him and to guarantee health care, welfare and maintenance for him and his dependants, on the initiative of, and in agreement with the Leader of the Party Chancellery, the following regulations have been issued by the *Reichminister* of the Interior, the Reich Labour Minister and the General Commissioner for Employment.

The following provisions result from these regulations:

I. With regard to the maintenance of his family, the following arrangements shall be made in respect of the *Volkssturmsoldat* enlisted for service in the German *Volkssturm*

1. For the first six weeks of his enlistment for service in the German *Volkssturm*

    a) if he is in employment, or is a home worker for only one employer, his remuneration shall continue to be paid by his employer;
    b) if he is a self-employed craftsman, a self-employed farmer, a member of one of the professions, a craftsman working at home or a home worker for more than one employer, an equivalent amount to his hourly wage rate shall be paid by the Labour Office.

    Official written certification of this enlistment must be provided to the employer or to the Labour Office by the Company Commander of the German Volkssturm. As an example of the kind of certification required, see the suggested format attached as Appendix 1,[100] which can be conveniently printed on a postcard. The certificate is to be handed out immediately following the enlistment of the *Volkssturmsoldat*, and is to be passed by him to his employer (or to the Labour Office).

    Any type of service which it is known shall be for a limited period or in respect of which it is intended that the individual shall be discharged after a certain period, shall, if at all possible, not to be extended beyond a period of six weeks.

    After the ending of any period of enlistment which does not exceed six weeks, a certificate (see Appendix 2[101]) for passing on to his employer is to be provided to the *Volkssturmsoldat* by the Company Commander indicating the duration of the period of his enlistment.

2. From the commencement of the seventh week onwards, family maintenance shall be paid in accordance with the relevant regulations of the law relating to the family maintenance of servicemen, insofar as the other conditions shall apply, and in particular wages and salaries shall not continue to be paid.

    The *Volkssturmsoldat* is to be provided by the Company Commander with official certification of any enlistment exceeding a period of six weeks. This certification is also, if necessary, to be issued immediately to the *Volkssturmsoldat* and to be passed by him to the *Stadtkreis* or *Landkreis*.

    Should such certification be issued, then, to avoid unnecessary administrative work, an indication should be given to the *Stadtkreis* or *Landkreis* should the period of the enlistment in the event not exceed six weeks.

    The Company Commander is further obliged immediately to inform the *Stadtkreis* or *Landkreis* which has approved the payment of family maintenance of all facts which may affect the continuation of the family maintenance, in particular of the discharge of the *Volkssturmsoldat*.

II.

1. Health care for the *Volkssturmsoldat* enlisted for service in the German and whose unit is under the command of the Wehrmacht or the Waffen-SS shall be provided by the units of the Wehrmacht and the Waffen-SS.

    During this period, family maintenance shall be maintained in accordance with the arrangements detailed under (I) above. In this connection, the regulations in Directive 10/45 issued on 26 January 1945 by the Leader of the Party Chancellery, provide that *Volkssturmsoldaten* wounded or becoming sick on active service in a combat zone shall continue to be regarded as being enlisted in the German *Volkssturm*.

2. Irrespective as to whether the *Volkssturmsoldat* is entitled to social insurance payments, health care which becomes necessary as the result of a period of training shall be provided to the *Volkssturmsoldat* by the general local health fund in accordance with the relevant social insurance provisions.

    The maintenance of the individual's family shall be guaranteed during this period by payment of sickness pay and domestic allowance, insofar as such payments are not being otherwise made.

    To permit health care to be provided by the local or rural health fund, a health care certificate (as detailed in Appendix 4[102]) is to be issued to the *Volkssturmsoldat*.

III. Should the *Volkssturmsoldat* suffer an injury which is materially connected with service in the German *Volkssturm*, irrespective as to whether such an injury is sustained on active service or in training, this injury shall be regarded as an injury sustained on military service within the meaning of the law relating to the health care and welfare of servicemen.

Physical injuries sustained on the way to and from service shall also be regarded as injuries sustained on military service.

IV.   All necessary certificates are to be immediately, carefully and conscientiously completed by the Company Commanders, to be signed, and to be stamped with the official service stamp.

The necessary printed forms are to be provided by the *Gaue*.

Signed: Friedrichs

7 Appendices![103]

Distribution: *Gauleiters, Gaustabsführer*.

For information to: *Reichsleiter*, Unit Commanders.

APPENDIX XVII

Recollections of Rudolf Pietsch regarding the *Volkssturm* in Oppeln, Upper Silesia

After the formation of the *Volkssturm* became law on its announcement in the Reich Legal Gazette, in the urban and rural district of Oppeln, men with dates of birth between 1885 and 1928 were called up for service in the *Volkssturm*.

I was appointed as *Kreisstabsführer* of the *Volkssturm*, urban and rural area, by *Kreisleiter* Pölsterl, the senior official of the NSDAP.

At a meeting of all the *Ortsgruppenleiter* in Oppeln, I presented them with a schedule for registration of the men. All the men in question were first to be registered on a list. Before doing so, all physically disabled men whose disabilities were obvious were to be exempted from the *Volkssturm*. These men received an exemption certificate from my office.

After the registration was completed in the urban district of Oppeln, the men were summoned to the Oppeln Stadium for assignment to units. Here, the men arrived by *Ortsgruppen* and were conscripted by their *Ortsgruppenleiter*. After this was completed, there was a certain filtering-out process.

The following were filtered out:

1.   All physically disabled and sick men were taken for examination to doctors in the castle. Anyone who was unfit for service immediately received his certificate of exemption.

2.   The entire staff of the *Reichsbahn* Works

3.   All staff of the *Reichsbahn* involved in technical services and in producing timetables.

4.   Technical staff of the *Reichspost* were temporarily exempted

5.   All the most important men with exemptions from industry and business, and also all doctors and care staff from the hospitals.

About 3,000 men had paraded. Of these, after others had been filtered out, there remained 1,600 to 1,800 men, of whom more were filtered out as a result of requests for various reasons

From the remaining men, I formed the following units in the City District:

1.   Mot. (motorised) Btl. 280
     Strength approx. 160. Commander: NSKK *Standartenführer* Domsch.
     Armament mostly Kar 98 rifle and *Panzerfäuste*.

2.   Vo. -Btl. 281
     Strength approx. 550. Commander: *Hauptmann der Reserve* Weinrich, Oppeln
     Armament Italian rifles, individual Dutch machine guns, *Panzerfauste* and hand grenades. Ammunition sufficient. After original shortage of equipment, this gradually became better to good.

Four companies.

3. Vo. -Btl. 282.
   Strength approx. 520. Commander: *Oberleutnant der Reserve* Neubert, Oppeln.
   Armament mostly Italian rifles with sufficient ammunition, also *Panzerfäuste*.
   Four companies.
   All companies possessed horse-drawn combat and/or baggage vehicles. The men had short entrenching tools.

4. Vo. -Btl. 283 in Krappitz
   Strength approx. 170. Commander *Oberleutnant der Reserve* Caja, Krappitz
   Armed by the *Wehrmacht* with Kar 98 rifle. Other equipment scanty.
   One company, commanded by Caja himself. It was later amalgamated into *Volkssturm* Battalion 281, the command of which was taken over by *Oberleutnant* Caja after *Hauptmann* Weinrich left.

Within the rural district of Oppeln, the following units were formed:

1. Vo. -Btl. 284
   Strength approx. 300. Commander: a Reserve officer. Five companies. Battalion HQ: Gross-Döbern – Kupp.

2. Vo. -Btl. 285
   Strength approx. 300. Commander: *SA-Obersturmbannführer* Jaenicke, Oppeln. Three companies. Battalion HQ: Initially Johannsdoef near Proskau (?), from February, Langenbrück, *Kreis* Neustadt.

These battalions were only formed on paper. It was not possible to arm and equip them, and this took place later. As a result of the rapid Soviet advance, the resulting confusion and the overloading of the telephone lines, maintaining telephone communications to commanders became impossible. Although the emergency plan had been thought-out to the smallest detail, emergency arrangements mostly failed.

Training of NCOs

As early as the end of September 1944, a start had been made with short training courses in the *Gaustabsführung* training school in Bad Schalkowitz, Upper Silesia. For NCOs who had previously had military experience, the courses lasted for a week, for NCOs without military experience they lasted for two weeks. But only in quite exceptional cases were NCOs who had no military experience assigned to units. They were trained as *Zugfuhrer* and *Gruppenfuhrer*. In detail, this included training with rifles, machine pistols, *Panzerfäuste*, and entrenching equipment. Even if in this short time it was not possible to give extensive training, at least the NCOs made a good impression after they had returned from their training courses.

The Volkssturm in combat

1. Vo. -Btl. 281

Mobilised for action on 15 January 1945 and sent into action on 18 January 1945 on the eastern periphery of the town of Oppeln by order of the Fortress Commandant. This action was intended to secure the routes Oppeln – Lenzen and Oppeln – Rosenberg.

On 21 or 22 January 1945, the Oppeln police battalion was deployed in this sector. This battalion had already withdrawn to Neisse and had been called back again.

In the night between 22 and 23 January 1945, the Soviets had worked their way up to the Oppeln – Illnau railway line, and Battalion 281 was under constant Soviet fire. The battalion then received orders to disengage from the enemy and to withdraw to the town. Here I should like to mention the action of *Luftwaffe Oberst* Rudel, who polished off one tank after the other and thus impeded the advance of the Soviets and made it considerably easier for our men to disengage from the enemy.

In the southern sector – the Oppeln-Lenzen road – the Soviets followed on only hesitatingly with weak forces, whereas in the northern sector – the Oppeln-Rosenberg road – pressure from the Soviets was strong, with the result that the withdrawal here did not pass off so smoothly.

After *Hauptmann* Weinrich had his battalion once again firmly under his control, they were sent into action again on the orders of the *Wehrmacht*, and then until the end of February were involved in a work detail, from which they were relieved by *Volkssturm* Battalion 282 so that they could to go to Langenbruck for refreshment and recuperation.

At the end of March, the battalion, together with *Volkssturm* Battalion 280, was back in action on the Neustadt-Wackenau road along which were pushing the 3 divisions encircled in the Steinau 'pocket', among which was *Volkssturm* Battalion 282. After they had successfully broken out, both *Volkssturm* Battalion 281 and *Volkssturm* Battalion 280 were deployed to secure the railway at the Langenbruck railway station. Battalion 281 was here until mid-April, and was then transferred with Battalion 280 into the Sudetenland. Nothing more is known of any other combat actions.

2. Vo. -Btl 282.

On 22 or 23 January, *Kreisleiter* Pölsterl was invited to meet a general in the Forms Hotel in Oppeln to discuss the deployment of the *Volkssturm*. I myself happened to be at the Oppeln railway station and in the town, and had not been invited to the meeting.

When I returned to my office towards evening, I learned that Battalion 282 had been sent into action, although it was unfortunately too late to do anything to stop it. Because the battalion was not yet fully equipped and had no machine guns of any kind, it was deployed without any kind of reconnaissance and it was unsuitable for a night action.

The battalion was deployed with its left wing on the Oder bridge near Niklasfähre and its right wing near the Halbendorf brickworks, that is, in a sector which required a combat regiment at full strength, but was in no way suitable for a battalion with a company strength of 125 men. The sector was about 21 kilometres long.

The 1st Company was able to take up position in the sector to which it had been assigned without any further ado, as was the 3rd Company.

But in the case of the 2nd Company, the following occurred: The Soviets had already taken the village of Eisenau which was located in this sector, but this fact was not known to the military authorities in Oppeln. When Battalion Commander Neubert had reached the centre of the village with his Staff he found himself suddenly completely surrounded by Soviets. With great presence of mind, he and his men fired *Panzerfäuste* into the ranks of the Soviets. In the resulting confusion the Battalion Staff was able to break through to the northwest and to escape to Fischbach where it was planned to locate the battalion command post. The 2nd Company, which similarly had taken up positions in Eisenau lost a few men in the process. According to eyewitness accounts, they were literally beaten to death by the Soviets.

Because of the combat alarms and the fires round about – the villages of Eisenau and Preisdorf had both gone up in flames – the Battalion was forced to withdraw through Dambrau to Volksmannsdorf, *Kreis* Neisse, and where I eventually found it after days searching for it.

The 4th Company got as far as Schurgast, where it was received by a pioneer unit of the *Wehrmacht*. The pioneer units had blown up the bridge over the Oder and then had withdrawn before the strong Soviet offensive to the north eastern edge of Schurgast. The 4th Company received German weapons from the pioneer unit and was sent off to Koppen, *Kreis* Brieg, with orders to secure positions there. The following report of their actions appeared in the *Oberschlesische Zeitung* War Issue, Series 15, Year 1, of 10 February 1945:

"In its passionate bond between a determined commander and fanatical men, the 4th Company of *Volkssturm* Battalion 282 Oppeln, whose combat stations were the villages of Schurgast, Eschenried, Koppen and Lossen, formed the core of the resistance which even the cold waters of the Neisse could not stop.

"This company had received orders in Koppen to secure the Oder crossing and the edge of the woodland into which the Bolshevists had penetrated. In Koppen, the men were under heavy artillery and mortar fire all day. Towards midday, the infantry fire also increased, and the position of the men became very dangerous, because connections to the units to the right and to the left of them had been lost. When the enemy succeeded in going round the village, the *Volkssturm* men were receiving considerable fire not only from in front of them but also from their flanks. The Company Commander, *Hauptmann* Gerke, recognised the danger of the situation and gave orders to withdraw to the Oder dam and to carry on the fight from there. After ammunition was almost exhausted and there had also been various casualties, the company's situation became so threatened that it was no longer possible to remain in this terrain without any cover. Therefore orders were given to cross over the dam and to disengage from the enemy while still fighting. Despite their considerable superiority in numbers, the enemy did not have the courage to mount an assault on the dwindling number of *Volkssturm* men.

"When, despite enemy fire from heavy weapons, the men had withdrawn some 300 metres from the village, the enemy began to bring artillery fire to bear on the western periphery of the village and were thus shelling their own people. The remnants of the company reached Schanowitz where they joined up with a pioneer unit and then continued the march to Lossen to place themselves at the disposal of the *Ortskommandant* there.

"During the night, suddenly Bolshevists in tanks broke in to Lossen, so that the *Volkssturm* men once again became involved in extensive fighting. An anti-tank gun which the men had with them received a direct hit and was put out of action. In the meantime, *Hauptmann* Gerke had fetched three *Panzerfäuste*, and soon the first tank had been immobilised. Soon after this, *Hauptmann* Gerke knocked out another enemy tank.

"The enemy was defied for another two hours, and then the battalion were instructed to withdraw to the safety of the railway embankment and then to make for Klein-Neudorf over open country. Scarcely had they reached the village when enemy tank fire began once more. In this action, Company Commander Gerke's hand was torn to shreds. *Oberleutnant* Sengenfeld from a Pioneer Battalion now took over the defence of the village. While the men were defending the village for some two hours, *Oberleutnant* Sengenfeld knocked out a tank. After further casualties, the *Volkssturm* men received orders to withdraw to the Neisse using the western exit from the village. Once again, they had to cover this distance of 2000 metres over open country.

"Despite the enemy pressing on behind, however, the men of the *Volkssturm* , carrying their wounded, managed to reach the Neisse safely. But the Michelau bridge had been blown up shortly before the men arrived. The attempt made by the pioneers to create an emergency crossing failed. So there was nothing left but to try and find a ford by which to cross the river. All difficulties were overcome and the opposite bank safely reached, and even the wounded which they had been carrying with them could be brought to safety.

"The never-failing daring and the exemplary commitment of the Company Commander had given the men and the tenacity and the strength to overcome the greatest difficulties with determination, although among the members of the unit were some men born in 1885 and 1886."

In Langenbrück, *Kreis* Neustadt, the battalion was reformed. It now received 200 German rifles and *Wehrmacht* clothing. One problem which could never be solved, however, was how to procure overcoats. It was no less difficult to obtain horse-drawn vehicles.

At the end of February or the beginning of March, Battalion 282 was ordered to march to Oppeln to relieve Battalion 281. Battalion 282 once more moved into the Artillery Barracks, the Reserve Company into the Gumpertsdorf tank factory, where the *Kreis* Staff, the *Volkssturm* Staff, and the local administrative offices for Oppeln were also located.

After the breakout from the Steinau pocket, which has already been mentioned, *Volkssturm* Battalion 282 remained missing. It is assumed that those parts of the battalion which did escape were incorporated within *Wehrmacht* units.

3. Vo. -Btl. 283

As has already been mentioned, this battalion consisted of only one company. Its first mission was to secure positions on both Oder bridges, in the course of which it had to undergo heavy fighting.

After the bridges were blown up, the battalion was relieved by a *Landesschützen* battalion from Prague, and employed on evacuation tasks. At the beginning of March it was brought back to Langenbrück and incorporated into *Volkssturm* Battalion 281.

4. Mot. Btl. 280

Apart from its two actions with Battalion 281, this battalion was only used for transport tasks. After its vehicles were finally out of commission despite constant repairs in its own workshops, at the beginning of April it was taken to eastern Sudetenland, where the few vehicles which were still usable were used to transport refugees.

To remember and to record the actions of my *Volkssturm* men is something I considered to be my duty. I am preparing these notes from memory almost without any supporting documents. If in doing so I have made individual errors, or should I not have mentioned important incidents, then I apologise. The brave actions of these men of the *Volkssturm* made it possible for countless women and children to flee from the endangered areas; countless refugee columns were enabled to move again.

APPENDIX XVIII

Extract from the account of Paul Flegel, former commander of *Volkssturm* Battalion Habelschwerdt

On 10 August 1944, about 1,000 men from the *Kreis* of Habelschwerdt/Silesia were brought by special train to Sterzendorf near Namslau within the framework of Operation Bartold. Trenches and anti-tank ditches were being built ...

In October 1944, the entrenching unit was transferred to Deutscheck near Schleiersee, where a new defensive line was being built. Intensive work continued on the organisation of the unit, with *Hundertschaften* and *Kameradschaften* being formed. After the general appeal for the formation of the *Volkssturm*, the *Hundertschaften* were changed into companies, which now together formed the *Volkssturm* Battalion Habelschwerdt. New company and platoon leaders were selected according to their suitability, confidence, and on military grounds. This reorganisation made discipline firmer, and the formal training which now began improved attitude, morale and commitment.

Under the pressure of the advancing Red Army, the battalion was withdrawn from Deutscheck to Freistadt in Silesia, which was being prepared for defence.

Using all available forces, anti-tank and street barricades were built, training in close quarters anti-tank warfare was hastily organised, rifles, hand grenades and *Panzerfäuste* handed out. In the base at Freystadt there was one *Wehrmacht Ersatz* Battalion, one Police Battalion and two *Volkssturm* battalions, Freystadt and Habelschwerdt. The *Wehrmacht* Command appointed the District Commander of Freystadt, *Oberstleutnant* Bannert, as Combat Commandant of Freystadt. He raised the Habelschwerdt Battalion to the status of a combat unit under the designation *Volkssturm* Battalion Flegel, and directed it into his own combat sector. From this point onwards, the two *Volkssturm* battalions were under the command of the *Wehrmacht*, and the battalion commanders swore the *Wehrmacht* oath.

It was not long before the combat actions began. Telephone and aircraft connections were broken. By setting up sentries and sending out reconnaissance units it was possible to re-establish communications with the troops which were holding up the enemy. Right in the last days before the attack, a consignment of assorted old grey-green uniforms arrived, which were distributed. Ditto armbands with the *Wehrmacht* insignia. There were no specific unit insignia.

The attack was carried out with the typical characteristics of Soviet armoured advances. Tank cannon, machine guns and mortars put the remaining inhabitants into a panicked flight. The roof slates rattling down into the streets as a result of mortar fire caused great confusion. Freystadt was able to hold out for three days, on the third day the enemy pushed into the town, moved in the direction of Nieder-Siegersdorf, and shelled the retreating units with artillery fire. My battalion and one company of Freystadt men were scattered. Scattered groups of men rejoined forces and together tried to get back to the battalion, other scattered men were sent by the *Feldgendarmerie* to collection points. In Guben I looked for and found again the Freystadt Combat Commandant. I obtained from him in writing the release of the unit from the regular armed forces, because the battalion was no longer capable of fighting.

From Guben, *Volkssturm* Battalion Habelschwerdt, now released from service in the *Wehrmacht*, marched through the Spree forest to Calau, where it was loaded onto trains and with around 500 men brought back through Saxony and Czechoslovakia to Gablon – zReichenberg – Tannwald. *Wehrmacht* lorries transported the battalion further over the mountain pass road to Hirschberg. From there the journey continued by rail to Glatz in Silesia. Every member of the battalion received a certificate of discharge and was allowed to return home. There was no room on the train for the battalion baggage train; it began the homeward march from Calau, because on the baggage carts there was a great deal of personal luggage which was able later to be returned to the *Volkssturm* men.

On arrival home, I declared the battalion to be disbanded. But the men were soon re-registered and assigned to the *Volkssturm* battalions in their areas of residence. I myself, after three days' leave, received orders to take over command of *Volkssturm* Battalion Mittelwalde, which had to defend the exposed sector in the area of the

Glatzer Schneeberg. There was no more fighting here, because the general surrender of 8 May 1945 also resulted in this battalion being disbanded.

During our combat action in Freystadt we suffered wounded and missing. The number of the latter was greater, some of them found their way home again. My deputy, Company Commander Georg Blaser, was later killed. As they marched into the Glatz area, the Soviets took many more people prisoner. I myself spent almost eight years in the prison camps of Glatz, Oppeln, Graudenz, Fünfeichen, Buchenwald, and Waldheim. A large number of my comrades went the same way.

Signed: Paul Flegel
Former commander of
Volkssturm Battalion Habelschwerdt
(now at Epe/Westf ... Füchter-Heide 3)

APPENDIX XIX

Report of a meeting of Defence District XVII, Vienna, 25 March 1945

Present:
General Kissel with accompanying officers
Staff *Oberst* Bachmaier, Chief of Staff, Defence District XVII
Staff *Major* Neumann, Ia, Defence District XVII

At the beginning of the meeting, *General* Kissel gave guidelines concerning the tasks and the deployment of the *Volkssturm*. He indicated that, on the basis of a report from Staff *Oberstleutnant* Thilo, OKH was of the opinion that not to occupy the frontier positions to the east of Vienna was not an option. He stated that we must manage to ensure that the process of issuing appropriate alerts and the occupying of the position could be completed within 24 hours at most.

Then we discussed details. This discussion was based on the fact that a first level alert (Tank Warning) had been passed on to Defence District XVII because of the dangerous situation in Hungary [Soviet breakthrough]. General Kissel emphasised that, apart from when something was 'going on' in the frontier positions, the *Gau* of Lower Danube had withdrawn all *Volkssturm* battalions.

Staff *Oberst* Bachmaier, Chief of Staff, announced that the A-battalions of the Defence District were being transferred to the eastern part of the Defence District. He said that a total of only 6,300 men were involved who had been trained up to 12 weeks. In addition, he stated, these battalions were to provide replacements for regular Army units. *Oberst* Bachmaier particularly stressed that on 15 February the number of *Volkssturm* battalions had been reduced to 10 and on 9 March they had been completely withdrawn from the frontier positions. He requested that the local garrison should obtain explosives and carry out necessary demolition. He stated that instruction and training in pioneer techniques had taken place.

Staff *Oberst* Bachmaier stressed that collaboration with the *Gaustabsführer* of Vienna and the Lower Danube was running smoothly and that he was receiving extensive support from the *Gau* of Lower Danube. *General* Kissel raised the question as to whether the German weapons should be passed to the Deputy General Command. He stated that the decision was a matter for the Deputy General Command. The Defence District Inspector explained that orders had been given for the 98k rifles to be handed over. All other weapons were to remain in the *Gau*. In response to this, *General* Kissel indicated that to hand over weapons in the way which had been ordered would immediately preclude in advance any occupation of the frontier positions, because it was only, of course, possible to defend a position with armed battalions. *Major* Neumann, Ia with the Chief of Staff, immediately supported the idea that the weapons should remain with the battalions. Orders were finally given that the battalions should retain their weapons.

APPENDIX XX

Report of Waldemar Magunia regarding the *Volkssturm* in East Prussia 1944/45

Former President of the Königsberg Chamber of Trade

In the middle of September 1944, the *Volkssturm* in East Prussia was called up. All *Volkssturm* units and all command authorities were under the command of *Gauleiter* Koch in his capacity as Reich Defence Commissioner.

Tactical command, recruitment, training and services were the responsibility of the *Volkssturm-Gauführung Ostpreussen*. Chief of Staff of this organisation was *Gau-Organisationsleiter* Dargel. Under his command were the Section Heads and the *Volkssturm* Sector Leaders in the *Gau*.

The *Volkssturm* Sector Leader was in charge of one *Volkssturm* Sector. This generally comprised several administrative *Kreise*. The *Gau* was divided into 12 Sectors.

In each *Kreis* there was a *Volkssturm* Sub-Sector. The Sub-Sector Leader (*Unterabschnittsleiter*) was usually the *Kreisleiter*. He was responsible for all the *Volkssturm* battalions formed within the *Kreis*. The strength of the battalions varied. The battalion consisted of 3–4 companies. Every *Ortsgruppe* provided one or more companies.

In East Prussia, about 67,000 men were called up for the *Volkssturm*, and these were divided into about 120 battalions.

Possible operational tasks envisaged for the *Volkssturm* were:

1.   Repulsing Soviet attacks, either in collaboration with the *Wehrmacht* or alone.

2.   Combating enemy paratroop units.

3.   Fighting partisans who had infiltrated or had been dropped into the area.

4.   Protecting specific targets within the *Kreis* area.

5.   Auxiliary police duties.

6.   Deployment against foreign workers in the event of unrest.

The operational area for deployment was generally the home *Kreis*. It was envisaged that larger *Volkssturm* units would be brought together to operate outside the home *Kreis*.

The armament of the East Prussian *Volkssturm* varied. A few battalions had German weapons, including the MG42 or other older German models. The majority of the battalions were armed with the French Lebel rifle and French machine-guns mounted on a tripod. Other units had Italian weapons. Within the individual battalions, there was the same kind of armament, but there was not always enough.

The *Panzerfaust* was issued as an anti-tank weapon. *Volkssturm* units from Königsberg had a number of so-called *Püppchen*, an adapted flare pistol which fired a 2cm explosive shell. This close-quarters weapons was very effective up to a range of 150 metres.

In the last two weeks of January 1945 the writer of this account encountered a horse-drawn *Volkssturm* battery with three French 155mm howitzers. This battery had taken part in the fighting in north-east Prussia.

The uniforms were mostly the brown Party uniforms. In addition there were also SA uniforms. But there were also units who wore grey-green uniforms. The overcoats were mostly brown-grey or grey-green.

Wearing Party uniforms had an adverse psychological effect. The men of the *Volkssturm* quite rightly feared that if they wore them they would receive particularly savage treatment if they fell into their hands of the Soviets. For this reason many *Volkssturm* men tried to join the *Wehrmacht*.

Eyewitness reports of the fighting in Königsberg between 7 and 10 April 1945 agree that a very considerable number, probably more than 2,000 *Volkssturm* men and members of the Party who fell into enemy hands while wearing brown uniforms, were murdered, often in a bestial way.

Most *Volkssturm* units had field kitchens; the baggage train was horse-drawn and equipped with agricultural vehicles.

Volkssturm commanders varied a great deal. There were company, battalion, sub-sector and sector commanders who led their units considerately and bravely, and others who were complete failures. The ratio between the former and the latter, seen overall, was 2:3.

The senior leadership of the *Volkssturm* placed particular emphasis on autonomy and shied away from any amalgamation with the *Wehrmacht*. One immediate command task of large *Volkssturm* units in the fight against the advancing enemy did not favour autonomous styles of leadership. In the face of the force of the enemy advance, they only had the opportunity to seek brief instructions from the sector leaders. The sector leaders had, for the most part, to rely on their own resources. *Gauleiter* Koch was unable to provide an example of recognisable confidence-inspiring leadership.

The East Prussian *Volkssturm* did its duty loyally, in spite of the momentum and speed of the Soviet advance into their homeland, the downfall of which was something that the men always had before their eyes. They stood their ground despite insufficient armament and equipment and often with inadequate leadership. The heritage of this ancient Prussian land of soldiers was in the very bones of these East Prussian *Volkssturm* men. Thousands of them fell, fighting with pitifully inadequate weapons, on their home soil.

The *Volkssturm* fought against overpowering enemy forces in the defence of Ortelsburg. There the sector leader, *Kreisleiter* Walter Schultz, was killed.

Under the command of its sector leader, *Kreisleiter* Lebrecht, *Volkssturm* from the *Kreise* of Tilsit, Elchniederung and Labiau mounted an assault on 19 January 1945 against the village of Kreuzingen which was held by the enemy. But in the face of the Red tanks the men could not hold their ground and had to withdraw.

The *Volkssturm* from Labiau, under *Kreisleiter* Karl Mikinn, a holder of the Prussian Golden Military Merit Cross from the First World War, defended the Deime crossing. Mikinn was killed on 23 January 1945 at the head of his men in Labiau.

In Elbing the local *Volkssturm*, with their comrades from Preußisch Holland and in concert with the *Wehrmacht*, defended the city until 23 January 1945.

Volkssturm units from south-east Prussia, together with the *Wehrmacht*, fought their way through from Schröttersburg (Plock) to Graudenz. They took part to the bitter end in the defence of this *Festung*. Their commander was Hermann Woelk.

The garrison of the fortress of Königsberg was significantly reinforced by about 10,000 men of the *Volkssturm*. From 25 January 1945 onwards they participated in the defence of the regional capital. On 26 January 1945, a small section of *Volkssturm* under the command of deputy *Gauleiter* Grobherr prevented the Soviets from capturing the Pregel bridge in Palmburg. In February 1945, *Volkssturm Bataillonsführer* Tiburzy destroyed several tanks with *Pänzerfauste* and was awarded the Knight's Cross. In Königsberg, mention should be made of *Volkssturm* battalions Gruber, Muss and Spielschen. All *Volkssturm* battalions played a large part in the eleven-week-long defence of the *Festung*. Most of the *Volkssturm* officers and NCOs, including seven *Kreisleiter*s, 60 SA commanders, *SA-Obergruppenführer* Schoene, deputy *Gauleiter* Grobherr and more than 3,000 *Volkssturm* men were killed or succumbed to the Red Death. In the Volksgarten, at the Sternwarte Bastion, at the Krauseneck Bastion and on the Erich-Koch-Platz, during the days of 7, 8, 9 and 10 April 1945, many hundreds of them fell victim to the awful fury of the Soviets.

Completed on 10 April 1955
Signed: Waldemar Magunia

APPENDIX XXI

Documents relating to the *Volkssturm* in the Wartheland

1. Account of *Gauleiter* and *Reichsstatthalter* Greiser concerning the formation and combat deployment of the *Volkssturm* in the *Reichsgau* of Wartheland, 20 February 1945

2. Comments on the account of *Gauleiter* and *Reichsstatthalter* Greiser by General Walter Petzel (ret'd), Hamel/Weser, former Commander of Defence District XXI in Posen, 6 March 1953.

3. Representative accounts of members of the *Volkssturm* and Party authorities concerning the deployment of the *Volkssturm* in the *Reichsgau* of Wartheland

1. *Account of* Gauleiter *Greiser*

Formation and combat deployment of the *Volkssturm* in the *Reichsgau* of Wartheland, 20 February 1945

I. *Introduction*

Only in the last four years of the war was the *Reichsgau* of Wartheland Germanised from 5% to about 23% of German ethnic origin. It is true that the last great migration of the approximately 300,000 Soviet Germans was, by the end of 1944, completed, at least in geographical terms, but, with a few exceptions, the migrants had not yet settled. The German governing class had to carry out all organisational tasks within the Party, the *Wehrmacht*, the State, agriculture, armaments, police, *Stadtwacht* and *Landwacht*, and latterly also in the *Volkssturm*. That this was very difficult in the extensive agrarian *Gau* of the Wartheland goes without saying. It was also by no means uncommon under these circumstances for many a German man in city, town or village to do a dozen or more different jobs. The *Gau* was the backbone of the nation's security in terms of food production, and numerous branches of the armaments industry were also based there. Every month, greater and greater responsibilities were laid upon the shoulders of the German men. This was not very much relieved when the new immigrants settled in the *Gau*, because the immigrants with their slow style of thinking were not able to keep up with the other Germans, and the difference between them could not be bridged by good will alone. Hundreds of thousands of migrants came from districts under the thumb of the Bolshevists with many women and children and very few men. If men did come along, they were immediately recruited and enlisted by the Waffen-SS. The Army soon latched on to this procedure so as to not lose out on the recruitment possibilities offered by the migrants. Those who remained behind had to get agriculture and armaments going at top speed using Polish workers, in addition they had to work in the Party and in many other honorary capacities, strengthen the police in the face of the threat of a Polish uprising and last but not least also form the *Volkssturm*. The *Reichsgau* of Wartheland, then, had a very different set of basic circumstances in which to form and organise the *Volkssturm* than any other *Gaue*. Thus, the general guidelines issued by the Supreme Command of the *Volkssturm*, which were applicable to most of the Reich, could not always be implemented by me in every detail. In particular, the question of leadership could not be solved without some difficulty. According to the existing guidelines, in my *Gau* I had no possible candidates for battalion or company commanders in the *Volkssturm*, because the few German men who might have been considered for these posts were already overloaded with duties and in actual fact belonged to the second levy.

In detail, the following figures relate to the German men within my *Gau*. I can only give these as approximate figures, because I do not have documents available at this time:

1.	Men fit for military service	265,000
2.	Ditto in the *Wehrmacht* and Waffen-SS	170,000
3.	Exempt	82,000
4.	Registered by the *Volkssturm*	100,000

In addition, two other orders had to be reconciled with the order to form the *Volkssturm*

a) The *Führer*'s order to keep armaments production running at top speed until the last possible minute (only possible by leaving German management staff in the factories)

b) the order to retain enough security forces to escort the refugee columns from the A-Zone through the B-Zone into the C-Zone. When the *Volkssturm* were deployed, refugee columns would certainly be created, but it would be impossible, without security forces, to escort the refugee columns through districts in which Polish uprisings might be expected.

II. *Organisation*

For the reasons mentioned above, the formation and organisation of the *Volkssturm* in the *Reichsgau* of Wartheland thus had to be regarded with a different set of standards than those which applied in the old Reich.

The majority of the first levy was composed of ethnic immigrants, corresponding to the structure of the German population of the *Reichsgau* Wartheland. The majority of them had never held a weapon in their hands or had served in foreign armies and been inadequately trained with foreign weapons. But one thing they all had at the beginning was enthusiasm and the firm intention to play their part in the *Volkssturm*.

That the planned organisation of the *Volkssturm* could not, in the short time available until they were deployed in combat, be carried out in such a way as to create combat ready formations, was not only due to the shortage of leaders and the structural composition of the population, but was due in the first instance to the extended nature of the individual *Kreise* in the agrarian *Gau* of Wartheland. Many villages, in which there were often only five to six men liable for service in the *Volkssturm*, were situated 6, 8, 10 kilometres from each other, but were 60, 80 and 100 kilometres away from the *Kreisstadt*, the seat of the *Kreis* leadership. Thus, with the best will in the world, an order from the *Gau* Staff Command only came into the hands of the *Ortsgruppenleiter* five to six days later, which made formation and weapons training very difficult.

In accordance with the first general directives issued by the Supreme *Volkssturm* Command, an immediate start was to be made with weapons training and above all with organisation, allocation to levies etc. But then, as time went on, there arrived large numbers of more specific instructions for allocating men to the levies from different industries. These instructions only arrived immediately before the *Volkssturm* were deployed in combat, and, in view of the relatively few available men liable for service in the *Volkssturm*, necessitated repeated reorganisations of the battalions and companies.

Despite this, the difficulties facing the formation of the *Volkssturm* under the unique conditions in the *Reichsgau* Wartheland would have been overcome if there had been enough time. It was evident again and again from the training plans, directives, orders and meetings, that 31 March 1945 was considered to be the deadline for the formation and the first period of training. This target could also have been achieved in the *Reichsgau* of Wartheland. The formation process was interrupted by the mobilisation of the first levy, which was deployed in action with 27 battalions from 18 January 1945.

In addition, special mention should be made to the fact that the *Gaustabsführer* nominated before me, *SS-Gruppenführer Pg.* Reinefahrt, together with his closest collaborator, *SS-Obersturmbannführer Oberstleutnant d. Schützpolizei* Fischer, had already, on the orders of the *Reichsführer-SS*, been on active service as the commander of a corps on the Western Front since November 1944, and thus was not available to supervise the formation of the *Volkssturm* in the *Reichsgau* of Wartheland. I myself had to take over the duties of *Gaustabsführer* at a few hours notice, and to charge my personal adjutant, *SS-Sturmbannführer* Harder, with the day-to-day administrative work. It is to *SS-Sturmbannführer* Harder's particular credit that, in the short time from November 1944 to the middle of January 1945, he successfully worked on the development of the *Volkssturm* in my *Gau* under the difficult conditions already outlined, effectively and with commitment.

III. Clothing and Equipment

The majority of the first levy was from the rural population and consisted for the most part of ethnic immigrants. Provision of clothing, uniforms and items of equipment, but especially provision of shoes, was very scanty, because these migrants had come with nothing into the *Gau* and had had to be provided with clothing by us. Despite the fact that the Party and its subsidiary organisations sprang to the rescue, as far as possible, with uniforms, overcoats and items of equipment, there was no question of the individual battalion being clothed and equipped in a uniform way, all more so since the scheme for dyeing Party uniforms had just been introduced but had not yet been implemented. Even more noticeable was the shortage of items of equipment such as haversacks, mess tins, ammunition pouches etc, because simply nothing was available and all our skills at improvisation failed because of the shortage of time and the lack of the most elementary raw materials and aids.

Recognising that coherence, discipline and fighting strength of a unit are significantly boosted by uniform clothing, from the first day my particular efforts were directed at providing uniform clothing – and, if possible, also equipment – for the *Volkssturm*. Since no significant deliveries from Berlin could be counted on, we got into contact with authorities in northern Italy and sent representatives there. The delivery of 13,000 metres of uniform material and items of equipment had been agreed and would have been made, if the *Gau* had not been overrun a few days before deliveries from Italy began. It had been agreed that the first levy would be provided with regular uniforms by February.

We were able to provide the battalions with 5,000 ammunition pouches from stocks in Warsaw. Provision of *Volkssturm* armbands by our own efforts had been completed. Every man throughout the *Volkssturm* had an armband. With the help of the templates sent to the *Kreise*, preparation of the caps was under way. Some *Kreise* which had their own clothing industry had already equipped their men using organised stocks of remnants of material. In other *Kreise* this was not possible because there was simply not a single piece of material to be had.

The uniforms and items of equipment promised by the *Wehrmacht* were not delivered. When I asked, it was explained to me that Berlin (OKH or BdE) had refused to issue them to the *Volkssturm*.

The factory of Die Deutschen Waffen- und Munitionsfabriken, A. G., in Posen, had promised to deliver identity discs made from leftover stocks. On the day that the *Volkssturm* was actually deployed, the identity discs had arrived, but it was too late to distribute them. The pay books, to the extent that it was possible to deliver them from Berlin, had all been issued to the battalions, but most of them remained without pay books.

IV. Armament

To reinforce internal security, to fight bands of partisans and possibly airborne troops, at the beginning of 1944, in conjunction with the *Wehrmacht*, I had set in train the Grolman Action. As part of this action, all men from the *Reichsgau* of Wartheland exempted from regular military service were brought together in the districts of Posen and Hohensalza into battalions and regiments. The men, the majority of whom later had to be assigned to the second levy of the *Volkssturm* because of their civilian occupations, were trained by the *Wehrmacht* on Sundays and holidays and called up to take part in one-day exercises. On 1 January 1945 the Grolman Action was carried over, together with the *Stadtwacht* and the *Landwacht*, into the *Volkssturm*. With the weapons lent by the *Wehrmacht* for the Grolman Action, the weapons already available in the *Gau* and the weapons made available by the *Wehrmacht* and the Supreme Command of the *Volkssturm*, it was possible to equip all the first levy with small-arms and Soviet light machine guns (but the latter were only delivered a few days before the *Volkssturm* was sent into action). The weapons were of Soviet, French, and Italian origin, some of them were even Mannlicher rifles. They were distributed throughout the *Gau*; there was very little ammunition available. On 1 January, 1945, an attempt was made to reorganise the weapons for the battalions and throughout entire zones within the *Gau*, because with the shortage of foreign ammunition it would be impossible to organise supplies before the battalions were deployed, never mind during the time in which they were actually in action, if the battalions all had different weapons. When all the preparatory work had been done, and the process of equipping the battalions with fresh weapons was about to begin, we were taken by surprise by the need to deploy the battalions immediately. Nevertheless, the battalions which were deployed all had the same weapons, and moved into their positions with sufficient numbers of Soviet light machine-guns, although they had not had the opportunity to receive a thorough training with these weapons.

The modern weapons provided by the Supreme Command of the *Volkssturm*, 98k rifles, MG42 light machine-guns and mortars (the latter arrived in Posen only 10 days before the *Volkssturm* were sent into action) were all immediately handed out. It was first intended to use them for training purposes within the units, so that all the men received a uniform training on German weapons.

Every battalion was equipped with between 50 and 100 *Panzerfäuste*, depending on its strength. During the night between 18 and 19 January, 1945, I personally agreed with *Reichsminister* Speer an additional delivery of 20,000 *Panzerfäuste* to Posen by special train. Of these, 15,000 arrived on 20 January 1945 and were handed over to the *Wehrmacht* to be passed on to the *Volkssturm* battalions which were already on the march, and some of which were in action, because we no longer had any means of transport to the combat areas.

The 80 12.2cm guns provided by the *Wehrmacht* at the beginning of January were, for tactical reasons, immediately sent to the battalions at the B–1 Line.[104] They were on the railway transports when the action began, but could not be used. Seven *Volkssturm* artillery battalions in the western area of the *Gau* were on the spot, but could not be used in this capacity because the *Wehrmacht* could not provide any support personnel, and the men themselves had, for the most part, never operated a gun before.

On average, for every small-arm of foreign origin there was about 60 rounds of ammunition, and for every light machine gun there was about 1,100 rounds of ammunition.

At the Deutsche Waffen- und Munitionsfabriken, A. G., in Posen, a contract was under way for manufacturing 2,000 2cm MG 151s with a carriage assembly specially constructed for my *Volkssturm*. The MG 151s were delivered, complete with ammunition, at the beginning of February. On 19 January, I was given the first *Volksgewehr* manufactured in Posen. The production and thus the actual provision of this armament to the entire *Volkssturm* could have then immediately shifted up to full speed.

V. Training

Training proceeded, strongly supported by *Wehrmacht* authorities. The following uninterrupted series of 8 to

10-day training courses was implemented:

1. Reich Training Course for battalion commanders in Grafenwöhr 8 participants

2. Battalion and company commander training course at the Infantry Officer Cadet School V in Posen-Kundorf 75 participants

3. *Zugführer* and *Gruppenführer* training course in Hohensalza 60 participants
   in Kosten 60 participants
   in Kalisch 60 participants

   The above training courses were carried out at the H. U. S. in Kosten and at the *Kommandantur der Panzertruppen* XXI/II in Kalisch.

4. Gunnery course at the *Kommandatur der Panzertruppen* XXI/II in Kalisch. 60 participants

5. Signals courses at *Kommandeur der Nachrichtentruppen* in Hohensalza and Posen 60 participants each course

6. Pioneer course at *Landes-Pionier Btl.* 508 in Posen 120 participants

7. In each *Kreis*, most often in the *Kreis* training centre or in other available accommodation, *Kreis* training courses for *Zugführer* and *Gruppenführer* provided using *Wehrmacht* training personnel 120 participants per course

8. To this should be added another series of individual training courses locally agreed and organised by the various *Kreisstabsführer* at the SS *Junkerschule* in Treskau near Posen and with *Wehrmacht* units

The training for officers and NCOs was planned in advance and organised in the form of courses lasting several days, whereas training for other ranks was carried out on Sundays and holidays.

Sufficient numbers of training personnel were provided by the *Wehrmacht*. Accommodation and food posed no problems. But the shortage of practice ammunition was a hindrance, especially since, with the exception of the few German weapons, the armament consisted of foreign rifles, the ammunition for which should and could not be obtained for firing practice. But if a soldier has not repeatedly practised marksmanship with the weapon that he is going to use, then he is inevitably not going to have a proper confidence in the weapon, and the effects on his shooting must be evident, and all the more so when the going gets tough.

The number of *Panzerfäuste* released for firing practice was so small that several platoons had to be assembled on those occasions when, from time to time, one of the *Panzerfäuste* which had been released was available for firing practice. At least enough of them should have been provided to ensure that in every group at least one man was a skilled marksman with the *Panzerfaust*. Immediately before the battalions of the first levy were marched off into action, orders were received by telephone from *SS-Obergruppenfuhrer* Berger that after units had taken up their positions, special training should be carried out on the *Panzerfaust* with the aim of ensuring that in every group at least one man became a marksman with the weapon. But as a result of the headlong development of military events, it was no longer possible to carry out further training in the positions.

VI. Combat deployment
On the basis of all tactical and strategic considerations to date, both the responsible political authorities and in particular the military authorities did not expect that the enemy would mount a direct assault on my *Gau*, but that rather it was likely that they would be following a strategic advance from a base on the Vistula to the southwest and north-west. But in any event the strongly developed B–1 Line in my *Gau* (which had taken a workforce of about 300,000 6 months to complete) had to be occupied in time to serve as an impregnable blocking line. To help achieve this, as the result of tireless and painstaking work (*Generalleutnant* Matterstock), the precise firing values for all weapons in this very deep system of positions, several hundred kilometres long, had been calculated and recorded. In addition to the blocking groups on the Eastern Front, it was planned to occupy the B–1 Line with 14 combat divisions. Thus, according to all the assurances given to me by the *Wehrmacht*, this line would be the obstacle over which neither a German soldier nor a Bolshevist could cross in an East-West direction.

Until the middle of January, the political view of the situation was based on calming assurances, which were underlined both publicly and in private as late as 12 January 1945. The responsible Supreme Commander of Army Group A, *Generaloberst* Harpe, declined to provide a military assessment of the situation either to me or to my representative, *Regierungsprasident* Dr. Riediger, Litzmannstadt. Thus, in order to get a clear picture, I had to rely on my own resources. I got that clear picture for myself on 17 January on a drive along the eastern border

185

of my *Gau*. Even so, the military commanders whom I visited could not give me a clear picture, and the response from Army Group A, which was in the process of changing its Supreme Commander, to my repeated telephone enquiries was also unsatisfactory.

I certainly did get a clear picture for myself when, on the afternoon of 17 January, I saw the first enemy tanks in operation at Löwenstadt, to the east of Litzmannstadt, and then towards evening at Görnau, to the north of Litzmannstadt, and well-equipped elements of the 9th Army (baggage trains, individual soldiers and fully motorised army units) fleeing westwards. Despite several attempts, I, as one individual, could not stop this headlong flight of ten thousand German soldiers who found themselves without officers (I only met two officers!!)

During that night and the next day in the eastern districts of my *Gau* I saw the same picture! So now I had that overall view of the situation which was so necessary! These impressions, while they were still fresh in my mind, I passed on that night (I telephoned from Kalisch to Oppeln) to the Supreme Commander of Army Group A, *Generaloberst* Schörner, who had just an hour before taken over as Supreme Commander of Army Group A, and, as he told me, was just in the process of being brought up to date on the situation by *General* von Xylander. I passed the same information by telephone to the Commander in Defence District XXI, *General der Artillerie* Petzel. In this situation, the *Volkssturm* of the Wartheland was moving up past the *Wehrmacht* in the direction of the B–1 Line and the front. It had been envisaged that, in addition to these units from the Eastern Front, 14 divisions should man the positions. The *Wehrmacht* provided just two battalions. Apart from these, it was the majority of the 27 *Volkssturm* battalions under the command of the *Wehrmacht* which moved into the B–1 Line as the combat garrison.

The HQ of XXI Corps had been repeatedly advised of the state of weapons training, the shortage of equipment and the still questionable fighting capability of these *Volkssturm* units whose training was only just beginning. But the *Wehrmacht* always stressed that the requirement for the *Volkssturm* was to act as a security garrison. In doing this, it would have had the opportunity, as had always been the intention before the *Volkssturm* were actually deployed, of immediately being able to carry out further training. But military events came head over heels one after the other, and, for the most part, the *Volkssturm* battalions were deployed alone. Some of them were assigned sectors within the positions some 10 to 12 kilometres long without any support from heavy weapons or anti-tank weapons. So the resistance they could put up against floods of tanks in strength between 50 and 60 with following infantry was only weak, and the battalions were simply overrun.

I also asked *Reichsminister* Dr Goebbels, in his capacity as *Gauleiter* of Berlin, by telephone to help me, and in the difficult situation in which we found ourselves, to assign 12–15 *Volkssturm* battalions from Berlin. The basic promise given by *Reichsminister* Goebbels was later extensively qualified by deputy *Gauleiter* Schach, who stated that Berlin was prepared to provide 12 battalions, but without weapons. I then telephoned *SS-Obergruppenfuhrer* Berger to ask him to intervene to help us, and then once again asked Deputy *Gauleiter* Schach to sort out the question of weapons directly with *Obergruppenführer* Berger. The battalions were supposed to be ready to march off in a few days. But the notice that they were ready did not arrive. By 23 January 1945, the *Gau* was overrun, so that it was too late for the intended deployment of the 12 Berlin battalions to take place in *Gau* Wartheland.

In total, the following battalions, with an average strength of 450 to 500 men per battalion, were placed under the command of the *Wehrmacht* on 18 January 1945:

> To *Kampfkommandeur* 1 in Dilltal (*Kreis* Welun)
> Btl. 35 from Birnbaum
> Btl. 37 from Eichenbrück
> Btl. 57 from Jarotschin
> Btl. 1 from Posen (city)
>
> To *Kampfkommandeur* 2 to Schieratz
> Btl. 69 from Kolmar
> Btl. 147 from Samter
>
> To *Kampfkommandeur* 3 to Schieratz
> Btl. 45 from Gostingen
> Btl. 47 from Oppenbach
> Btl. 169 from Wreschen
> Btl. 19 from Posen (city)
>
> To *Kampfkommandeur* 4 to Schwarzau (*Kreis* Kalisch)
> Btl. 61 from Kalisch

To *Kampfkommandeur* 4 to Wandalenbrück (*Kreis* Turek)
Btl. 9 from Posen (city)

To *Kampfkommandeur* 4 to Turek
Btl. 137 from Obornik

To *Kampfkommandeur* 5 to Warthebrücken
Btl. 161 from Warthebrücken
Btl. 41 from Gnesen
Btl. 73 from Konin
Btl. 81 from Kosten

To *Kampfkommandeur* 6 to Babenwald
Btl. 29 from Dietfurt

To *Kampfkommandeur* 7 to Grünholm
Btl. 55 from Hohensalza

To the *Kampfkommandant* of the Leslau-Schröttersburg blocking line
Btl. 99 from Leslau

To the *Kampfkommandant* of Schröttersburg
Btl. 31 from Gombin

On 20 January 1945, the following additional *Volkssturm* battalions were placed under the command of the *Wehrmacht*:

Btl. 27 from Seenbrück (*Kreis* Posen-Land)	Btl. 43 from Wittingen (*Kreis* Gnesen)
Btl. 49 from Oppenbach (*Kreis* Grätz)	Btl. 65 from Reichtal (*Kreis* Kempen)
Btl. 77 from Hinterberg (*Kreis* Konin)	Btl. 135 from Moglino
Btl. 155 from Schroda	Btl. 71 from Scharnikau
Btl. 15 from Posen (city)	Btl. 167 from Wollstein
Btl. 139 from Ostrowo	

Some of these battalions (certainly Battalions 27 Seenbruck, 65 Reichtal, 77 Hinterberg, 135 Moglino, 139 Ostrowo) were not able to reach their assigned deployment areas, because they were on the train for days, were re-routed, and the sectors which it had been planned they would occupy had already been occupied by the Soviets. They were then deployed on my orders to provide security for the columns of refugees which were particularly threatened.

At the present time there is still no reliable documentation relating to the fighting undertaken by those *Volkssturm* battalions which did manage to get to their deployment areas in time. According to credible statements made by men of the *Volkssturm* who came through the fighting, Battalions 55 Hohensalza, 169 Wreschen, 35 Birnbaum, 57 Jarotschin, and probably also Battalions 1, 9, and 19 from Posen City were wiped out, leaving only a few survivors. Large numbers of them were treated as partisans and shot by the enemy infantry.

The men of the *Volkssturm* from my *Gau* who were ordered to escort the columns of refugees had, just like all other men fit for military service, come to the *Volkssturm* from the Party, the State and industry, and had been instructed, insofar as the limited communications through the *Gau* of Mark Brandenburg to my headquarters would allow, to report once their column of refugees were safely through the area, immediately for further orders to the nearest the *Wehrmacht Ersatz* authority, *Volkssturm* collection point or Party *Ortsgruppe*.

VII. Lessons and Conclusions

1. *Volkssturm* battalions should never be deployed alone as combat troops. Should the situation require that the *Volkssturm* be deployed as combat troops, then, if at all possible, this should only be in association with *Wehrmacht* units.

2. *Volkssturm* battalions are principally security garrisons for their home territory and not intervention units.

3. Soldiers from the Great War can be good commanders. But in most cases, because of their lack of combat experience in the present war, command would be very difficult for them, even if they are the best kind of National Socialists. Training courses meet this lack of experience only to a very limited extent.

4. In combat, the strongest way of ensuring that *Volkssturm* battalions fight well is to provide them with young, politically educated officers from the *Wehrmacht* or the *Waffen-SS*.

5.   If it is planned to evacuate a district at the same time as the *Volkssturm* is mobilised, then it would be good to detail elements of the *Volkssturm* to help with the evacuation. If there is a shortage of men, the men of the second levy would be suitable for this, even if they were unarmed.

6.   The command arrangements for the *Volkssturm* must be established before they are sent into action. In my opinion, the moment they are deployed in action, command authority must lie with the appropriate *Wehrmacht* commander.

7.   In my experience, unclear perceptions, misunderstandings and mistrust have apparently not allowed the perception to grow among *Wehrmacht* authorities, commanders, and staffs that the *Volkssturm* and the *Wehrmacht* belong together. Despite all success in improvisation in forming, organising and equipping the *Volkssturm*, we should not be deceived that the bloody casualties of the *Volkssturm* will be all the greater the less individual Army authorities are prepared to understand the great principle behind the *Volkssturm*.

8.   But we should also not forget to recognise that whole series of *Wehrmacht* commanders in my *Gau* have selflessly and with great commitment supported the formation of the *Volkssturm*.

Signed: Greiser
Gauleiter and *Reichsstatthalter*

2: Account of General Petzel

Petzel
General (retd.)

Hameln, 6 March 1953
Ostertorwall 40

Subject: Account by *Gauleiter* Greiser on 'Formation and combat deployment of the *Volkssturm* in the *Reichsgau* of Wartheland', 20 February 1945.

I have the following comments to make on the above account:

On 20 January, 1945, Greiser had fled his *Gau* with his Staff and all his colleagues, and travelled to Frankfurt-an-der-Oder and later to Landsberg-an-der-Warthe. Because the situation very soon became unsafe there too, the *Gauleiter* and his staff were offered accommodation in Potsdam. Hitler was very angry at Greiser for fleeing, and reproached him very severely. That no criminal charges were brought against him he owes to Himmler, who went to Hitler and said that Greiser was acting on his orders. Greiser was told to stay in Karlsbad. It was there that he now wrote the above account. Overall, no material objections can be made against the account, but in some places it is clear that Greiser is anxious to portray the situation in such a way as to excuse what he did.

I have the following more detailed comments:

1.   The settlers had been assured that initially they would not be conscripted for military service, in order to give them time to take over and organise the farms which they had recently acquired. Unfortunately, as was customary with them, the SS did not hold to this undertaking, but sought, often using force, to pressgang young men into the *Waffen-SS*. The *Wehrmacht* did not follow this behaviour. I myself also tried, through the Supreme Commander of the Reserve Army, to bring about a change. Himmler promised to do what I asked, but nothing was changed. After the Defence Recruitment Authorities had been set up on 1 February 1940, organised registration of the male population took place. The first organised enlistments took place very much later. Even then, account was taken of the special circumstances of the settlers by granting exemptions from military service to many of them.

2.   Organisation: The difficulties are accurately described. But it is unfortunately not the case, as Greiser suggests, that weapons training began immediately. Because *SS-Gruppenführer* Reinefarth was engaged on other duties, there was no leadership by a person who could drive the scheme forward with energy. *SS-Sturmbannführer* Harder had far too many other claims on his time to be able to carry out this extensive new task in the way which was required. That he did his best, and that what he did achieve deserves special recognition, is something which is beyond doubt, even with me.

3.   Sector IV/Armament: The 'Grolmann Action' goes back to a suggestion made by Staff *Oberst* Hassenstein, Chief of Staff of Defence District XXI in Posen. Greiser stated that he was in agreement with implementing this action in accordance with the plans proposed by the Defence District Command. For more details, see my account 'Military preparations for the defence of the *Warthegau*', dated 10 April 1950.

4.   Combat deployment: Greiser's account suggests that he had been promised that the B–1 Line would be manned by 14 fresh divisions. But this is not the case, and could not have been the case, because these

divisions were simply not available. The position had been built to accommodate 14 divisions, but it was planned to use them as rearward positions for the frontline troops who were withdrawing.

With regard to the deployment of the units set up by the Defence District Command, I refer to my account of 10 April 1950: 'The Soviet advance through the *Warthegau* in January 1945'.

How the *Volkssturm* battalions actually fared in action can be seen from the attached individual accounts. That things went very differently than the authorities had originally planned is only to be expected in the light of the rapid development of events. No *Volkssturm* battalions "marched past the *Wehrmacht*" on their way to the front". Apart from Battalion 'Altburgund', which saw action near Mühlen, all *Volkssturm* battalions fought in connection with elements of the Army, insofar as they managed to get to the

B–1 positions at all.

Signed: Petzel

3. Representative accounts written by members of the Volkssturm and Party authorities concerning the deployment of the Volkssturm in the Reichsgau of Wartheland

All the accounts were written on the orders of the Deputy General Command, XXI Army Corps, Posen, in March 1945 while the experiences were still fresh in the writers' minds.

List of Accounts

Writer:	Kreis:	Volkssturm Battalion:
Kreisleiter Zülch	Altburgund	29
Ernst Gräber, Battalion Adjutant	Birnbaum	35
Commander *Kreisleiter* Streckert	Eichenbrück	39
Btl. Cdr. Stolpe	Gostingen	45
Parteigenosse Schimmel, Btl. Adj.	Jarotschin	57
Kreisleiter Orlowski	Jarotschin	57
NSDAP *Kreisgeschäftsführer* Schäfer	Kolmar	69 and 71
Btl. Cdr. *Freiherr* von Lüttwitz	Kolmar	69
Volksturmmann Franz Hoffart	Kosten	81
Volkssturmmann Eduard Geissler	Kosten	81
Hauptgemeinschaftsleiter Wallrodt	Krotschin	83
Volkssturmmann Obst	Posen (City)	19
Emil Niesbruch	Posen (City)	19
Hauptgemeinschaftsleiter Eppert	Schroda	155
Company Cdr. Robert Fuhrmann	Wollstein	167

The last account which is attached, taken from other documents, is that of the commander of *Volkssturm* Battalion 36/137, Obornik, dated February 1945.

Kreis *Altburgund:* Vst. *Btl. 29*
Account of: Kreisleiter *Zülch*

The battalion was marched off from Dietfurt on 17 January with 3 companies each of 140 men, 1 Staff Company, 90 men. It was taken by rail to Babenwald.

Btl. Cdr. *Hauptmann* Möller. Armament: 450 Italian rifles with 27,000 rounds of ammunition, 27 Soviet MGs with 12,000 rounds of ammunition, 240 *Panzerfäuste*, 5 boxes of hand grenades, six agricultural vehicles. In the positions it was discovered that the hand grenades had no detonators and that the MG ammunition consisted of blanks.

Combat mission unknown. Deployment in positions near Mühlental, about 20km from the railway station at Babenwald. Arrived 18 January in the afternoon. Introduced into the sector by the *Wehrmacht*. The older men so exhausted by marching on foot that they could do no more. On 19 January, first frontal attack by Soviet tanks, which turned round when they met countering fire. Heavy enemy casualties. Because the crossing points over the anti-tank ditches had not been blown up, the tanks went round Mühlental to the south and to the north. When darkness fell, battalion withdrew westwards. At Petrikau, once again contact with enemy armour. In Strelno finally encircled and wiped out. Several Soviet tanks said to have been knocked out, 5 of which were destroyed by *Zugführer* Kunder alone (a clerk in the *Landratsamt* in Altburgund, 54 years old). Apart from 5 anti-

189

tank guns, which never fired a shot, no *Wehrmacht* were involved. The soldiers manning the anti-tank guns were described by the *Volkssturm* men as second-rate soldiers.

Kreis *Birnbaum: VSt. Btl. 35*
Account by: Ernst Gräber, Btl. Adjutant

17 January battalion ordered to Birnbaum. Battalion strength 206. Armament and equipment: 206 Soviet rifles, 75 *Panzerfaust*. Loaded onto trains at Birnbaum station to Wilhelmsbrück on the Prosna, where we were unloaded on 19 January, 7:30 am. Battalion commander von Jägow, who at first had to act on his own initiative, because he had no telephone connection. Battalion deployed at Wilhelmsbrück from 19 January, 9:00am. Scattered officers from Welun reported approaching enemy tanks.

On 19 January, 8:00pm Soviet tank attack. Six tanks knocked out by battalion commander von Jägow, 4 by Company Commander Voss. On 20 January, 5 am., von Jägow wounded in head by a shell splinter. Battalion command taken over by Company Commander Voss. Withdrew to Kempen, where on 21 January we were placed under command of *Wehrmacht* and sent into action.

On 22 January, 9 pm, ordered by the *Wehrmacht* to Gross-Warthenburg. From there marched into the positions at Schreibersdorf, where we were placed under command of 3rd Company, Gnesen Officers' School . Many men reported sick. On 23 January, 8:00pm, on orders of the *Wehrmacht* marched back to Gross-Warthenburg. From there with remaining six *Volkssturm* men via Namslau, Öls, to collection point in Breslau. Battalion commander Voss arrives there with 13 men.

Kreis *Eichenbrück: VSt. Btl. 39*
Account by: Commander Kreisleiter Streckert

VSt. Btl. 39, Eichenbrück, set off on 17 January by rail in direction of Welun. Details of fate of battalion not known. The battalion was completely scattered before reaching its planned destination. A large part of it was re-registered in Breslau. Some of the men discharged on account of their advanced age. Contact with battalion commander von Heyden not possible. Combatants' papers issued, but instead of these pre-printed forms. These were supposed to be completed and handed in while on the march.

Kreis *Gostingen: VSt. Btl. 45*
Account by: Btl. Cdr. Stolpe

Battalion 45, 1st levy, mobilised on 15 January. This order then changed to say that the battalion was to assemble from 7 pm on 16 January in the fire service school in Gostingen. On 17 January at midday the battalion stood ready with Staff Company and two companies – total strength c. 280 men.

Armament: Italian rifles, each with 70 rounds, 60 *Panzerfäuste*, 3 Soviet light MGs per platoon. Equipped in normal SA overcoat over civilian clothing, footwear very poor; identity discs, paybooks and combatants' papers not available. Baggage train: 9 agricultural vehicles with 20 draft horses and one horse for riding.

17 January, 7 pm, loaded on to train at Gostingen station bound for Schieratz, to report to *Kampfkommandant* III. Arrived there on 18 January about 3 pm. Company commander reported to *Kampfkommandant* Neumüller. Immediate orders for defensive action in the southern sector of Schieratz under *Oberstleutnant* von Zülow, Sector Commandant South. "Soviet breakthrough to be prevented at all costs".

Towards 2300 hours, battalion commander reports that the position, which in the north extended as far as Osmolin and was about five kilometres wide, has been occupied as ordered. On 19 January regular training. Until 22 January battalion in positions. Receiving withdrawing *Wehrmacht* forces and reinforcement action. Thus shortening the defence sector of Schieratz battalion and preparing for all-round defence, the more necessary because strong Soviet forces already reported to the west of the town in the direction of Kalisch. Frequent strafing attacks by aircraft. On 20 January parts of the baggage train blown-up in heavy air attacks and withdrawn to the west, apparently to Blaski, later came under two strong tank attacks in Blaski and in Kalisch.

On 23 January, 0700 hours, orders given by the new *Kampfkommandant*, General Daniels, to withdraw and to get to the Prosna to the south of Kalisch. Protection by withdrawing *Wehrmacht* troops. Vehicles could not be provided. The daily marching goal had to be reached, because it was only possible to keep open one last bridge over the Prosna, which was to be blown up that night. Withdrawal, 80 kilometres, across country and on field paths with steady infiltration of enemy tanks. At the Prosna, where it was originally planned that we would have a few hours' rest, orders received from *Oberstleutnant* von Zulow to immediately march on westwards, because Ostrow and Krotoschin had in the meantime been occupied by the enemy. Marching on until 24

January, 2000 hours, as far as Raschkau. There battalion discharged by *Oberstleutnant* von Zulow with orders to report back to the *Kreisleiter*. In the next few days retreat through Horleburg, Gostingen, Lissa and Fraustadt. From 26 January retreat via Glogau, Sagan, Forst, Cottbus to Luckau, where battalion arrived on 1 February.

In his general assessment of the action in which the battalion was involved, the battalion commander refers to the following : Because of 'Action Grolmann', within the *Kreis* there were no fit men available for the *Volkssturm* first levy. For training purposes there were only a small number of rifles without ammunition, but no machine guns and *Panzerfauste*. When 'Action Grolmann' was incorporated into the *Volkssturm* on 1 January, only a small number of men were incorporated into the first levy. The majority of men fit for military service were in second levy for occupational reasons. Thus, in the first levy there were only old men, sick man and unfit men, plus uneducated Black Sea ethnic Germans who could not speak German. From 1 January until we went into action, shortage of time and constant change of battalion strength meant that it was not possible to properly form and train the battalion. In Schieratz it became evident the that within the battalion there were a whole series of amputees, men with heart disease and men with all sorts of other complaints. Most of them had no military training, with the result that they didn't understand any military commands.

Kreis *Jarotschin: VSt. Btl. 57*
Account by: Btl. Adj. Parteigenosse *Schimmel*

Battalion alert on morning of 16 January. On morning of 17th January, 374 men loaded on train at 09 30 hours to Trummerfeld, arrival there on 17 January, 2100 hours. Shown to barracks quarters, which at the same time were occupied by *Ostarbeiter* and refugees, by a battalion of infantry regiment 378.

In the night between 17 and 18 January, the ammunition store of Regiment 378, housed in a barracks, is blown sky-high. After this, the *Volkssturm* battalion commander had the battalion vehicles unloaded and had the battalion withdraw from the barracks. The battalion commander of Regiment 378 apparently refused to deploy the *Volkssturm* Battalion, because it was not sufficiently trained. Rather, the battalion, he said, should be marched off towards Dilltal. Then, battalion marched back to Baumbach and awaited further orders. Then the entire battalion was ordered to turn round and go back to Trummerfeld. The second and third company were deployed within the positions to reinforce the said infantry regiment. The baggage train and Staff company remained in the village, at the railway station one company was assigned to a company of Regiment 378. The situation was quiet and it was possible for training to take place.

Then, after a successful Soviet attack, the battalion adjutant was sent back to the baggage train and Staff company, to bring forward all available men from there as reinforcements. According to the battalion commander, the 2nd Company has already suffered considerable casualties because of its lack of training. The battalion adjutant was to remain with the baggage train. He was later forced by enemy tanks to withdraw with the baggage train, left the baggage train vehicles where they were and lost communication with the battalion. Many people were managing entirely on their own initiative. He went on foot through Kempen and from there by rail via Ostrovo to Jarotschin, where he arrived at noon on 20 January.

Account by: Kreisleiter *Orlowski*

On 15 January, 1700 hours, *Volkssturm* Battalion 57, at a strength of 386 men, loaded on train to Dilltal, *Kreis* Welun. Battalion deployed in Trummerfeld together with remnants of an active battalion, no supporting units on either side. Bolshevist attack with 18 tanks and about fourfold superiority in infantry. Knocked out from 7 to 8 tanks. The rest of them overran the position; the *Volkssturm* battalion was scattered. About 50 men later reported back to the *Kreisleiter*. They explained that the *Panzerfäuste* were without detonators and the Soviet machine guns were only provided with practice ammunition. The *Kreisleiter* had given the battalion all available weapons. In response to his repeated requests for new weapons, *Sturmbannfuhrer* Harder promised him 200 *Panzerfäuste*, but these did not arrive.

Kreis *Kolmar: VSt. Btl. 69 and 71*
Account by: NSDAP Kreisgeschäftsführer *Schäfer*

Volkssturm Battalion 69 loaded onto train at Kolmar station on 18 January, 1000 hours; *Volkssturm* Battalion 71 at Scharnikau station on 19 January, 1500 hours. Weapons per battalion 520 Soviet rifles, 48 Soviet automatic rifles, 30 Soviet machine guns, 45 *Panzerfäuste*. Ammunition with *Volkssturm* Battalion 69: 115,000 Soviet cartridges; with *Volkssturm* Battalion 71: 85,000 cartridges. Each battalion about 20 stick grenades. In addition, each battalion had five vehicles, 10 draft horses, two horses for riding.

Account by: Battalion Commander of VSt. Btl. 69, Freiherr von Lüttwitz

Left from Kolmar station 18 January. Arrived 19 January in Spatenfelde, to the east of Kalisch. Problems with the railway meant that it was not possible to travel on to Schieratz. Agreed this by telephone with *Kampfkommandant* II. Ordered to march to Burcenin, about 20 kilometres south of Schieratz. Battalion arrived at Suchy on evening of 20 January. News concerning the dangerous situation on the Warthe and outflanking by Soviet tanks at Warta and Welun. Asked Adjutant Warmbier to try to get through to Schieratz. Because of heavy traffic westbound, Adjutant did not reach Schieratz, but obtained sufficient clarification of the situation on the way there at various command posts. Therefore decision taken by battalion commander on 21 January, 0200 hours, to march to Schwarzau. There were placed under command of 25th *Panzer* Division and ordered to securing positions at Schwarzau. Also assigned to *Kampfgruppe* 'Natsch'. Building security positions round Schwarzau. 2 Soviet tanks, with infantry seated on them, turned up at the edge of the town, and pushed on into the town. Heavy local fighting. One tank destroyed by *Volkssturmman* Hadel, who was killed by the back flash of his *Panzerfaust*. This followed by withdrawal of the second tank and the Soviet infantry. Establish that large numbers of the battalion had fled in panic. Weak elements were brought back the next day.

On 23 January to the east of Schwarzau, Soviet motorised infantry turned up before 3rd Company. Artillery firefight with German assault guns and flak. Enemy movements south of Schwarzau. Enemy attack on 1st and 2nd Company at northern exit to town. Took several prisoners and 2 vehicles. Town was encircled. In the meantime, Kalisch taken by Soviets to the rear of Schwarzau. Combat mission of the battalion, hold open the road to Kalisch. Discussion of situation with *Kampfkommandant*. Decided to evacuate the area under cover of darkness. Retreat through Josefovo to Raschkau. Constantly being outflanked by enemy armoured point units to the south and to the north. Lack of food became noticeable. Built a potato steamer on a vehicle, so as to be able to cook while on the march. Marched again out of Raschkau on 25 January, 1000 hours. At Krotoschin, road to the west blocked by Soviet tanks . Attempts to fight free by our own tanks did not succeed. Therefore, marched on by side roads. Reached our own lines at Koschmin-Krotoschin. Further march through Guhrau. Arrival in Glogau 29 January. On 31 January once again to Buntzelwaldau, where we were placed under command of XXXX *Panzerkorps*. Battalion remained here in local accommodation. 51 men who had lost contact with 4 Company here rejoined the battalion.

Note by the Kreisgeschäftsführer re VSt. Btl. 71

Not possible to date to link up with VSt. Btl. 71. It was deployed south of Hohensalza and is said at the moment to be in action around Küstrin.

Kreis Kosten: VSt. Btl. 81
Account by: Volkssturmmann Franz Hoffart, 1 Company

Transport of Battalion 81, during the night between 16 and 17 January, to Warthbrucken. Composition of the battalion: Staff company and 3 infantry companies. Total strength: 561 men.

19 January unloaded in Warthbrücken. Overnight quartered in barracks. On 21 January, 0400 hours, issue of 72 rounds of ammunition per man. At 1400 hours a sentry reported that the Soviets were approaching. The company attacked the enemy, but was pushed back in a counter-attack. Ammunition soon exhausted, many men left without permission, some of the company taken prisoner. Hoffart, with a few remnants of the company, joined a refugee column.

Account by: Volkssturmmann Eduard Geissler, 2 Company

Geissler also reports that on 20 January the battalion was sent into action at Warthbrücken. Towards 1600 hours, some of the company came into contact with the enemy and were overrun. Probably all were taken prisoner. Orders to retreat. On 21 January at 0700 hours, remnants of the company encircled in some woodland and broke out. Geissler was later wounded on the Warthe.

Kreis Krotoschin: VSt. Btl. 83
Account by: Hauptgemeinschaftsleiter Wallrodt

The *Volkssturm* of the *Kreis* received no combat orders, because they had no weapons. Afterwards, *Volkssturm* 1st levy was detailed to escort columns of refugees …

Kreis *Posen – Stadt: VSt. Btl. 19*
Account by: Volksturmmann *Obst*

Marched out from Bienen 18 January. On 20 January to Ostrovo. On 22 January building barriers in Ostrovo. 23 January towards noon, retreat from Ostrovo. Fired on by Poles on the railway embankment. *Wehrmacht* fleeing in complete disorder. The formation of a *Kampfgruppe* under Major Luckow, consisting of about 50 members of the *Wehrmacht* and 150 *Volkssturmmänner*. From 24 January retreat past Krotoschin, through Gostingen, Lissa, Fraustadt. One *Kampfgruppe* of the battalion, reinforced by *Wehrmacht*, mounted an assault on the village of Heiersdorf. Four men killed. Continued march while still fighting through Schlichtenhain, LIchtenberg, Zedlitz and Seehagen. From 10 to 11 February in action at Oberquell. Loss of the entire combat baggage train at Haselquell as a result of artillery direct hit. 13 February retreat through Beuthen to Neustadtel. 14 February in action again in Herzogswalde. 15 February retreat through Nauenberg to Benau. There, once again in action at the front. Battalion was the last to evacuate the position under heavy infiltration by enemy, after *Wehrmacht* had already withdrawn. During the next days further retreat to Cottbus.

Account by: Emil Niesbruch

On 21 January in Ostrowo, *Wehrmacht* streaming back in retreat. Army quartermaster stores plundered, with officers and Poles taking part. Impression extremely shaming. *Volkssturm* had no food. Marched to Adelnau. On the way, short training session on the *Panzerfaust*. Mounting guard on eastern periphery of Adelnau. *Gendarmerie* post already deserted. At night Soviet tanks from south to Adelnau. No alert. One tank stood in the courthouse square. On 22 January in the morning, bridge blown up by pioneers. Soviet attack from south and east. Great confusion. Attack by Soviet tanks and Polish insurgents with white and red armbands. Complete failure of our own weapons. Retreat, because no ammunition. Fired on from the flanks. General disintegration. Through Schönfeld to Krotoschin. Crazy confusion in the town. The companies are beginning to join up together again. On 23 January to Koppelstadt. From there by rail on 24 January to Lissa. Many *Volkssturmsoldaten* , including battalion commander Kreuz, simply travel on in the direction of Glogau. The people with a certain degree of discipline look for their companies in Lissa. Parts of the battalion brought together again under Company Commander Gutsche. Spent the night in Lissa. *Kreisleitung* already evacuated, therefore no assistance, particularly re food. *Wehrmacht* said that they were not responsible. In the town a general picture of retreat. On 25 January and March to Fraustadt. On 26 January in the morning announcement that we were going into action again in the town of Lissa. On the march to Lissa the incredible image of soldiers throwing entire boxes of ammunition away into the ditches. Outside Lissa an air-raid. The writer was run over by a *Wehrmacht* motorcycle and was detached from the unit.

Kreis *Schroda: VSt. Btl. 155*
Account by: NSDAP Hauptgemeinschaftsleiter *Eppert*

German male population of the *Kreis* about 1100 men, of which 850 registered for the first and second levies of the *Volkssturm*. Strength of battalion (first levy): 200 men. Mainly Black Sea ethnic Germans, without military training, low combat value. Clothing not possible, badly tattered civilian clothing, unusable footwear. Armament: one light machine gun MG42, Soviet, Italian and Mannlicher rifles. Ammunition for the light machine gun 2,000 rounds, for the rifles 30 rounds each, for available German 98k rifles no ammunition at all. In addition 60 machine pistols, apparently also without ammunition. Sufficient numbers of *Panzerfäuste*, but these were never used.

On 20 January, orders from the *Kampfkommandant*, to Schroda for all-round defence of the town, battalion deployed for this purpose. On 21 January, orders from the *Gaustabsführer* to load the battalion for Moschin. In Moschin, established contact with *Kampfkommandant*. Combat mission: "Defence of Moschin against enemy who are expected from the West, Schrimm and Karlshausen. But enemy attack later came from the East. Battalion was turned round and sent into action, after the *Luftwaffe* company from Schroda aerodrome had withdrawn. More of our own forces in the town of Moschin: *Kampfkommandant Hauptmann* Springer with 60 men from a survey unit and about 30 men who had lost their units. Strong, well equipped and armed elements of *Wehrmacht* and police "streaming back westwards", which badly affected the mood of the *Volkssturm* men in action. Orders from the *Kampkommandant* to clothe and equip the members of the *Volkssturm* Battalion from the stocks of the gigantic store of winter clothing in the church at Moschin. This store was set on fire on 24 January. The efforts of the writer to provide clothing for the battalion from a store in the Schroda

Cathedral failed because the responsible *Wehrmacht* officials refused to release it, explaining the that issue of clothing could only be made "by orders from higher authority".

On 25 January, 1200 hours, Moschin said to be already encircled by the Soviets. Then, orders from the *Kampfkommandant* to evacuate the town and to retreat across the lakes at Seenbrück. Next day, after a 56 kilometre night march, the battalion reached Oppenbach with 34 men, who were loaded on trains from there to Neu Bentschen. The writer indicates that the rest of the battalion was killed or missing.

Kreis *Wollstein: VSt. Btl. 167*
Account by: Robert Fuhrmann, Company Commander in the battalion

Half of *Volkssturm* Battalion 167 consisted of ethnic Germans, and half of settlers. 20 percent of the battalion could not speak German. Another part with serious head injuries was discharged by the medical officer. Armament: one rifle and 30 rounds of ammunition per man. Two models of rifle, lots of problems in loading them. Equipment scanty, only one company was fully equipped with SA overcoats. Footwear some boots, some ordinary shoes or shoes with wooden soles. 15 haversacks and water bottles per company. Most people showed a dislike of the idea of the *Volkssturm*. The ethnic Germans would rather fight as soldiers, the settlers show themselves to be uninterested and passive. 20 percent deserters.

First action in Lissa. Guarding provisions stores, then manning key points on the western edge of the town. Shortly before Lissa was encircled, the battalion was relieved and marched to Neusalz. There, guard and sentry duty, unloading Oder barges, construction of positions at the bridgeheads. After completing entrenching work, assignment of one platoon from each company to the *Wehrmacht*. Manning key points. Our people, being farmers, felt uncomfortable and unsafe in the city. The rest of the battalion built defensive positions in the city centre.

Next deployment on the Bober, supported by police units on both sides. Enemy approach on 13 February could not be prevented, because the weapons, Italian rifles and machine guns, did not work. On the morning of 14 February, Soviet attack. The battalion was literally overrun and wiped out. No resistance, great fear of being taken prisoner. In a counter-attack by the second company with elements of the police battalion, the position was mostly retaken. The battalion was once again scattered at the collection point by Soviet tank fire. On 18 February the there were only 44 men left.

The battalion was under the command of the responsible *Wehrmacht Kampfkommandant*. He regarded it almost always as a fully-fledged combat unit. When the *Wehrmacht* withdrew, the battalion was always deployed to cover their withdrawal.

Account by the battalion commander of Volkssturm *Battalion 36/137, Obornik, written in February 1945:*

The commander of *Volkssturm* Battalion 36/137, who was in action with his battalion in Schieratz, strongly drew the attention of the *Kampfkommandant* to the fact that his battalion, which only had 250 Italian rifles with 30,000 rounds of ammunition and 1 MG42, and whose men had not yet received any training on these weapons, was not ready for combat in this state. Despite that, he received orders to deploy his battalion to secure the Posen, Turek, Deutscheneck and Tönningen roads. When he received the orders he was told that, before the Soviets came, he would have time to familiarise his men with the weapons.

The battalion commander then explains how on the roads leading westwards, *Wehrmacht* vehicles, fully loaded with soldiers, police vehicles with items from headquarters, and columns of refugees were moving westwards at top speed. Then he continues:

On 20 January, towards 1215 hours, as I was coming from the most forward position to the battalion command post, I met a runner who was bringing me from the *Kampfkommandatur* the news that the battalion should load its baggage onto the vehicles and prepare to retreat. While this was going on, a platoon from the NCO school at Jauer were actually engaged in fighting. In this position, heavy fighting with tanks had flared up.

When towards 1330 hours no orders to withdraw had arrived, I sent two runners to the *Kampfkommandant's* command post. They came back with the news that the command post was deserted. Then I sent the runners to the *Ortskommandatur*. But even this had already been abandoned. After lengthy efforts, through a *Wehrmacht* telephone connection I got an *Oberleutnant* on the telephone who, when I asked him when we should withdraw, stated that anyone who left the position before being ordered to would be shot. I asked him who was supposed to do that, since the *Wehrmacht* had already withdrawn. To that I got no answer. Then I gave the order to withdraw. At this time, Warthbrucken was under heavy fire from the Soviet tanks which had crossed over the

Warthe at Eichstedt. The defence had been left to the *Volkssturm* from Posen, Warthbrücken, Konin and Obornik. The Obornik *Volkssturm* left the town long after the *Wehrmacht* and the police had left.

Extracts from the account of Friedrich Helmigk relating to the fighting in the Obrastellung between Schwerin/Warthe and Schwiebus,

21 January–28 February 1945
(at that time commander of a Volkssturm *company)*

Towards half-past seven we are in Starpel, we stop in front of the inn. We go in, we are allocated and shown into the various bunkers ... The bunker is hidden underground three stories deep.

The new day brings allocation of weapons, some of the company move into the neighbouring bunker to the south ... Between the village of Starpel and Burschen is a wooded mountain ridge, on the highest point of which the command bunker for our sector is located. It is the best armed and has underground connections running northwards with a long series of other bunkers ...

Towards 9 o'clock we sight the first Soviet tanks, 13 fairly heavy tanks rolling up from Calau to our anti-tank barriers ... Now the first tank comes out of the sunken road, then the second and third. They stop in front of the barrier. Besides my hunting glass I have my a telescopic rifle with which I've just been shooting The leading tank opens its hatch and some Soviets clamber out. A fat officer with a walking stick goes with two men to the barrier and inspects the obstacles. The fellows behave as if it was deepest peacetime. A couple of words with the *Feldwebel*, then I get the officer in my sights, pull on the trigger and fire. The man folds up like a penknife, we are only 150 metres away. When they hear my shot the Soviets shoot apart. Our machine-gun is now hammering away. Our mortar peppers a series of 10 to 12 rounds on to the tanks. We both slide quickly as we can into our foxhole. Scarcely are we back in there again and the armoured turrets are bolted shut than we get 5 to 6 15-centimetre shells planted against our doors. Our machine gun falls silent. The gun is completely shot up, one man's slightly wounded. Whether there are any Soviet casualties, and, if so, how many there are, we can't tell. They have disappeared. Only the tanks are still standing there.

Soon we see infantry approaching; not very many of them, but still at least a good 100 men. They are firing from all the bushes and from the small area of woodland which lies in front of us in the direction of Calau. At last our own machine gun has been changed and we're able to fire with it. To and fro our little mortar shoots out a series of rounds. The Soviets then disappear immediately from the place where they fall. In return, we get a few shells on the turret, so that the whole bunker shakes, but the Soviets can do us no serious damage, because our armoured dome is 22 centimetres thick. And so the hours pass.

At 3 o'clock in the afternoon, the tanks suddenly start moving and roll back the way that they came. We're beside ourselves with joy that the Soviets are retreating. When everything is quiet, a patrol is sent out to see whether the anti-tank barriers are still intact. They are not fired on. We pass a report on to the sector bunker. Other bunkers also have contact with the enemy. The Soviets are said to have broken through at a place to the north of us. Towards evening, you can see everywhere in the sky the reflected flames from burning farms. Night falls. Towards 8 o'clock in the evening, we can hear noises at the barrier. We fire several bursts of machine-gun fire at short intervals. Suddenly, the there is a powerful explosion. The Soviets have blown up the barrier. It doesn't take long before vehicles are rolling continuously along the road to Starpel.

Otherwise, the night remains quiet. By morning the road is again fairly empty. Only now and then does a lorry drive quickly westwards. The *Feldwebel* still doesn't give the order to fire. We're not here to quietly watch the Soviets advancing further westwards. I threaten to report him to the sector commander. Just at that moment a lorry drives through. The neighbouring bunker fires with his machine gun over us at the lorry. Then the *Feldwebel* also gives our machine-guns the order to fire. In a few minutes the lorry stops. It was filled with 16 to 18 Soviets. The fellows run across a field of oats to the nearby woods. Several of them, however, fall before they get there, some are lying beside the lorry. The Soviets fire at us with machine gun and rifles from the wood. We give answering fire. Now nothing else comes along the road to Starpel, but further south behind our neighbouring bunker, in which there were comrades from our company, there is no more firing, although the Soviets are moving past it very closely. Soon we hear that the bunker has been abandoned during the night. The people have legged it.

We are really depressed. Our people are cursing loudly, and it's only with difficulty that we can persuade them that they must continue to hold out. The day remains quiet. We bring potatoes from a potato store not very far away, get rations from the command bunker and cook our meals outside the back door of our bunker.

Towards evening I am ordered to a meeting in the sector bunker. It is about 1½ kilometres away. I take one man with me. But to get there is no longer dangerous, because within our bunker line scarcely any Soviets are to be expected. Nevertheless, of course we take our rifles with us. I give my report on what has happened today and yesterday and on the mood of the men. I hear that the two bunkers in Starpel and Burschen have been encircled by the Soviets. Even telephone connections have been broken. The sector commander is planning a surprise attack on the Soviets in order to release the bunker, but still wants to wait for a section of *Waffen-SS* which he has been promised from the northern bunker. When after two hours we stroll back home, you can see the light of burning even in the West. Almost every village is burning. We get back safe to our bunker.

Next morning nothing more is to be seen of Soviets, the lorry is still on the road to Starpel. During the morning there is suddenly an alarm. A column with several horse-drawn vehicles with Soviets is coming past us on a country road which leads 6–700 metres to the east of us. The machine gun is already set up. When the Soviet column is right in the field of fire in front of us, we open fire. Over there there's a hell of a panic! The horses take off, our tracer ammunition flashing between them. Horses fall over each other, wagons turn over. After a few minutes the fun is over. There are some wagons with dead horses still on the stretch of road. A haystack which stands right by the road and which the Soviets have used as cover, is brightly aflame. Also, not far away from our bunker, a small haystack now begins to burn brightly.

In the afternoon, a patrol goes to the lorry, I go with them. Carefully, we creep up, if possible under cover. Something's going on, but everything is still quiet. The dead Soviets who yesterday evening were lying around on the ground and on the lorry have gone, but there are bloodstains everywhere. We find on the lorry lots of provisions, above all several hundredweight of dried bacon, then a good 60 pairs of good boots. Untouched, we bring our booty back to the bunker. We can make good use of it all, especially the bacon.

The next morning I decide to inspect the vehicles on the country road to the east of us. Bragulla goes with me, sure, it's a bit far outside our bunker line, but yesterday's loot makes us hope to find something even better. Our MGs should give covering fire and keep us always in sight. So we both set off. Everything stays quiet. The haystack is still smouldering, behind it there's a half-toasted Soviet, but only the two vehicles with the two dead horses are up there in front. The vehicles are loaded up with 8cm mines. On one of them we find several unopened boxes of cigars. They were also good pickings. Then we turn round and report the 8cm mines to the command bunker. They are brought in straight away, because the sector bunker can make good use of them.

A few days pass without anything particular happening. I am at the sector commander's almost every evening, urging that we try to free the two bunkers in Burschen and Starpel. Finally it's over. Unfortunately we can't go along. The SS is to make the attempt alone. When I get back in the evening, the operation is already under way. I hear that there are only 50 men with three machine guns. I'm really sceptical whether they'll be able to achieve anything. If they had let rip against 400 to 500 men with all their *Panzerfauste*, rifles and machine guns blazing, then perhaps the Soviets might have been fooled, because the *Panzerfäuste* make a terrible din, and at night you could perhaps have freed the bunker for a short time. For the next morning we hear that the attack failed, 15 men are killed or missing, one machine gun is done for. A serious loss! The bunkers haven't opened up. No one knows anything about the people inside. I stand on the turret and look in the direction of Starpel. Suddenly, a great black mushroom cloud of smoke rises over the wood and a heavy detonations shakes the turret. That can only be the bunker at Starpel being blown up.

Further south, too, we see another bunker go up. It must be the one at Wutschdorf. Once again the black mushroom cloud of smoke, then the explosion . . .

And so the days pass; it's dreadful being certain that the Soviets have now occupied your homeland, and not knowing yourself whether your nearest and dearest were able to get away in time. What's going to become of us? In our positions we don't even have a radio. There are rumours that the Soviets are already at the Oder. You can also hear continuous artillery fire from the West. And to the north of us too there's the continual thunder of heavy guns. Now and again you here a heavy gun a few kilometres away. If the Soviets bring up artillery, we're dead meat.

I inform the sector commander that we men of the *Volkssturm*, least my company, don't want to be taken prisoner. We will try to make a breakthrough at the last minute. I know the terrain pretty well from my earlier military exercises and I can trust myself to be able to guide people home at night through the woods. We are dressed in civilian clothes and we don't want the Soviets to stick us up against a wall if they nab us with our weapons in our hands. The commander lends me a map, which I memorise exactly. Things haven't got to that point yet, but I'd like to be prepared for every eventuality.

With my telescopic rifle I now often go hunting to get some meat. I've already shot six deer, one buck and a hare. There are many deer round about our bunker; shooting them is not all that difficult. My hunting bags are always greeted with jubilation. One time we make an armed advance to our deserted neighbouring bunker, from which we have to drive a few Soviets with machine gun fire. Some SS people are the main instigators of this action. We get from the bunker various different rations, a few hundred bread rolls and meat conserves. A few kilometres from us in the woods there is a mill. We take an armed walk there too. We get fired on a few times, and we return the fire, and then things go quiet. We purloin a fairly fat sow weighing about 4 hundred-weight and several cows. Amazingly, the Soviets haven't yet taken the cattle. We receive great praise from the sector commander, because the meat is urgently needed.

One day, a few Soviets are again milling cheekily around the deserted neighbouring bunker. We send over a series of rounds from our mortar, which explode bang in the middle of them. It's as if the Soviets vanished off the face of the earth.

… We hear bad news. The Soviets are said to have brought up artillery to the north of us and are blowing one bunker after another to bits. There are also said to be some of them in parts of the underground tunnels. If that's the case, things will soon be all up for us. After a few days it happens. The Soviets are working with the civilian population on building trenches on the slopes to the east of us. We can't stop them, because we can't fire on the German women who are being forced to work there.

One morning people came with a white flag and asked us on behalf of the Soviets to surrender. We send them to the sector commandant, but he, to my great delight, chases them away. Then there is suddenly the rumour that the commander is negotiating with the Soviets. Now things really will be at all up for us soon! I can see right in front of the bunker, it must be 6 o'clock, and there comes the SS *Scharführer* with his men, with whom we brought the cattle from the mill, and says that the Soviets are already in the command bunker. He only just managed to get away. He says that the bunker has already surrendered.

Since he knew from me that I wanted to break out, he came with his people to go along with us. I sound the alarm and call the men together. Then by telephone comes the order that we should gather together without weapons on the Burschen – Kalau road east of our positions at 7 o'clock, because the position had been surrendered to the Soviets. I inform the men of this order and tell them straight away that I do not intend to obey it. We will try to break out in secret. Anybody who wants to come along should be immediately pack the most necessary things, get iron rations, and meet together in the woodland south of the Kalau – Starpel road, where the anti-tank barrier was. I said that we would set off at the latest at 7 o'clock.

To a man, the *Volkssturm* company followed my suggestion. And about 12 of our *Landsers* joined us. When I went to the *Feldwebel*, he was already standing in his room in his civilian clothes. He was quite out of his mind with fright. A dreadful chap …

As I leave the bunker with Bregulla, the last to leave, we can see many people coming towards us from the command bunker with torches. In the meantime it has got quite dark, and we disappear quickly in the opposite direction behind the railway embankment, and soon afterwards we're at the meeting point in the wood. I give orders to form up, forbid any loud speaking and smoking. And then we're off …

History of *Volkssturm* Battalion 22/I 'Oberdonau'

by Leutnant *Hans Rödhamer (retd), Linz (Austria)*

On 20 January 1945, the 560 *Volkssturm* men who had been called up within 24 hours had gathered together at the collection points in Ried/I., Schärding, Braunau a. I., Gmunden, Vöcklabruck, Wels, Kirchdorf, Perg, Enns and Steyr in the *Gau* of Oberdonau. They were then brought to Linz by scheduled trains, where they were provided with the Auhof barracks for accommodation. The following days were devoted to very hard training under the command of experienced front-line soldiers and officers. Marches and combat exercises at a temperature of minus 20 degrees centigrade were the order of the day. The final division of the battalion into companies, platoons and groups, and the assembly of the Staff Company and the Battalion Staff took place on 26 January.

On 27 January, at 1900 hours, the battalion marched to the station at Kleinmünchen to be loaded on to trains. *Gauleiter* Eigruber bade farewell to the assembled battalion, and assured them that he would do his best for every member and take care of their families.

The battalion staff was embarked on two express train coaches, the men and the baggage in closed goods wagons. The baggage train consisted of 16 agricultural vehicles with 30 horses and one lorry, which had had to be surrendered by a Linz butcher. The equipment of the pioneer, signals, and anti-tank platoons was accommodated in the last wagons. In the first and last wagon, telephones were installed; the telephone line ran loosely along the outer walls of the wagons. The kitchen was well equipped and had brought plenty of food along. During the journey, the destination of which was unknown to the men, the men continued to receive weapons training. The journey went from Linz through Freistadt, Budweis, Prague, Aussig, Dresden and Cottbus to Frankfurt-an-der-Oder, from where the transport train was directed southwards again. One part of the battalion was unloaded at Lossow and another at Wiesenau. The following day, 2 February 1945, the battalion marched into its assigned positions on the Oder, where the first wounded had been sustained through Soviet artillery fire.

Since the defensive sector to which the battalion had been assigned was not yet built, the *Volkssturmsoldaten* of the Upper Danube immediately set to work building the earthen bunkers. The whole terrain was covered with pine trees so that there was no shortage of timber. Here, during the icy nights, the *Volkssturmsoldaten* stood on sentry duty and watched the other bank, where the Soviets were.

On 6 February, at 8 o'clock in the morning, there broke loose a hurricane of fire such as the men of the *Volkssturm* had never experienced. And the first Soviets were already on the peninsula. Nevertheless, the *Volkssturm* didn't let themselves be driven out so quickly, they only withdrew slowly. Particularly hard pressed was the 3rd Company, whose commander was seriously wounded and all of whose *Zugführer* were lost. *Zugführer* Hüthmayr from Gmunden, who had already been decorated many times during the First World War, was the first man to be killed in the 3rd Company. In the afternoon the battalion moved over to counter-attack and threw the Soviets back across the Oder.

On 7 February towards midday, the enemy attacked again with redoubled strength across the Oder. But their attack didn't get anywhere because the *Volkssturmsoldaten* didn't budge. It is true that the battalion had to pay a heavy price for this behaviour. A fifth of them were dead, wounded or missing.

Overall, February passed quietly. The weather was, as can be imagined, unfavourable. Rain and snow storms blew and transformed the ground into a morass. The population of the villages of Lossow, Brieskow, Finkenheerd, Wiesenau and Ziltendorf had already been evacuated. Only a few people had remained behind.

In the night between 1 and 2 March a heavy snowstorm raged. 3 March brought icy wind and once again a lot of snow. On 8 March there was collection for the *Winterhilfe*, to which the battalion contributed 4,000 *Reichsmarks*. On 10 March the battalion finally received its field post number 36120. Until then organising the post had been very difficult. Only once had a courier been sent home with post and had returned again. On that day the Soviets mounted an attack. On 11 March there was an unexpected issue of beer. On 16 March, after the men had already been in the positions for six weeks, they had their first chance to change their underwear and to have a wash.

The following days again passed off quietly. The first field post letters and parcels arrived. Also, on 19 March, a courier arrived from Linz with 12 Hitler Youth who brought sacks with them. The people at home had not forgotten their *Volkssturmsoldaten*. For every man there were 20 cigarettes, chocolate, underwear and other things.

For days on end the Soviets – apart from a small amount of artillery fire – remained quiet; during the night they set up loudspeakers which encouraged people to desert. They also dropped leaflets which were specially printed for the *Volkssturm* of the Upper Danube.

At the end of the month the battalion spent a few days' rest to the rear. Then it had to go back to the front again and relieve the *Volkssturm* from Dresden.

On 11 April, the Soviets played music and then fired wildly around the area. Then there were another three quiet days. On 15 April the Divisional Chaplain, Rolf Otto, visited the battalion and heard confessions and gave Communion.

But only a few hours later, on 16 April at 5 o'clock in the morning, all hell broke loose. Over the front there beat a maelstrom of fire from which nobody thought they would escape. Everyone had resigned themselves to dying. On the stroke of 9 o'clock, the Soviet artillery fire ceased. All around everything was on fire. Then, often at hourly intervals, enemy attacks and pauses in the fighting alternated. The intensity of the fighting increased more and more. For three days, *Volkssturm* Battalion 22/I held out against the continuous attacks of the Soviet 362nd Rifle Division. A whole division against one battalion! But despite this the Soviets could not make any headway. Courage, bravery, commitment and good leadership of the battalion brought this about.

Only when at dawn on 19 April the battalion commander, *Hauptmann der Reserve* Ferdinand Lichtenberger, was killed by a shell during a Soviet attack and at the same time units to the left and the right of the battalion were retreating, had the time come for the men of the Upper Danube to leave their positions. At Schlaubehammer, Kaisermühl and Müllrose the battalion put up determined fighting as they retreated against the Soviets pushing on behind them. On 21 April, *Volkssturm* men from the Upper Danube destroyed 17 Soviet tanks.

At Müllrose, about 40 *Volkssturm* men were pushed back and were fighting a few days later in Fürstenwalde. The majority of the battalion under the Adjutant, retired *Major* Dr. Petritsch, withdrew from Müllrose through Beeskow, Glienicke, Storkow and Friedersdorf to Konigswüsterhausen, which they passed through on the morning of 24 April. Then the march headed for Berlin. With difficulty, the battalion snaked through the city area which was under Soviet fire to Potsdam, and thus at the last moment escaped the inferno of the Battle for Berlin. Outside Potsdam it was once more split into two parts. One part marched southwards under *Major* Petritsch and was taken prisoner by the Americans at Rosslau-Dessau. A few days later they were handed over to the British, who, as early as June, let them go home. The other, stronger part of the battalion under Company Commander Hofmüller marched westwards to Brandenburg, where they turned northwards through Rathenow, Kyritz, Perleburg and Ludwigslust to reach Hagenow. This part of the battalion was taken prisoner here on 3 May, was brought to camps in Schleswig and in August to East Frisia, from where the men were released in December 1945.

Bravely, loyally and tenaciously was how the *Volkssturmsoldaten* from Upper Danube fought for three months against a vastly superior enemy, until they had to withdraw in the face of overwhelming odds.

Battalion Commanders:

1. *Hauptmann d. R. z. V. Ferdinand Lichtenberger*
    killed in action 19 April 1945 at Müllrose.

2. *Hauptmann N. N.*, assigned from Divisional Staff
    killed in action 21 April 1945 at Müllrose.

3. *Major d. R. Dr. Fritz Petritsch,*
    from 21 April 1945 until taken prisoner.

    Battalion Adjutant:
    Major d. R ... Dr Fritz Petritsch, until 21 April 1945

    Battalion Medical Officer:
    Dr. Walter Pösch

    Supplies Officer:
    Ing. Franz Bernard

    Staff Company Commander:
    Andreas Nehr

1 Company Commander:
Karl Hofmüller

2 Company Commander:
1. Eduard Lindner, wounded.

2. Fritz Besemer, killed in action 21 April 1945 at Müllrose

3 Company Commander:
Franz Schwaiger, killed in action 16 April 1945 at Unterlindow

APPENDIX XXIV

Memoir of Rudolf Hönicka (born 14 December 1890), *Volkssturmmann* in *Volkssturmbataillon* z. b. V. Hessen II

As far as I can recall, towards the end of 1944, we employees of I. G. Farben Industries, Frankfurt A. M., insofar as we were not physically disabled and not aged over 60, were required, as future men of the *Volkssturm*, to take part in a form of pre-military training. The exercises usually took place on Sundays and were limited in practical terms to forming up, dismissing, counting off and mostly marching. Once, under the direction of experts, there was some small-calibre shooting, with each man having 3 shots. I myself had never been a soldier, even during the First World War, during which I was interned in Canada.

Although nobody assigned any great significance to this training, on 8 February 1945 things suddenly got serious. Towards 6 pm, many of us received from the NSDAP *Blockwart* a request to present ourselves at 2200 hours at the Party *Ortsgruppenstelle* in Ffm-Eschersheim for front-line active service in the *Volkssturm*. The selection of these men had doubtless been made by the NSDAP representatives who were in all offices and industries and, in the case of larger companies such as I. G. Farben, also in each department. These Party representatives were perfectly in a position to assess whose services could be dispensed with. I was dispensable, because the business contacts with the countries with which I had to deal (Greece, Bulgaria, Turkey, Syria) had been broken by the events at the front.

At 2200 hours, some 200 to 300 members of the *Volkssturm* from the most varied industries and authorities were gathered together. Then followed the recording of personal details, the issue of pay books, and the issue of SS or SA uniforms. The uniforms lay in a big pile, in which every man had to rummage around to find himself something which more or less fitted him. There was no medical examination. The whole procedure lasted until about 3 o'clock in the morning. Then came orders for us to report the following day, 9 February, at a certain time to the Ffm-Rodelheim railway station, where the journey to Weilburg/Lahn was to begin.

In Weilberg, the SS and SA uniforms were left behind; in their place we received used *Wehrmacht* uniforms, plus a rapid-firing rifle with – I think – 32 rounds. Then, together with *Volkssturm* men from other areas, including even 17 year-olds, we were divided into battalions. Besides officers, the backbone of battalions was formed by experienced front-line soldiers of the Second World War, mostly NCOs.

On the afternoon of 11 February, the whole transport was taken from a railway station 14 kilometres away through Giessen, Gottingen, Berlin to somewhere near Küstrin. The transport included about a hundred horses, which we had to lead on foot during the night from Weilberg to the said that railway station, and which then had to be loaded onto the train. During the journey, in our cattle wagon there was some necessary instruction on the rapid fire rifle, which was unknown to us. But this instruction only consisted of showing how to load and how to dismantle and re-assemble the rifle.

At our destination railway station, where we arrived on 14 February, the transport was unloaded. After several hours' march, our battalion reached a lonely, isolated village, the name of which I have forgotten. There we spent the night. The following day, 15 February, at 1700 hours we began our march to the front. This much lasted all night and led over footpaths and softened fields.

On 16 February about 10 o'clock we arrived in a smaller village. Here we got an hour's rest with food, and then came the order: Off with your overcoats, prepare to attack! Then, in loose groups, we moved forwards. Nothing was to be seen of the enemy. Only the enemy bullets were whistling around us, and from time to time shells exploded. One of them sent a splinter through my right hand and one into my right ankle. Thus my combat service came to a relatively happy end.

Then there followed emergency dressings in the field hospital, transfer via an intermediate hospital in to the Wunsdorf Military Hospital near Potsdam. My barracks burned down during an air-raid. They had left me in there as are the only non-walking wounded, but at the last minute they got me out. But I lost my papers, money and spectacles; only the hospital clothes remained to me. For the lost paybook there was the attached replacement card. In total I was sluiced through three other military hospitals. Finally I came to Strolberg in Saxony, which I left on two crutches in July, as the Soviets were beginning to throw their weight about. On goods trains, the journey went in the direction of Bavaria and on foot over the "green" border to Hof and thus to home in the neighbouring district.

Enterbach b. Rottach/Obb., 2 May 1960

Signed: Rudolf Hönicka

APPENDIX XXV

Actions of the *Volkssturm* in the Neisse *Stellung* near Guben

*by ***, Bevensen, Kreis Uelzen*

In Guben things were very lively, provisions, as earlier, were only issued in exchange for vouchers. Just after we had left our quarters in the Hindenburg School on 21 February, the first shell hit it. On the march through the town to the village of Gr. Breesen, things already looked very different. The evacuation had apparently begun. The town was already being shelled by artillery from the high ground to the east. We arrived without casualties in the village of Gr. Breesen on the Neisse, about four kilometres below Guben. There our company, which at that time only had a combat strength of about 50 men, was deployed to defend the river on its left bank. We built ourselves firing trenches in the bank and already on the next day (22 February) we could see that the Soviets were occupying the aerodrome opposite our position, which until 25 February was only occupied by one battalion of *Volkssturm*, to which we had in the meantime been assigned. If the Soviets weren't attacking, they shot at every man they could see; we did the same. Even in those first days, mostly as a result of enemy mortar fire, we had several dead and wounded. On 26 February infantry occupied our position, which was further extended by them. Our company had to bring the material to extend the positions into the positions by night, and in addition had to build a communications trench from Gr. Breesen to the positions. Particularly during the night, the positions and the ground between them and the village (1 kilometre) were constantly under infantry fire and also being shelled by mortars. The *Volkssturm* Battalion Kolmar, whose commander, *Freiherr* von Lüttwitz, and some NCOs, I knew, was also assigned to Guben.

On 5 March I was appointed by the Staff of the 35th SS Police Grenadier Division as the *Volkssturm* liaison officer, with the task of communicating and representing the particular requests of the two *Volkssturm* battalions and one *Volkssturm* Regiment. At the end of March until they surrendered the Gr. Breesen position on 23 April, all the *Volkssturm* were deployed north of the Neisse. I rode almost every day up close to the positions, left my horse at a farm to the rear and then reported to the battalion or regimental Staff. After discussing the tasks of the Divisional Staff and receiving requests or suggestions, I went through the positions speaking with the men and officers, who, at ages up to 60, were bravely doing their bit. There was never any peace there. The Soviets had installed snipers on the other side of the Neisse, who, at the relatively short range of 100 metres, shot several sentries in the trenches. No one could show themselves out of cover.

On 15 or 16 April in the evening, first the tanks and artillery of the division withdrew westwards, on the following evenings the two infantry regiments were also withdrawn and marched off in the same direction; their positions were occupied by *Volkssturm*.

On 17 April, the Divisional Staff Headquarters was transferred from Sembden to Krayne. On 18 April I rode from there back to the positions on the Neisse near Coschen. When I came back, my horse had been taken, because half the Staff was also withdrawing. The command of the Staff had now been taken over by an *Oberstleutnant* who had arrived from an *Ersatz* unit ...

On the evening of 22 April, the rest of the Staff marched away, myself with a small section on foot through Pinnow, on 23 April through Syskadel, Lamsfeld to Liebenrose ...

Notes

1. *Kolberg 1806/07* pp. 24 and 95.

2. Nettelbeck, pp. 40–45.

3. *Kolberg 1806/07* pp. 24 and 95.

4. Nettelbeck, pp. 40–45.

5. Bischoff, p. 194.

6. Barclay, p. 64–65.

7. Kalinow, p. 89ff.

8. *Der Größe Vaterländische Krieg der Sowjetunion*, p. 60.

9. Von Tippelskirch, p. 431.

10. *Wedemeyer Reports*, p. 197.

11. Guderian, pp. 326–328.

12. Guderian, pp. 326–328.

13. Guderian, pp. 326–328.

14. Guderian, pp. 326–328.

15. Clausewitz, *Vom Kriege*, Book 3, Chapter 11.

16. *Bilanz des Zweiten Weltkrieges*, p. 219.

17. Berlin Document Center.

18. Berlin Document Center.

19. Bundesarchiv documents *Reichskanzlei*, letter from Himmler to *Reichsminister* Dr Lammers.

20. American Microfilm Project T–81, roll 94.

21. Bundesarchiv documents *Reichskanzlei*.

22. Jacobsen, p. 402.

23. American Microfilm Project T–81, roll 94.

24. Bundesarchiv, *Der Deutsche Volkssturm*, pp. 5 & 6.

25. NSKK = *Nationalsozialistisches Kraftfahrkorps* (National Socialist Motor Corps), a special unit of the SA 1931–34, and thereafter a subordinate section of the NSDAP.

26. NSFK = *Nationalsozialistisches Fliegerkorps* (NS Flying Corps)

27. Berlin Document Center.

28. American Microfilm Project T–81, roll 94.

29. American Microfilm Project: T–81, roll 94.

30. Berlin Document Center.

31. American Microfilm Project T–81, roll 94.

32. [Publishers' note: However, since this work was originally published evidence has come to light that a small number were indeed modified].

33. Berlin Document Center.

34. Bundesarchiv, Abt. Zentralnachweisstelle: *Der Deutsche Volkssturm*, p. 12.

35. American Microfilm Project T–81, roll 94.

36. Bundesarchiv, Abt. Zentralnachweisstelle: *Der Deutsche Volkssturm*, pp. 21–25.

37. Berlin Document Center.

38. American Microfilm Project T–81, roll 94.

39. American Microfilm Project T–81, roll 94.

40. Bundesarchiv-Militärarchiv, Koblenz, Akten H 10–11/1–3 & H 15–9/1–5.

41. American Microfilm Project T–81, roll 94.

42. American Microfilm Project T–81, roll 95.

43. Dieckert & Grossmann, p. 116.

44. Dieckert & Grossmann, pp. 63–65.

45. Dieckert & Grossmann, pp. 63–65.

46. Dieckert & Grossmann, pp. 50–52.

47. Berlin Document Center.

48. Bruno Just, former Adjutant of *Volkssturm* Btn 25/235, diary entry from 9 May 1945.

49. Lasch, p. 134.

50. Lasch, p. 43.

51. *Dokumentation der Vertreibung der Deutschen aus Ost-Mitteleuropa*, 3. Beiheft.

52. Dieckert & Grossmann, pp. 105–107.

53. Material from the Bundesarchiv "Vorwürfe gegen *Gauleiter* Forster bzgl. der Aufstellung des *Volkssturms*".

54. *Dokumentation der Vertreibung der Deutschen aus Ost-Mitteleuropa*, Band I/1, pp. 40–45.

55. Diary of Schulze-Cassens, entry from 14 January 1945.

56. *Deutsche Soldatenzeitung* Nr. 10 from 5 March 1953.

57. Material from the Bundesarchiv, "Organisation und Einsatz des *Volkssturms* um Landsberg/Warthe 1944–1945".

58. Material from the Bundesarchiv, "Einsatz des *Volkssturm-Bataillons* Küstrin 1945".

59. Material from the Bundesarchiv, "Die Kämpfe in der Obrastellung zwischen Schwerin/Warthe und Schwiebus, 21. Januar bis 28. Februar 1945".

60. Busse, p. 151.

61. Material from the Bundesarchiv, "Einsatz des *Volkssturm-Bataillons* Küstrin 1945".

62. Bernau, pp. 90–105.

63. Willemer, p. 43.

64. Willemer, p. 25.

65. Schulze-Cassens diary.

66. Material from the Bundesarchiv: "Zivile Verteidigungsmaßnahmen u. a. Aufbau des *Volkssturms* in den Kreisen Arnswalde und Friedeberg 1944–1945".

67. Material from the Bundesarchiv: "Militärische Vorbereitungen zur Verteidigung Pommerns – Aufstellung des *Volkssturms* – Räumung des Kreises Naugard 1944 bis 1945".

68. Material from the Bundesarchiv: "Der Kreis Pyritz im letzten Kriegsjahr – Aufstellung des *Volkssturms* – Räumung der Stadt Pyritz 1944–1945".

69. Material from the Bundesarchiv: "Versagen der Pommernstellung und Einsatz des *Volkssturms* 1945".

70. Voelker, pp. 14, 73, 81, 98, 106, 143, 147, 148.

71. *Dokumentation der Vetreibung*, Band I/1, p 239.

72. See footnote 5.

73. See footnote 5.

74. See footnote 5.

75. See footnote 5.

76. Schulze-Cassens diary, entry for 10 February 1945.

77. Percy Ernst Schramm, section "Der russische Großangriff aus dem Brückenkopf von Baranow", p. 311ff.

78. See footnote 2.

79. Von Ahlfen & Niehoff, pp. 26, 27, 28, 30, 40, 48, 81, 82, 83.

80. See footnote 1.

81. See footnote 1.

82. C. H. Kühn, *Der Frontsoldat erzählt*, 3/1952, p. 68.

83. H. E. Niehoff, "Über den Ruinen von Breslau" in *Deutsche Soldatenzeitung* 17/1954.

84. Statement of the former Chief of General Staff of the 19th Army, *Oberst i. G. Brandstaedter, 14 April 1947*.

85. Blumenstock, p. 22, 23, 24, 25, 26, 57, 107, 170.

86. Letter by *Mitteilung Oberstudiendirektor i. R. Dr Kurt Jacki, Freiburg i. Br. from 27 September 1956.*

87. See footnote 2.

88. See footnote 2.

89. See footnote 2.

90. See footnote 2.

91. See footnote 2.

92. Information from the author.

93. See footnote 2, chapter 17.

94. Information from the author.

95. Percy Ernst Schramm, section "Der *Volkssturm*", pp. 25/26.

96. Busse, p. 157.

97. By a veteran: "Das *Volkssturm*-Bataillon 591" in ASMZ, pp. 232–234.

98. Letter from *Oberstleutnant a. D. Joachim Leder, 9 August 1960.*

99. Hans-Jürgen Eitner, p 318.

100. Not included in this translation.

101. See footnote 1.

102. See footnote 1.

103. See footnote 1.

104. These would have been captured Soviet 122mm M1931/37 guns.

Glossary

Abteilung	Battalion
Alarm	Emergency
Alarmeinheiten	Emergency units, i.e. units formed at very short notice from stragglers, etc. and thrown into battle in emergency situations.
Allgemeine Heeresamt	General Army Office
Armeeoberkammando / AOK	Army HQ, although often used simply to refer to an Army
Bataillonsarzt	Battalion surgeon
Bataillonsführer	Battalion commander
Blockwart	Block warden (NSDAP rank)
der Reserve / d. R.	Reserve
Ersatz	Reserve
Feldausbildungs	Field Training
Feldgendarmerie	Field Police
Feldwebel	Sergeant
Festung	lit. 'fortress', although in 1944/45 Hitler frequently applied this term to towns which lacked any real defences
Gau	Nazi administrative district
Gauleiter	High-ranking Nazi official responsible for a Gau
Gau-Organisationsleiter	Organisational head within a Gau
Gaustabsführer	Gau Chief of Staff
Gaustabsführung	*Gau* leadership/staff
Gebirgsjäger	Mountain troops
Generalfeldmarschall	Field Marshall
Generalleutnant	Lieutenant-General
Generaloberst	General
Gruppenführer	Section leader
Hauptgemeinschaftsleiter	Senior-ranking NSDAP official
Hauptmann	Captain
Heerespersonalamt	Army Personnel Office
HJ Gebietsführer	High-ranking Hitler Youth official, responsible for approx. 100,000 boys
Junkerschule	Officer training school
Kampfgruppe	Battle group
Kampfkommandant	Battle commander

Kompanieführer	Company commander
Kreis	Administrative region, approximately equivalent to a county in size
Kreisgeschäftsführer	Regional-level NSDAP official
Kreisleiter	Nazi Party official in charge of a *Kreis*
Kreisstabsführer	Kreis staff commander
Kriegsmarine	Navy
Landser	Nickname for the German soldier, similar in meaning to the British 'Tommy' or US 'GI'
Landsturm	Territorial militia
Landwacht	Auxiliary police force established in 1942 to protect the population from threats posed by foreign workers, escaped POWs etc.
Nachbarschaftshilfe	lit. 'neighbourly help', programme designed for the population to lend assistance to one another
Nachrichtentruppen	Signals troops
NSDAP	Nazi Party (standing for *Nationalsozialistische Deutsche Arbeiterpartei* or National Socialist German Workers' Party)
NSKK	*Nazionalesozialistiches Kraftfahrkorps* or Nazi Party Motor Corps
Oberbauleiter	Senior construction leader
Oberbefehlsleiter	Senior NSDAP official
Oberkommando der Wehrmacht (OKW)	Armed Forces High Command
Oberleutnant	Lieutenant
Oberst	Colonel
Oberstleutnant	Lieutenant-colonel
Ordnungspolizei	Order Police
Ordonnanzoffizier	Orderly officer
Organisation Todt	Nazi organisation responsible for constructing defensive and other structures
Ortsgruppe	Nazi administrative unit below a *Kreis*
Ortsgruppenleiter	Nazi Party official responsible for the political and administrative affairs of a small town or district of a larger city
Ortsgruppenstelle	HQ of an *Ortsgruppe* (see above)
Ostarbeiter	lit. 'eastern workers', labourers working in Germany from occupied territories
Panzerkorps	Tank corps
Panzerjäger	Tank hunter
Parteigenosse / Pg.	lit. 'party comrade', a form of addressing Nazi Party officials
Pionier	Pioneer/Engineer
Reichgesetzblatt	Reich Law Gazette
Reichsarbeitsdienst / RAD	National Labour Service
Reichsbahn	National Railways
Reichskanzlei	Reich Chancellery
Reichsstatthalter	Highest civil authority within a *Gau*

Reichswehr	German Armed Forces 1918–35
Rüstungskommandatur	Armament Command
Sanitätsdienstgrad	Medical Orderly
SA-Obergruppenführer	SA Lieutenant General
SA-Obersturmbannführer	SA Lieutenant Colonel
SA-Wehrmannschaft	SA militia
Schutzpolizei	Protective Police
Sicherheitsdienst/SD	Security Service
SS-Gruppenführer	SS Major General
SS-Hauptamtes	SS Head Office
SS-Obergruppenfuhrer	SS General
SS-Obersturmbannführer	SS Lieutenant-colonel
SS-Scharführer	SS Staff Sergeant
SS-Sturmbannführer	SS Major
Stadtwacht	Equivalent organisation to the *Landwacht* for urban areas
Standartenführer	Colonel
Standschützen	Territorial militia
Stellung	lit. 'position', usually used in reference to defensive positions
Technische Nothilfe	Technical Emergency Service
Transportkorps Speer	Breakaway transport organisation from the NSKK under the auspices of *Reichsminister* Speer
Unterabschnittsleiter	Sub-sector commander
Verwaltungspoliei	Administrative Police
Volksgewehr	'People's gun'
Volksmaschinenpistole	'People's machine-pistol'
Volksopfer	Programme for collecting winter clothing etc to send for use at the front
Volkssturmmann	Private soldier within the *Volkssturm*
Volkssturmsoldat	Name applied to all members of the *Volkssturm* regardless of rank
Waffenmeister	Armourer
Winterhilfe	Similar programme to the *Volksopfer* scheme (see above)
z. b. V.	For special purposes
Zahlmeister	Paymaster
Zelle	Cell (NSDAP administrative unit)
Z-Karte/Zuteilungskarte	Allocation card
Zugführer	Platoon commander

Bibliography

Documents and unpublished material

Reichsgesetzblatt 1944, Teil I, pp 253, 343, 344.

Reichsgesetzblatt 1945, Teil I, pp 5, 15, 24, 34, 35.

Reichshaushalts- und Besoldungsblatt 1945, p 23.

Heeresverordnungsblatt 1944, Teil B, pp 205, 260, 371.

Heeresverordnungsblatt 1944, Teil C, p 313.

Heeresverordnungsblatt 1945, Teil B, pp 5, 38.

Allgemeine Heeresmitteilungen 1944, p 279.

Verfügungen, Anordnungen, Bekanntgaben der Partei-Kanzlei, 2. Teil 1944, VII. Band. *Verfügungen, Anordnungen, Bekanntgaben der Partei-Kanzlei* Jan-April 1945.

Akte „*Reichskanzlei*" 692, Stichwort "*Volkssturm*" Bundesarchiv Koblenz.

Akte *Generalinspekteur für den Fiihrernachwuchs des Heeres* Bundesarchiv-Militärarchiv Koblenz.

Documents regarding the *Volkssturm* at the Berlin Document Center U. S. Mission Berlin, APO 742, U. S. Forces.

Documents regarding the *Volkssturm* in the American Microfilm-Project (Exhibits and Publications Branch, National Archives, Washington 25, D. C./National Archives Microcopy No. T – 81, rolls 94 und 95).

Bundesarchiv, Abt. Zentralnachweisstelle, Kornelimünster: Ausarbeitung "Der Deutsdie Volkssturm" (Az.: II 19 Nr. 247/56).

Professor Dr. Percy Ernst Schramm: various recollections as well as *Das Kriegstagebuch des Oberkommandos der Wehrmacht (Wehrmachtführungsstab)*, Band IV. Bernard & Graefe Verlag für Wehrwesen, Frankfurt am Main 1961.

Private diary of the Ia, "Führungsstab Deutscher Volkssturm", Major i. G. Günther Schulze-Cassens, November 1944 to Mai 1945.

"Werwolf" documents, Institute für Zeitgeschichte, München 1956.

Wilhelm Willemer: "Große Flußübergangsunternehmen durch russische Streitkräfte und deutsche Abwehrmaßnahmen gegen solche Unternehmen", unpublished manuscript.

Documents and papers of the author

Material in the Bundesarchiv Koblenz regarding the *Volkssturm* in the Wartheland, East Prussia, Pomerania, Danzig-West Prussia, Brandenburg, Lower- und Upper Silesia including the following:

1. *Beitrag zur Frage des Osteinsatzes – Stellungsbau 1944, Beitrag zur Geschichte des Volkssturmbataillons Goldap 1944.*

2. *Mein Volkssturmeinsatz 1945.*

3. *"Kennwort Gneisenau für Allenstein" – Verteidigung von Allenstein durch eine Volksgrenadierdivision und Volkssturm 1945.*

4. *"Vom Pregel z. Elbe" (Einsatz von Jagdkommandos d. Volkssturmes) 1945.*

5. *Der Volkssturm in Ostpreußen 1944–1945.*

6. *Der Ostwall, seine Entstehung, sein Verlauf und seine Bewährung – dazu kritische Stellungnahme des Generals a. D. Dr. rer. pol. Walter Grosse.*

7. *"Gauleiter Erich Koch und die Räumung Ostpreußens 1944/45".*

8. *Einsatz des Volkssturms in Königsberg 1945.*

9. *Kriegstagebuch d. Bat-Adjutanten d. Volkssturrm-Einsatz-Bataillons Goldap (15/235) über die Kriegsereignisse vom 17.10.1944 bis zur Auflösung des Volkssturms in Flensburg 2.5.1945.*

10. *"Meine Tätigkeit im Volkssturm".*

11. *"Deutscher Volkssturm des Kreises Darkehmen".*

12. *Sechs Berichte über den Einsatz beim Volkssturm in Ostpreußen.*

13. *Bericht über den Einsatz d. Volkssturmbat. Zempelburg i. Bromberg vom 21–26.1.1945.*

14. *Der Durchbruch v. Thorn (Westpreußen) (Versuch des Volkssturms d. Einschließung d. Stadt Thorn zu durchbrechen).*

15. *Vorwürfe gegen Gauleiter Forster bzgl. der Aufstellung des Volkssturms.*

16. *"Einsatz d. Volkssturms !m Wartheland, in Schlesien u. in der Mark 1945".*

17. *"Militarische Vorbereitungen f. Verteidigung des Warthelandes – Aufstellung des Volkssturms 1944–1945".*

18. *Volkssturm/Wehrkreis XXI Sonderbeilage I zum Kriegstagebuch d. Stellv. Generalkommandos XXI A. K. – hierin Bericht d. Gauleiters u. Reichsstatthalters Greiser über Aufstellung und Einsatz des Volkssturms vom 20.2.1945.*

19. *Einsatz des Volkssturms i. Reichsgau Wartheland (47 Berichte von Volkssturmangehörigen u. Parteidienststellen).*

20. *Räumung der Stadt Rawitsch u. Einsatz des Volkssturms 1945.*

21. *Bericht über meine Erlebnisse als Volkssturmmann in Pommern 1944–1945.*

22. *"Zur Vertreibung der Deutschen a. d. Osten – Ostpommern (Pommernwall), Räumung der Stadt Pyrit – zEinsatz des Volkssturms 1944–1945".*

23. *Der Kreis Pyritz im letzten Kriegsjahr – Aufstellung des Volkssturms der Stadt Pyrit – z russische Greuel bei Besetzung der Stadt 1944–1945.*

24. *Versagen der Pommernstellung und Einsatz des Volkssturms 1945.*

25. *Militärische Vorbereitungen zur Verteidigung Pommerns – Aufstellung des Volkssturms – Räumung des Kreises Naugard 1944–1945.*

26. *Bau des Pommernwalles – Aufstellung des Volkssturms in Stargard – Raumung der Stadt u. a.*

27. *Aufstellung des Volkssturms und Räumung von Belgard 1944–1945.*

28. *Dokumentation z. d. Geschehnissen vom Sommer 1944 b. z. 3.3.1945 in und um Köslin (Aufstellung des Volkssturm, Räumung der Stadt).*

29. *Zivile Verteidigungsmaßnahmen u. a. Aufbau des Volkssturms in den Kreisen Arnswalde und Friedeberg 1944–1945.*

30. *Organisation und Einsatz des Volkssturms um Landsberg/Warthe 1944–1945.*

31. *Einsatz des Volkssturmbataillons Küstrin 1945.*

32. *Ostwallbau und Volkssturm in Ostbrandenburg – Gauleiter Stürtz als Reichsverteidigungskommissar 1944/45.*

33. *Maßnahmen ziviler Dienststellen zum Schutze der Heimat und ihrer Bevölkerung – Aufstellung, Ausbildung und Ausrüstung des Volkssturms 1944–1945.*

34. *Einsatz des Volkssturms in Polen 1945.*

35. *Die Kämpfe in der Obrastellung zwischen Schwerin/Warthe und Schwiebus, 21. Januar bis 28. Februar 1945.*

Published material

Absolon, Rudolf *Das Wehrmachtstrafrecht im 2. Weltkrieg* (Kornelimünster: Bundesarchiv Abt. Zentralnachweisstelle, 1958).

Ahlfen, General von & General Niehoff *So kämpfte Breslau* (München: Gräfe und Unzer Verlag, 1959).

(Anon.) "Die letzten Tage von Kolberg" in *Deutsche Soldatenzeitung*, München, 12/1954.

(Anon.) "Im Inferno des Endkampfes, von den Abwehrkämpfen im Raume Schneidemühl", in *Deutsche Soldatenzeitung*, München, 8/1954.

Barclay, Brigadier C. N. "Englands Bürgerwehr" in *Wehrwissenschaftliche Rundschau*, Frankfurt/M., 2/1960.

Baum, Walter "Vollziehende Gewalt und Kriegsverwaltung im Dritten Reich" in *Wehrwissenschaftliche Rundschau*, Frankfurt/M., 9/1956.

Baumann, Günther "Der Kampf urn Posen erforderte Übermenschliches" in *Deutsche Soldatenzeitung*, München, 10/1953.

Bernau, Fritz "Erinnerungen eines Küstriner Volkssturmmannes" und "Die letzten Tage an Oder und Warthe" in *Küstrin und Umgebung*, (Wolfsburg: Selbstverlag Wilhelm Fitzky, 1952).

Bischoff, *Hauptmann* Helmut "Kampfgrundsätze des Gebirgskrieges, Durchbruch des Marschalls Ney durch die Scharnitz-Klause anno 1805" in *Truppenpraxis*, Darmstadt, 3/1959.

Blumenstock, Friedrich *Der Einmarsch der Amerikaner und Franzosen im nördlichen Württemberg im April 1945* (Stuttgart: W. Kohlhammer Verlag, 1957).

Bundesministerium für Vertriebene (eds.) *Dokumentation der Vertreibung der Deutschen aus Ost-Mitteleuropa*, Band 1/1 & 2, Band IV/1, 2 & 3 (Berlin: Bernard & Graefe, 1955–57)

Busse, Theodor "Die letzte Schlacht der 9. Armee" in *Wehrwissenschaftliche Rundschau*, Frankfurt/M., 4/1955.

Dieckert, Major & General Grossmann *Der Kampf um Ostpreußen* (München: Gräfe und Unzer Verlag, 1960).

Eckhart-Morawietz *Die Handwaffen des brandenburgisch-preußisch-deutschen Heeres* (Hamburg: Verlag Helmut Gerhard Schulz, 1957, S. 217–219).

('einem Mitkämpfer') "Das Volkssturmbataillon 591" in *Allgemeine Schweizerische Militärzeitschrift*, Frauenfeld (Switzerland), 3/1948.

Eitner, Hans-Jürgen "Die 'Kampfgruppen der SED' – die Bürgerkriegs-Miliz der SU" in *Wehrwissenschaftliche Rundschau*, Frankfurt/M., 6/1960.

Förster, Otto-Wilhelm *Das Befestigungswesen* (Neckargermünd: Kurt Vowinckel Verlag, 1960).

Grieger, Friedrich *Wie Breslau fiel* (Stuttgart: Kulturaufbau-Verlag, n. d.).

Großen Generalstab, Kriegsgeschichtliche Abteilung II *Urkundliche Beiträge und Forschungen zur Geschichte des Preußischen Heeres*, Heft 16 bis 19 *Kolberg 1806/07* (Berlin: Ernst Siegfried Mittler & Sohn, 1911).

Guderian, Heinz *Erinnerungen eines Soldaten*, (Neckargemünd: Kurt Vowinckel Verlag, 1950/1960).

Haken, J. C. L. (ed.) *Joachim Nettelbeck, eine Lebensbeschreibung, von ihm selbst aufgezeichnet* (Leipzig: F. A. Brockhaus, 1821 & 1823).

Heinrich, Johann "Die letzten Tage des Deutsch Kroner Volkssturms", Ausgabe 5/1952 & Leo Gramse "Das Ende des Deutsch Kroner Volkssturmes", Ausgaben 3, 4, 5 & 6/1954 of *Deutsch Kroner Heimatbrief*, Springe/Deister, Mittelweg 30.

Hopffgarten, Hans-Joachim von "Der Kampf um die Oderbrückenköpfe Lebus und Göritz (Februar/März 1945)" in *Wehrkunde*, München, 11/1955.

Jacobsen, H. A. *Der Zweite Weltkrieg in Chronik und Dokumenten* (Darmstadt: Wehr und Wissen Verlagsgesellschaft, 1959).

Jedlicka, Ludwig "Das Milizwesen in Österreich" in *Wehrwissenschaftliche Rundschau*, Frankfurt/M., 7/1959.

Just, Bruno "Auszug aus dem Kriegstagebuch des Goldaper Volkssturm-Bataillons 25/235" in *Die Heimatbrücke*, Leer (Ostfriesland), 21, 22, 23, 24/1952 & 1/1953.

Kalinow, Kyrill D. *Sowjetmarschälle haben das Wort* (Hamburg: Hansa-Verlag Josef Toth, 1950).

Kühn, C. H. "Der letzte Kampf um Breslau" in *Der Frontsoldat erzählt*, Pressa-Verlag, Flensburg, 3 ff./1952.

Lasch, General Otto *So fiel Königsberg: Kampf und Untergang von Ostpreußens Hauptstadt* (München: Gräfe und Unzer Verlag, 1958).

Lechthaler, Alois *Heimatland Tirol, Geschichte* (Bozen: Verlagsanstalt Athesia, 1959).

Nusser, Albuin *Südtirol* (Buchenhain vor München: Verlag Volk und Heimat, n. d.).

Tippelskirch, Kurt von *Geschichte des Zweiten Weltkriegs* (Bonn: Athendum-Verlag, 1956).

(Various) *Bilanz des Zweiten Weltkrieges* (Oldenburg: Gerhard Stalling Verlag, 1953).

(Various) *Der Große Vaterlandische Krieg der Sowjetunion* (Berlin: SWA-Verlag, 1947).

(Various) *Große Sowjet-Enzylclopädie, der Große Vaterländische Krieg der Sowjetunion 1941 bis 1945* (Berlin: Verlag Rütten & Loening, 1953).

Voelker, Johannes *Die letzten Tage von Kolberg* (Warzburg: Holzner-Verlag, 1959).

Wedemeyer, Albert C. *Der verwaltete Krieg (Wedemeyer Reports)* (Gütersloh: Sigbert Mohn Verlag, 1958).

Wolf, P. "Küstrin vor dem Sturm 1945", in *Heimatzeitung des Kreises Königsberg-Neurnark*, Braunschweig, 9/1956.

Additional material

Verbal and written responses to questionnaires from numerous people as well as the personal recollections of the author.

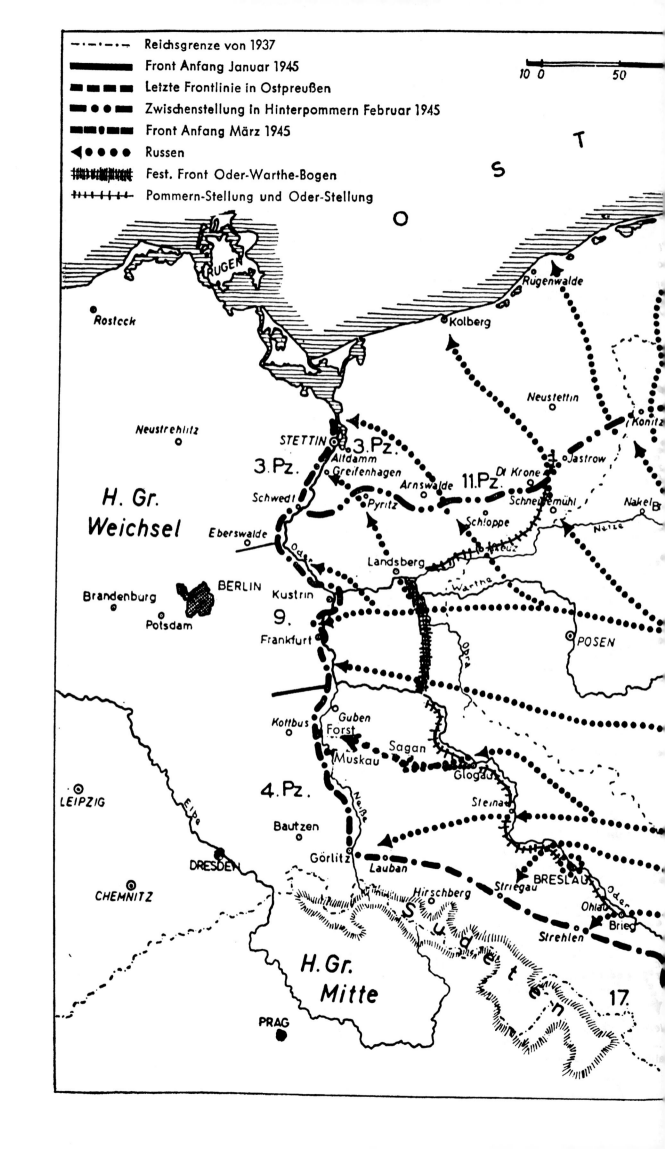

10 0   50

Rostock

RÜGEN

O S T

Rügenwalde

Neustrehlitz

Kolberg

Neustettin

STETTIN 3. Pz.

3. Pz.

Konitz

Altdamm

Greifenhagen

Jastrow

Dt. Krone

H. Gr.
Weichsel

Schwedt

Arnswalde

11. Pz.

Schneidemühl

Nakel

Pyritz

Schloppe

Netze

Eberswalde

Oder

Landsberg

Kreuz

Warthe

Brandenburg

BERLIN

Kustrin

Obra

Potsdam

9.

POSEN

Frankfurt

Kottbus

Guben
Forst

LEIPZIG

Muskau

Sagan

Glogau

4. Pz.

Neiße

Steinau

Bautzen

Elbe

Görlitz

Lauban

DRESDEN

Striegau

BRESLAU

CHEMNITZ

Hirschberg

Oder

Ohlau

S u d e t e n

Brieg

Strehlen

17.

H. Gr.
Mitte

PRAG

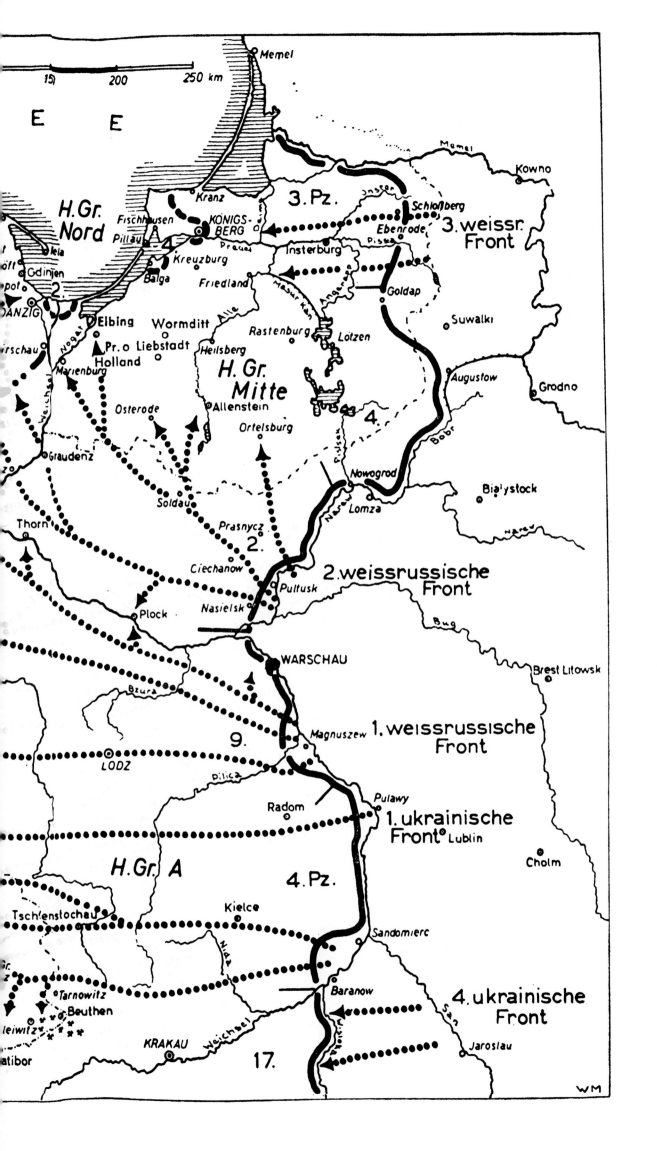

Also available from 🌞 Helion & Company Limited

The Black Devils' March – A Doomed Odyssey. The 1st Polish Armoured Division 1939–45

Evan McGilvray – 160pp, 94 photos, 9 maps.

Hardback – ISBN 1-874622-42-6

Twilight of the Gods: A Swedish Waffen-SS Volunteer's Experiences with the 11th SS Panzergrenadier Division 'Nordland', Eastern Front 1944–45

Thorolf Hillblad – 144pp, 16 photos
Hardback – ISBN 1-874622-16-7

For Rex & For Belgium: Léon Degrelle and Walloon Political & Military Collaboration 1940–45

Eddy de Bruyne & Marc Rikmenspoel – 304pp, 400+ b/w photos, ills, maps, docs
Hardback – ISBN 1-874622-32-9

Hitler's Miracle Weapons. The Secret History of the Rockets & Flying Craft of the Third Reich Volume 2 – from the V-1 to the A-9: Unconventional short- and medium-range weapons

Friedrich Georg – 148pp, 16 pages colour plates, 31 b/w photos, diagrams, docs. Hardback – ISBN 1-874622-62-0

A selection of forthcoming titles

To The Bitter End. The Final Battles of Army Groups North Ukraine, A, Centre, Eastern Front 1944–45
Rolf Hinze, ISBN 1-874622-36-1

Under Himmler's Command. The Personal Recollections of Oberst Hans-Georg Eismann, Operations Officer, Army Group Vistula, Eastern Front 1945
Hans-Georg Eismann, edited by Fred Steinhardt, ISBN 1-874622-43-4

Penalty Strike. The Memoirs of a Red Army Penal Company Commander 1943–45
Alexander V. Pyl'cyn, ISBN 1-874622-63-9

Some Additional Services From Helion & Company

BOOKSELLERS

- over 20,000 military books available
- four 100-page catalogues issued every year

BOOKSEARCH

- Free professional booksearch service. No search fees, no obligation to buy

Want to find out more?
Visit our website – www.helion.co.uk

Our website is the best place to learn more about Helion & Co. It features online book catalogues, special offers, complete information about our own books (including features on in-print and forthcoming titles, sample extracts and reviews), a shopping cart system and a secure server for credit card transactions, plus much more besides!

HELION & COMPANY

26 Willow Road, Solihull, West Midlands, B91 1UE, England
Tel: 0121 705 3393　　　　　　　　　Fax: 0121 711 4075
Email: publishing@helion.co.uk　　　　Website: http://www.helion.co.uk